Dog Talk

ANNIE

Photographs by James Parker and Cathrin Cammett

Illustrations by Jocelyn Sandor

John Ross and Barbara McKinney

Dog Talk

Training Your Dog Through a
Canine Point of View

St. Martin's Press

New York

This book is dedicated to my parents, Jean and
Joseph Ross, and to my grandmother, Rose
Torcaso, for the many years of emotional and
financial support that allowed me to pursue a career
I love. Without them this book would not exist.

—J.R.

To the memory of my mother.

—B.M.

NOTE TO READER

The information in this book is intended to guide dog owners in the
training and handling of their dogs. As different dogs have different
temperaments, results from employing the methods in this book may
vary. These techniques are meant to be used humanely and carefully,
and the authors do not condone or take responsibility for training
excesses that may harm a dog.

Library of Congress Cataloging-in-Publication Data

Ross, John.
    Dog talk : training your dog through a canine point of view /
John Ross and Barbara McKinney.
        p.   cm.
    Includes index
    ISBN 0-312-11778-7
    1. Dogs—Training.   2. Human-animal communication.
I. McKinney, Barbara. II. Title.
    [SF431.R65   1995]
    636.7′0887—dc20   94-45117
                                                            CIP

First published in the United States by St. Martin's Press

First U.S. Edition: March 1995
10 9 8 7 6 5 4 3 2 1

Contents

Part Three: The Dog Talk *Training Program*

Part Four: *Household Manners*

Part Five: *What Every Dog Owner Should Know*

Foreword

I sometimes wonder how people live without the joys of good canine companionship. Perhaps it is because my own dogs bring such joy into my life. Their affection and playfulness remind me time and again that a good dog is a true treasure.

The key to this wonderful relationship is good canine manners. If your dog is out of control, his freedom is restricted, and your joy is diminished. In fact, an out-of-control dog is a downright nuisance. Herein lies what you need to understand your dog, to become the owner he will respect and love, and to have a pet you can be proud of.

As founder and director of "Camp Gone to the Dogs," a summer camp for people and their dogs, I have the opportunity to meet and observe many, many dog trainers. John Ross is a real find. I hired him to teach pet-oriented obedience at camp, and my "campers" from all over the United States couldn't say enough about him. They loved him, immensely enjoyed his classes, and could really understand what was behind everything he taught. They were able to apply what they learned in everyday situations and feel good about it. They had never met a trainer like him. I agree! John's love of people and dogs is evident in all he does. His approach to training through a canine point of view makes *sense*.

I also have the pleasure of knowing John and Barbara on a personal level. They truly love and spoil their dogs. One of my favorite memories is John showing off how he had taught Byron to eat corn on the cob. No force methods of domination here—love, humor, and "talking dog" are what it's all about.

Enjoy this book. It will surprise you, make you laugh, and teach you how to train your dog to be the canine companion you have always hoped for.

Honey Loring, M.A.Ed.
Founder and Director, "Camp Gone to the Dogs"
Putney, Vermont

SAM

Preface

Well-trained dogs are not created with magic. Such dogs are the product of an important investment made by their owners—an investment in time, patience, and a proven training program. If you are willing to set aside some time and can be patient, you now have all the ingredients that are needed.

Dog Talk will change the way you and your dog live together. This book will open your eyes to some untraditional ways of looking at your dog. It will show you why obedience training is the very best thing you can do for a dog—especially the family pet. It also will surprise you, because *Dog Talk* training is a lot of fun. You will realize that you and your dog can have a great life together—now that you have a training program to show you how.

The focus of *Dog Talk* is on raising a young dog to be a well-behaved adult. Preventing undesirable behaviors during the formative first two years of a dog's life is more effective than trying to undo those behaviors many years after they have become bad habits. However, the training techniques in *Dog Talk* are effective on a dog of any age. We have had students with ten-year-old dogs make remarkable accomplishments using this program.

Whether you have a new puppy, an "unruly" young dog, or an untrained middle-age pet, you can start improving your dog's behavior immediately. Through training, your dog's life will be changed for the better. And as a result, so will yours.

Acknowledgments

Special thanks to: Chuck Noonan, D.V.M. & Chris Benyei, D.V.M. for years of support and encouragement; Brian Silverlieb, D.V.M. for consistent support and the use of his beautiful farm for our photographs; Al Reuben for his friendship and help in getting this project off the ground; Bob Weil, our great editor, for his expertise and faith in our idea; and Jocelyn Sandor, James Parker, and Cathrin Cammett for their artistic talents.

We also thank Joyce Jaskula, Ted Godfrey, Cork, and Glin for their hospitality, friendship, and excellent adventures; Richard, Gail, and P. J. Stieglitz for their friendship and moral support; the Brotherhood of Thieves for chowder and curly fries; and the Atlantic Cafe for apple streudel with ice cream. Thanks also to Jim Dasbach, D.V.M., John Rae, D.V.M., Judy Clarkson, and the entire staff of the Nantucket MSPCA veterinary hospital, and to Ann VanArsdale and her great dogs for their courageous efforts at an attempted cover shot during a Nantucket nor'easter.

From John: Special thanks to Carolyn Stauffer, who sold me my first dog, Jason, and who gave me the dog bug; and to Travis McGee, Jimmy Buffett, and Captain Augustus McCrae for inspiring me to follow my own path.

From Barbara: Warm thanks to Julie Starkweather for showing me how much fun it is to share my life with dogs. Thanks also to Jeff

LaCroix, D.V.M., for always taking time to teach me points of canine medicine.

Special love to dogs of the past: Jason the Irish setter, Jena the German shorthaired pointer, Woody the golden retriever, Joslyn the standard poodle, and Michelle the miniature poodle, chaser of bunny rabbits and polar bears.

Special thanks to our students and their dogs for their help in demonstrating Dog Talk *training techniques:*

Jordana Bloom and Remington & Riley, Jack Russell terriers
Cathrin Cammett and Barclay, dalmatian
Debbie Corcione and Joshua, husky-shepherd mix
Carolyn Crabtree and Shannon, terrier mix
Susan Dale and Raven & Brucie & Scruffy, three great mixed-breeds
Karen DiMargo and Sam, cairn terrier
Cheryl Dixon and Owen, Welsh springer spaniel
Rich Duncan and Whitnall, yellow Labrador retriever
Martha Ewbank and Winston, shepherd mix
Michael Feely and Casey, English cocker spaniel
Rose Fogelman and Turbo, Belgian Tervuren
Robin Henner and Max, Bouvier des Flandres
Stephen Herman and Holly, golden retriever
Judith Hibbard and Murphy, Irish setter
Susan Hubregsen and Captain, Australian shepherd
Beverly Kessler and Buddy, Lakeland terrier
Carol Martin and Spencer, Old English sheepdog
Barbara & Mindee Reuben and Sneakers, golden retriever
Bill & Lori Streaman and Casey, beagle
Pamela Wienski and C. B., Bermuda fox terrier
Edward Wienski and Molly, flying squirrel
(a.k.a. tiny Bermuda fox terrier)
Barbara Yarbrough and Janus, American foxhound

SNEAKERS

Part One

Before You Begin Training

One

The *Dog Talk* Approach

A well-trained dog is a dog that a person lives with for up to fifteen years and loves and enjoys. It is a dog that an owner can bring anywhere and have under control. A well-trained dog is not a nuisance to his owners, to house guests, or to the neighborhood.*

The training techniques in *Dog Talk* are pet-oriented. The exercises will help you teach your dog how to become a well-behaved canine companion. By working through the exercises in this book, you can expect to gain a happy and obedient pet.

The exercises in *Dog Talk* are *not* designed around the skills needed for the artificial world of the obedience competition ring. I place no emphasis on military-style precision. Insisting that dogs sit straight and work like American Kennel Club competition dogs adds stress to their lives. In my opinion, it takes the fun out of obedience training. The emphasis of *Dog Talk* training is on attentiveness, responsiveness, and a happy working attitude.

*For ease of discussion, dogs are referred to by the male pronoun throughout. In addition, authors John Ross and Barbara McKinney use the voice of John Ross to present much of their information. The word "I" refers to John Ross.

The *Dog Talk* Training Philosophy

A sound training philosophy is the foundation for all good dog training. It provides a framework for each of the training exercises and establishes guidelines for daily interactions with your dog. Before you use this book, you should clearly understand my approach.

The training philosophy of *Dog Talk* is based on a combination of common sense and a thorough understanding of dogs. I have spent many years gaining dog training experience and developing this program. One phrase I hear repeated over and over by people who take my training course is "It makes so much sense!"

In short, my approach is *training through a canine point of view*. This even has become the motto of my dog obedience school. Why? The reason is simple. I do not know whether your dog thinks he is a human . . . or that you are a dog! However, I strongly believe that he thinks he is the same kind of creature you are.

Unfortunately, your dog cannot think and learn like a human. But this book can teach you *how to think like a dog*. It will show you how to train through a canine perspective. Only when you teach on a canine level will your dog clearly understand what you want.

The training approach in this book also relies on the commonsense idea that dogs must be *shown* what we want them to do. You are

The *Dog Talk* approach is based on communicating with your dog from a canine point of view. Successful training depends on it.

taught how to break obedience exercises down into small, simple steps. First you show the dog a simple step, then you practice it many, many times. Then you add another simple step, building toward an end result.

Simple training steps make it easy for owners to succeed in carrying out obedience techniques. Simple steps also make it easy for dogs to succeed in learning the exercises. I have found that success is, by far, the greatest motivator in dog training. The more owners succeed, the more they want to train their dogs.

Whenever possible, dogs should not be corrected for not responding to an exercise they have not been taught. Too many trainers—both amateurs and professionals—make this mistake.

The corrections that I teach are never violent. I never advocate abusive techniques, such as hitting, kneeing, or choking dogs. Beware of any training program that does. There is absolutely no reason in the world to abuse your dog in order to train him.

You *will* learn how to correct your dog with a growl-like tone of voice. This will be one of your most important training tools. Another will be the training collar, sometimes mistakenly called a choke collar. A training collar becomes a choke collar only when it is misused. You will learn to give gentle jerks and releases with this collar rather than to pull on it, which produces a choking effect.

I put a lot of emphasis on enthusiastic praise in this book. This is where your voice is once again a useful tool. Warm pats and hugs are also greatly encouraged! And food is a perfectly acceptable motivator in my approach to training. It is one of the many items that I use to focus a dog's attention, cause him to do a behavior, reward him for complying, and so on.

Owner Qualifications

Owners must have two basic qualifications to successfully train their dogs. The first is common sense. Owners who have the ability to use common sense when teaching their dogs are a giant step ahead of the game. If you never have owned or trained a dog before, you will find this book filled with commonsense advice about dogs.

The other ingredient, but perhaps the more important, is that owners must love their dogs. Loving a dog means being willing to spend time with the dog. It means viewing the dog as an important member of the family. It means caring for the dog to the best of your ability from the day you bring the pup home until he reaches old age. The dog must always be high on your priority list regardless of what happens in your life. I truly believe that a person who cannot make this commitment should not own a dog.

Even dog owners who have common sense and who love their dogs often make mistakes in training. One common mistake is training haphazardly; another is not being aware of training techniques that have been tested and proven to work. This book provides owners with practical information about canine behavior, proven training techniques, and a step-by-step training program.

What This Book Is Not

This book is not a magic wand. You cannot wave it over your dog's head and expect him to become a model canine citizen overnight. Wouldn't it be great if it were that easy! Unfortunately, there is no such thing as a magic-wand solution to dog training. The amount of time and effort you put into your dog corresponds exactly to the level of obedience and reliability your dog is capable of giving.

This book is not filled with hype and buzzwords. Some training books on the market state that they do not train dogs, they teach dogs how to think. Then the authors proceed to offer standard stimulus-response training methods used by every other dog training book. Other books are little more than collections of useless gimmicks assembled by people with few dog-training credentials. *Dog Talk* is not a con job. It is based on many years of successful pet-oriented training.

There are no celebrities' names in this book, although I have worked with several internationally known people. How well did they do? No better or worse then my clients who have been housewives, executives, schoolteachers, artists, and mail carriers. Celebrities have no special ability to train a dog. Having them as clients adds nothing to my credentials as an obedience instructor. If you are more impressed by name-dropping than by a training program that works, this is the wrong book for you!

Still other books tell you, "Just loving your dog is all it takes. You *never* have to correct your dog." While love is an essential part of successful training, so is correction—when it is used fairly. When you view training from a canine point of view, you realize that a wolf pack leader does not maintain order and harmony in his pack simply with affection. There are occasions when a well-timed growl or a bite are necessary.

Some trainers will tell you that they can perform a miracle with dogs and that you can have a trained dog in thirty minutes. Can anyone teach a child to be a responsible adult in thirty minutes? Dog training takes time! If it was easy, *everybody* would have a well-trained dog, and millions of dogs would not be abandoned to dog pounds and euthanized every year.

You *Are the Trainer*

There is one final but important aspect of *Dog Talk* training. I strongly advocate that dog owners train their own dogs. I sometimes wear a T-shirt when teaching a group class that says "I am the instructor, you are the trainer." Nothing says it clearer than that!

I feel this way for several reasons. I have years of experience with the two approaches to training dogs: owners training their own dogs and owners sending their dogs to a professional for training. I have found that the best results are achieved when owners learn to train their own dogs—using the guidelines of a proven training program. Although I could make a lot of money if I convinced people to send me their dogs for train, I don't do it. I truly believe that having others train your dog does not work well in the long run. All it does is teach the dog to be obedient to that trainer. Dogs respond reliably only to whomever trains them. If you want your dog to respond to you, *you* must train your dog.

In addition, training your dog while he lives in your home teaches him to fit into your life. When you "send the dog off to be trained," he usually lives in a kennel. Even if the trainer works with your dog for a full hour every day, what is your dog doing for the other twenty-three hours? He is probably in a kennel crate or a dog run. He is certainly not learning how to live with you.

If you want your dog to fit into your life, *you* train the dog. Use the step-by-step training approach outlined in this book. Follow the advice on how to teach good household manners. Most important, read the chapters on canine behavior and learn how to train from a canine point of view. With a little time, patience, and effort, you can accomplish more than any other trainer. That's because you will be using "dog talk" to build a relationship between your dog and the most important person in his world—you!

Two

Should I Obedience Train My Dog?

I receive many phone calls from people who are interested in gaining control over their dogs but are not sure that obedience training is for them. Here are some of the questions and concerns these people have. Maybe you have wondered the same things.

"I have heard horror stories about abusive trainers who choke dogs and intimidate handlers. Is that what I must experience in order to train my dog?"

There is no place for mental or physical abuse in dog training. A qualified obedience instructor does not have to rely on hanging, hitting, or kneeing dogs in order to achieve results. These are techniques used by people who do not know what they are doing.

Qualified obedience instructors also understand their role. Their role as instructors is to provide information and a sound training program to their students. Their job is not to badger, bully, or humiliate people into training their dogs.

While experience is essential to a good instructor, longevity alone does not make someone competent. Whether the instructor has been training dogs for four years or four decades, he or she has the responsibility to help people, not harass them. A good dog trainer provides a program that is a fun and productive experience for both dog and handler. (See Chapter 28, "Choosing a Qualified Dog Obedience Instructor.")

"Would my dog prefer not to be trained?"

I don't know whether a dog would prefer to be trained or not. I'm sure many dogs would prefer to do whatever they feel like doing. I have one dog, Drifter, who would love to spend the day "doing his own thing." If he had his way, he would roam the neighborhood, chase cars, raid garbage pails, and bite kids on bicycles. However, I prevent him from doing these things for his own safety and because I love him. I want him in my life as long as possible.

I do know that a dog can *enjoy* obedience training. Drifter loves when I practice obedience exercises with him, and he is a very well-trained dog. That's because I make training a fun experience.

Unfortunately, my dog will never understand why I train him. But *I* know why. Training not only keeps him safe, it enhances *his* enjoyment of life. If Drifter did not come when I called him, he would not get to go for his daily run on the beach. If he did not understand controlled walking, he would not get his walks into town. When guests come to visit he would be exiled to the bedroom or garage if he did not do a reliable down-stay. My dog accompanies me on vacation every year because I know he will not chew up the hotel room. These are just a few of the things in life my dog can experience because he is obedience trained.

Is it natural to train a dog?

In one sense, yes. It is very natural. It is natural for a dog to use his brain and to follow direction from a pack leader. Granted, many of the obedience exercises we train dogs to do are not things they would do in the wild. However, canines in the wild do not live in houses, ride in cars, or have dinner fed to them every day.

In many ways our dogs are like their wild canine cousin, the wolf, but the major difference is that they are *not* wild. They are domesticated creatures who are dependent on humans for their welfare. A dog who has been trained through a canine point of view—using commonsense methods—is a mentally balanced and contented animal.

In addition, dogs are creatures of habit. They seek out structure in their lives. Training not only provides structure, it provides dogs with stimulating behaviors. When a dog has a sense of structure and a job to do, he is most content. A dog who lives his life chained in the backyard and does not get proper exercise and social interaction—because he is not under control—is a sad individual living an unnatural life.

Will training break my dog's spirit?

Only abusive training can break a dog's spirit. Positive training is mentally healthy for a dog and will even bolster the dog's confidence.

Fortunately, dogs are such resilient creatures that, even when exposed to bad training, it is not easy to break their spirits. However, some individual dogs have very sensitive personalities—just like some people have. These are the ones who suffer the most at the hands of bad trainers. Even though the majority of dogs in the world are not overly sensitive, it is imperative that owners carefully screen what type of training (and trainers) they expose themselves and their dogs to.

Should only one person in the family train the dog?

Not at all. Anyone who wants the dog to respond to him or her should work with the dog. A dog is not a computer that can be programmed to respond to just anyone! Dogs respond well only to whoever trains them. If just one person in the family does the training, the dog will respond reliably just to that person.

By the same token, no one can undo your training. When you train a dog, you develop a relationship and establish a form of communication with the dog. No one can do these things for you (that's why I recommend that owners train their own dogs)—and no one can take them away. If you are consistent and carry out the training techniques properly, your dog *will* respond to you—even if everyone else in the family does it wrong.

If you want your dog to obey all the members of your family, show each individual how to carry out the exercises. Take turns practicing with the dog. It is equally important that every family member convince the dog that they are higher than the dog in the "pecking order of the pack." (See Chapter 6, "Pack Leader.") Keep in mind, however, that most children under the age of eight do not make effective dog trainers. Children between the ages of eight and sixteen should be allowed to *help* with training, as long as they are closely supervised by an adult.

Training Is for Everyone

You probably realize by now that I strongly advocate obedience training for all dogs. However, training a dog is hard work. It requires time, patience, and expertise. As I've said, if training was easy *everyone* would have well-trained dogs. But most people don't. And because many people find it too difficult—or too inconvenient—to train their dogs, millions of dogs are abandoned or given to pounds every year where a majority are killed.

Were I not convinced that *Dog Talk* training did not greatly enhance my dogs' lives, I probably would not to do it with them. I find it much more fun to play Frisbee or go swimming with my dog than to practice controlled walking and come-on-command training techniques. However, I know that an educated dog is a happier dog, so I make training fun by keeping it lively and interesting. My demeanor is always pleasant and enthusiastic whenever I work with my dogs.

Think back to your school days. Good teachers try to do the same thing. They try to help their students enjoy learning to read, write, and understand math. But even the best students would prefer to be at the beach, at the fair, or listening to music—as opposed to sitting in a classroom. However, nobody can deny that their lives are enhanced by the hard work of a good education.

This is very true of our dogs. The trained dog gets to go places and do things that the out-of-control individual is denied. I feel it is our responsibility when we bring a puppy home to help him enjoy the fullest and most wonderful life he can have. Good obedience training is really the only way to make that happen.

Three

How Dogs Think and Learn

Dogs learn simply by doing behaviors. If a behavior is agreeable to them *as they are doing it,* they will repeat that behavior in the future. If the behavior is disagreeable *as they are doing it,* dogs will develop an avoidance to that behavior. After repeating the behavior X number of times, dogs develop a habit, or a conditioned response. Formally speaking, a conditioned response is a consistent reaction that someone—or some pet—has in relation to a specific signal or signals.

Humans react with conditioned responses every day. For example, you may be reading a book and the telephone rings. The sound of the bell is your signal. Your conditioned response is to pick up the telephone and say hello. You may be driving your car down the road when a traffic light turns red. The red light is your signal. Your conditioned response is to stop your car. You also have conditioned avoidances, such as keeping your hands away from a hot oven. After one or more occasions of burned fingers, you learn to keep your hands away.

An obedience-trained dog has conditioned responses to many specific signals. For example, the sound *"Sit"* is a signal. The trained dog's conditioned response is to put his rear end on the floor. When given the *"Stay"* command, the trained dog has a conditioned avoidance to movement. That's because whenever he did move, he received a tough *"NHAA"* from the handler. Before long the dog learns to avoid movement in response to the *"Stay"* command.

Your dog may also exhibit conditioned responses that you did not intentionally develop. For example, every afternoon you pick up your dog's Frisbee and take him outside for a game. After several days or weeks you will see that when you pick up the Frisbee, your dog runs to the door anticipating a game. Picking up the Frisbee has become your dog's signal. Running to the door is now his conditioned response.

Your dog also may develop conditioned avoidances on his own. If he were to put his nose on the hot oven door and burn himself, you would see that after one or several experiences he would avoid the oven door.

Forming Conditioned Responses

What does it take to form a conditioned response in a dog? One important criterion is to repeat the behavior consistently. Dogs rarely develop a conditioned response without many repetitions. But how many repetitions will it take? Quite a few factors influence how many. One important factor is how agreeable or disagreeable the experience was. Another factor is how closely aligned to the dog's selectively bred instincts the behavior was. A playful dog with a strong retrieving instinct and chase reflex will pick up on the routine of the backyard Frisbee game very quickly.

Other factors that influence how fast a dog develops a conditioned response include the dog's individual intelligence, physical and mental health, and physical stoicism.

The subject of stoicism deserves some explanation. Selective breeding of dogs over many years has developed various genetic traits in different breeds. Some traits are simply an enhancement of a canine instinct, such as chasing or retrieving. Other traits relate only to the dog's physical appearance, such as an Irish setter's red coat. One trait that particularly affects canine learning is stoicism, or what could be called pain tolerance. A good example of stoicism is the springer spaniel charging through pricker bushes to flush out a pheasant. He certainly doesn't mind—or even notice—the sharp thorns. This dog will learn the behavior of flushing birds much more readily than a pain-sensitive dog who is hurt and/or frightened by the prickers against his skin.

These various factors make an important point: Just like people, all dogs learn different things at different rates of speed. Also keep in mind that one or even several repetitions of a behavior do not mean that the dog has a conditioned response. Most habits take days, weeks, or even months to develop. You are setting yourself up for disappointment if you think your dog has a reliable behavior when he does something two or three times. Help yourself and your dog by giving good habits time to develop. When you do so, training will be a much more positive experience for both of you.

Timing

Timing is probably the most important factor in how fast the dog learns something. What I mean by timing is this: Let's say that your dog put his nose on the hot oven door. A few moments later he walked into the family room, looked at the TV, and *then* felt the burning sensation on his nose. He would associate the burning sensation with the TV. Because of the lapse in time, he would never in a million years associate the disagreeble experience of his burned nose with the oven door.

Timing is vital when teaching your puppy the rules around your house, such as not to chew the rug. For example, say you walk into the living room five minutes after the puppy has finished chewing the rug. You find him sleeping in the corner and drag him over to the rug. You point to the rug and scold him. Your correction is too late. Your pup will never figure out that the disagreeable experience he is having *now* has anything to do with what he did five minutes before.

Correcting a dog more than a few seconds after he does a behavior is too late. He will no longer associate your correction with his previous deed. Of course, if you come into the room even many hours later ranting like a maniac, your dog is going to cower and act apprehensive. Do not misinterpret apprehension for "guilt" (See Chapter 10, "Guilty or Not Guilty.") To help your dog learn rapidly and efficiently, it is up to *you* to develop good timing.

So what is good timing? Good timing is correcting or praising your dog as he is *thinking* about doing a behavior. That's the best way to get a dog to associate your correction or praise with the behavior you are trying to influence. You do not have to be a doggie mind reader to know what your dog is thinking. Canines are open, honest creatures. Everything they are about to do is written all over their faces.

The ability to anticipate a dog's next move is called "reading the dog." It's not as hard as it may sound. The more time you spend with your dog, the better you will become at "reading" him. Imagine this scenario: You are expecting company and put out a plate of cheese

The ideal time to correct a dog is when he is *thinking* about doing an unwanted behavior.

The next best time to correct a dog is just as he is in the act of doing something wrong.

The worst time to correct is when you arrive on the scene and find that the deed has been done.

and crackers on the coffee table. Your dog looks at the cheese and takes a few steps toward the table. *Now* is the time to tell him "NHAA." Chances are good that he was thinking about taking the cheese. Well-timed corrections will teach your pet to avoid stealing food.

The next best time to correct your dog is just as he is doing the unwanted behavior. Using our example, this means a tough "NHAA" just as the dog's mouth is reaching for the cheese. The worst time to correct is ten seconds after the dog has done the unwanted behavior. Yelling at the dog when you discover an empty cheese plate will not effectively teach him to avoid stealing the cheese in the first place.

As an owner, it is very simple to shape your dog's behavior if you closely watch your pet and ask yourself "Is this a behavior that I want my dog to do for the rest of his life?" If the answer is yes, then find a way to cause the dog to repeat the behavior. If the answer is no, then do not let the dog repeat the unwanted behavior. You can shape canine behavior most effectively by observing your dog!

Canine Thinking

Dogs have active brains and can think about their actions. In fact, their ability to think never ceases to amaze me. I have witnessed many, many examples of canine behavior that have me convinced that dogs think and reason. I don't believe they have the same mental skills as humans, but I know that something is going on inside their heads. Consider these two stories.

Byron is a black Lab who loves squeaky toys, natural bones, tennis balls, et cetera. Even at age seven he loves a good game of fetch or a good chew with one of his toys, which are kept in a big basket on the family room floor. Many times he walks over to the basket and begins rooting around for a while. He is clearly after something in particular. One time it may be the squeaky gorilla, another time the new orange tennis ball, another time a natural bone. What amazes me most is that when he wants the gorilla, he doesn't want the squeaky turtle or squeaky pig. He doesn't want the old frayed tennis balls when he is after the new one. And most noticeable of all (because all the hard, white natural bones look alike to me), he roots around for many minutes going after the particular bone that he is in the mood to chew.

Now some sort of thinking was going on when he decided to walk over to the toy basket. And he certainly had something in mind by fishing around in the basket until he found what he was looking for. What were his actual thoughts? We will never know. If I had three wishes, one of them would be to be a dog for one day so that I *really* knew what was going on in their heads.* Their actions certainly show that thinking of some sort is taking place.

Now consider this story: My dog Drifter loves to raid my cat's food dish. As a puppy Drifter would attempt many times to get into the cat dish. I would growl *"NHAA."* The first couple times Drifter ignored my correction, so I accompanied a louder, stronger *"NNNHHAAA"* with a

---

*Just to be clear about this statement, being a dog for a day would be third on my list of three wishes. Hitting the lottery and living on a tropical island would be first and second!

firm shake at the scruff of his neck. After a couple of these corrections Drifter avoided the cat dish . . . when I was standing nearby. When I was not in the room, Drifter repeatedly raided the dish. After not being able to think of an effective way to correct my little gremlin humanely when I was not in the room, I decided to alter the environment.

I lived at the time in a split-level house, so I moved the cat's dining quarters to the downstairs family room. I would keep the door between the two levels closed. When the cat wanted to eat he would tell me by meowing at the door. When he wanted to come back upstairs he would scratch at the door. Until I was conditioned to keep that family room door closed, Drifter would slip down the stairs and steal cat food. It took me about a week to remember consistently to close the door. The system seemed to work fine—for a while.

At the bottom of the family-room stairs, to the left, was a laundry room. Many times while doing laundry, I would happen to look over my shoulder to see Drifter virtually tiptoeing down the stairs trying to sneak by me. When he noticed that I was aware of him, he would turn and bolt up the stairs. On other occasions I would return upstairs after doing laundry and look around for my lovable pup. I would call his name, "Drifter! Oh, Drifter!" and get no response. My sneaky little couch coyote had snuck by me and gotten to the cat food. He was now trapped downstairs behind the closed family room door.

I believe that Drifter's actions entailed more than rote conditioning. There was a thought process going on. However, unlike humans, canines are not capable of projecting thought into the future. *This is an important distinction.* I do not believe that Drifter woke up in the morning and thought to himself, "Oh, boy, it's Friday. Laundry day! This afternoon when the pack leader is doing laundry, I think I'll raid the cat food." But when the opportunity arose, *that's* when Drifter's wheels began to turn. Keep in mind that canines are the world's greatest opportunists.

That fact is important to remember when you try to teach your dog the rules around the house. Your dog is incapable of thinking "I better not chew this rug now because in two hours Mom will be home and I will be corrected." A dog will learn to avoid doing a behavior only if the action he is doing is unpleasant *as he is doing it.*

On the other hand, dogs have great memories. A disagreeable experience in the past can have a strong influence on the dog's behavior in the future. He will remember that yesterday, when he sniffed a strange cat and received a painful scratch, it was very disagreeable. He will probably avoid doing it again.

A dog also may continue to do a behavior that only *appears* to us to have a disagreeable result. It is important to analyze the behavior closely and see what the dog is gaining through his actions. A dog may continue to chase porcupines even after repeatedly being quilled in the nose. The dog's apparent pain may make us wonder why he does not learn to avoid this behavior. If the hunt, chase, and pounce behaviors are more agreeable to the dog than the quills in the nose are *disagreeable*, he will continue porcupine chasing. Dogs will always choose what is most agreeable—to them.

Dogs have no "moral code" of right and wrong, as humans do. Humans know that it is wrong to kill, steal, lie, and so on. We know that it is right to help a friend, care for the sick, pay off a loan. Dogs do not know that it is "wrong" to urinate on your Oriental rug or eat the cat's food. Dogs do not know that it is "right" to sit on command or come when called. All they know is that if something tastes good, smells good, or feels good *as they are doing it,* then it is okay to do it again. If something tastes bad, smells bad, or feels bad *as they are doing it,* then it is something to avoid. This is the canine "moral code" of behavior. The only way for you to shape your dog's behavior (that is, train him) is to make a behavior agreeable (through praise) or disagreeable (through correction) *as he is doing the behavior.*

A Perfect Dog?

As discussed previously, canine learning is based largely on repetition. When a behavior is repeated enough times, dogs develop habits, or conditioned responses. Assuming that those habits are positive ones—such as eliminating outside, coming when called, lying down and staying when told, and others—you will have what you want: a trained dog. That's because dogs are creatures of habit. Once you set up a routine of various signals and conditioned responses (sit, down, stay), the dog will do *exactly* what you tell him every time. Right? Wrong.

No conditioned response is infallible. Creatures with advanced brains can think. They can defy conditioning. They also can make mistakes. Think about two of your own conditioned responses. You have a habit of answering the telephone when it rings, but one day you decide not to take any calls. The telephone rings but you keep reading your book. You know what you usually do, but today you decide not to do it. You also have a habit of stopping your car at a red light. But one day you are tired or distracted and you roll through an intersection. Even the most experienced drivers sometimes make mistakes.

Similarily, there will be times when even the best-trained dog will either defy conditioning or make a mistake. Therefore you must avoid becoming complacent or overconfident about learned behavior. Do not rely on conditioned responses in potentially dangerous situations. For example, I would never unleash even the best-trained dog near a busy road. One mistake could result in injury or death to my dog.

Owners need to reinforce their dog's conditioned responses. Certainly the more practice and proofing you do with a dog, the more reliable his response will be. Skilled human beings, from tennis pros to typists, need practice to stay in top form. This is because all learned skills need reinforcement.

When you feel you have achieved a well-trained dog, continue to practice obedience exercises once in a while. It can be fun for both you and the dog. Plus it reinforces the good behaviors you worked so hard to achieve. When you need to call on those skills in real situations, such as doing a stand-stay at the veterinarian's office, you will be more confident that your dog will comply. Your dog will be more confident by doing something that is familiar—and for which he can earn your praise.

Four

Developmental Stages: Puppyhood to Old Age

Puppies experience developmental stages as they mature in much the same way that human children do. In some ways, the stages they experience are very similar. As you read this chapter, you will begin to realize how many similarities in development that humans and canines have.

Although the parallels between puppies and children are interesting and educational, these parallels are not comparisons in intelligence. They are comparisons of maturity levels. Children will be able to do a multitude of things at a comparable maturity level that a dog will never be able to do. These include reading, writing, and speaking. If you keep this perspective in mind, you will find the parallels between puppies and children quite enlightening.

"You Have to Live Through Puppyhood"

Child rearing takes time and effort. Some parents do a wonderful job. But regardless of the skills good parents possess, there is no way for them to bypass their child's developmental stages. There is no way to get a two-year-old child to behave like a five-year-old. There is no way that a twelve-year-old child can have the life experience and mature behavior of a twenty-one-year-old. Still, good parents do not ignore their children, waiting for them to reach adulthood. Rather, these parents begin teaching their children as toddlers so that by the time they become adults, they have good habits formed. Only time and supervision on the part of the parents will turn children into mature, respectful, well-mannered adults.

This fact is also true of puppies. The ideal time for owners to begin training their puppy is at seven weeks old. Yet no type or amount of training will turn the pup into a mature, well-behaved adult dog instantly. To achieve this, time and consistent training on the part of the owner are required.

I receive phone calls on a regular basis from highly frustrated puppy owners. The usual conversation goes something like this: "I took Rover to kindergarten puppy class when he was ten weeks old. I work with him almost every day. Now he's five-and-a-half months old, but he still has a ton of energy. He doesn't always listen and he won't respond to commands consistently."

My answer is always the same: "Of course he has lots of energy; he's a puppy! Responding consistently to commands means that the dog has good habits formed. It means that when the dog hears a command he reacts with a conditioned response. Your puppy is only five-and-a-half months old! He has not been on earth long enough to have formed any strong habits or conditioned responses."

Owners *have* to live through puppyhood. There is no way to circumvent a dog's developmental stages. Two key ingredients go into creating a well-trained dog. One is allowing the puppy to grow up. The other is working to develop reliable conditioned responses through consistent repetition. Although living through puppyhood can at times be trying, being aware of a dog's developmental stages can ease some of the frustration. What follows is a brief description of what you can expect at each stage.

Birth to Three Weeks Old

The first developmental stage in your dog's life begins at birth and lasts until the puppy is three weeks old. During this period the puppy is incapable of any learned behavior. The puppy's major functions are nursing, sleeping, and eliminating. Mother dog takes care of all the puppy's needs. Between ten and fourteen days, the puppy's eyes and ears begin to function. Although the eyes and ears are open at this point, sight and hearing are limited.

Three Weeks to Seven Weeks Old

A significant developmental stage occurs between the ages of three and seven weeks old. After three weeks of age, puppies' eyesight and hearing strengthen daily. Puppies start to crawl around. They start to become aware of their environment.

Most significant at this stage is the puppy's ability to learn. The experiences and learned behaviors acquired now will influence the puppy's future life. During this stage puppies learn the rules of how to fit into a pack. Although it is instinctive for dogs to be pack animals, the rules of fitting into the pack are learned behaviors.

Canine pack rules are learned through interactions among the puppy, its litter mates, and the mother dog. During this stage puppies wrestle and chew on each other. They experiment with being assertive and submissive. By the seventh week, experienced dog breeders can recognize a hierarchy among their puppies. The breeder can point to the puppies in a litter and tell you where each one fits in. Although the role may vary from day to day, the breeder can tell you who is the puppy pack leader. That particular puppy growls the toughest and bites the most. He or she is always first in line to eat and bosses litter mates around much of the time.

I once asked a friend, who is an excellent, experienced breeder of Labrador retrievers, which sex is most often the puppy pack leader. She said that it is either the biggest male or the female with the biggest mouth! Regardless of who the puppy pack leader is, the mother dog is the undisputed pack leader. She doles out discipline to the entire pack.

It is here, with mother dog and young litter mates, that puppies learn the give and take of pack life. Puppies learn that when they encounter another puppy who displays signs of dominance, they should submit. When they encounter submissive puppies, they can push these creatures around and dominate them.

Seven Weeks to Six Months Old

Seven weeks of age is the ideal time for the puppy to leave the litter and come to live in your home. Because the puppy thinks that he is the same kind of creature as you, he will view your family as his brand-new pack. He will use the same techniques that he learned in his first pack experience with his new human pack. He will do this to determine where he fits into the hierarchy of your household. This is the time for you to begin establishing yourself as your puppy's new pack leader. Success with obedience training depends on it. (See Chapter 6, "Pack Leader.")

The seven-week-old puppy's maturity level is comparable to that of a human infant. Your seven-week-old puppy will be very dependent on you. For example, when you take the pup out for a short walk in the woods, he will stay right by you. If he is particularly bold, he may stray a short distance away. By simply squatting down, clapping your hands, and making appealing sounds, you will cause even the bravest young puppy to run back to you quickly. Sticking close to pack members is instinctive at this stage of puppies' lives.

Like children, puppies become more and more independent as time goes on. With puppies this happens very quickly. The independence phase begins at around four months old. Some behaviorists refer to this period as the flight instinct period. I call it the "Terrible Twos of Doggiedom."

A statement I hear from puppy owners at this time is "My puppy was so good. I used to let him out in the backyard and he never left. Now when I let him out he takes off and I find him down the street in my neighbor's yard. Why is he doing this?"

Up until about four months old, it is instinctive for puppies to stick close to the den, which is your house. Then suddenly the big, scary world is not so scary. The puppy picks up a scent and off he goes. Greater supervision is *imperative* during this phase. Do not let bad and

That blur is a puppy! Puppy crazies, or "the zooms," are a normal part of growing up.

dangerous behaviors, such as leaving the yard, develop into habits.

Before puppies reach four months old, they do very little destructive chewing. However, at about four months puppy teeth begin to fall out and adult teeth start to come in. This is when unwanted chewing becomes more frequent. Puppies want to get into everything at this stage. You will need to watch your puppy very closely in the house. Supervision at this time is also important to continue the housebreaking process. (See Chapter 22, "Dealing with Housebreaking and Unwanted Chewing.")

The ideal time to begin formal obedience training is four months old. Training will begin to give you control mechanisms and allow you to shape your dog's behavior. Both are necessary for you to cope effectively with the independence phase. (However, it's never too late. If you adopt an older dog, begin training right away.)

Another behavior that develops at around four months old is what I call the "puppy crazies." I have heard other dog people refer to it as the "zooms." The puppy may run around in circles, over furniture, under tables, around trees, up and down the yard, and so on. This may be accompanied by growling. The fur on the puppy's back may bristle. The tail may be tucked between the legs. The puppy may shake or toss his toys. Owners seeing this behavior for the first time think their puppies are possessed. Do not despair; this is normal puppy exuberance. Unless a puppy is knocking the house down in the process of the puppy crazies, I stand back and let him do it. Actually, it's a lot of fun to watch. Your dog is having a great time. Do not try to inhibit this behavior. As puppies grow up the frequency of this behavior decreases.

Six Months Old to One Year Old

Six-month-old puppies are about as mature as five- or six-year-old children. These older puppies have a *lot* of energy. The more you can tire them out physically, the easier they are to live with. At this age when you growl *"NHAA,"* you must be able to get their attention.

At six months old, all the puppy teeth have fallen out and all the adult teeth are in. However, dogs at this stage still have a strong compulsion to chew, because the adult teeth are shifting and settling into the jaws. Close supervision should continue through this stage. Be sure to provide the dog with acceptable objects to chew. (An old shoe or glove are not acceptable objects—unless you don't mind a new

Puppies will chew on anything. You must supervise at all times.

shoe or glove being chewed. Dogs don't know the difference.) By one year old, the dog's adult teeth will be in their permanent positions, and chewing will slow down considerably. Unwanted chewing *may* continue if you have allowed it to develop into a bad habit.

The dog matures quickly between the ages of six months and one year. Daily obedience training sessions are imperative at this time. As I mentioned, dogs form habits by repeating behaviors consistently. The behaviors that you want your dog to respond to reliably as an adult must be reinforced at this stage.

One Year to Two Years Old

The year-old dog has the maturity level of a thirteen-year-old human. Dogs at this age are calmer and easier to live with than six-month-old pups. At last, you do not have to supervise your dog's every move.

Although dogs are considerably more mature at a year old, they still have their moments. They are teenagers! They still want to spend time playing. A case of the puppy crazies is not uncommon. Plenty of exercise and daily training sessions bring out the best behavior in the "teenage" adolescent dog.

Most dogs' adult personalities are fully developed at about two years. Like humans, however, individuals grow up at different rates of speed. In fact, some particular breeds, such as the Bichon Frise and poodle, tend to be slower to mature than others.

At two years old, subtle behaviors that the puppy had previously displayed can become pronounced. To the dog owner with an untrained eye, some of the undesirable behaviors that the two-year-old dog is exhibiting may seem to have appeared out of nowhere.

An example of this is a two-year-old dog who suddenly bites the family's teenage son as the boy was simply trying to remove the dog from the sofa. The bewildered owners call me, giving me the famous line: "He never did anything like that before." After interrogating the owners, I find out that the dog frequently mouthed their arms and hands. "But he was just playing," the owners explain. I then learn that in the past the dog growled whenever they tried to clip his toenails. "That's because he doesn't like his feet touched," they say in his defense. "Did he ever bite before?" I ask. "Well, he did snap a couple of times when we tried to take his rawhide bones away. But he didn't actually bite. We stopped giving him rawhide bones, so it hasn't been a problem."

The experienced dog trainer would have noticed that this dog exhibited all the signs that he would have a biting problem as an adult. In general, there are *always* subtle clues throughout puppyhood indicating potential behavioral problems in the adult dog. These behaviors are simply not as pronounced as they will be once the dog's adult personality is achieved. It is up to the owners to put a stop to undesirable puppy behavior so that they do not have a problem on their hands in the adult dog.

Two Years Old and Beyond

I do not believe the cliché that you can't teach an old dog new tricks. There is no age at which a dog's brain shuts down and becomes incapable of absorbing information. However, training is more difficult once a dog attains his adult personality at about two years old. Training is extremely difficult (if not impossible) if the adult dog has achieved the status of pack leader within the family (See Chapter 6, "Pack Leader.")

Although you can teach your older dog new tricks, you will have a tougher time extinguishing his bad habits. Dogs are very routine-oriented creatures. Once they develop a behavioral pattern, it becomes ingrained in them. Follow this rule of thumb to extinguish an unwanted behavior: First, find a way to stop the dog from repeating the behavior. Second, substitute the unwanted behavior with a desirable behavior. Third, the dog must repeat the new, desirable behavior for the same length of time as the old behavior existed.

When Is the Ideal Time to Begin Teaching My Dog?

Behaviorists have determined that the optimum learning period in a canine's life is between the age of seven and sixteen weeks. This means that by the time your seven-week-old puppy arrives in your home, he is ready and eager to learn. The major thing the pup is lacking is experience, which he gains on a daily basis.

If your dog was a wild canine, such as a wolf, he would start following adult pack members into the woods during this phase in his life to learn behaviors essential to survival. For example, he would learn to avoid porcupines and poisonous snakes and to trail rabbits. It is *instinctive* to follow direction at this point in a canine's life.

The same is true of your domestic dog. He is going to learn during this period, whether you supervise what he learns or whether he learns haphazardly on his own.

Unfortunately, many trainers, breeders, and veterinarians still recommend waiting until a dog is six months old to begin obedience training. By the time puppies reach this age, the instinctive, optimum learning period has passed, and canines are in a phase in which they begin to assert their independence.

In the wild, six-month-old wolf pups begin wandering off with litter mates to explore their environment without adult supervision. Domestic puppies of this age become less and less dependent on the security and safety of the den (your home) and on the guidance of adult pack members (you and your family).

In addition, by allowing six months or more to pass before your dog's training begins, you run the risk of letting unwanted behaviors, such as chewing furniture and jumping on people, develop into bad habits.

Clearly, it is to your advantage to start obedience training early— even if it is the informal training for very young puppies described in Chapter 7, "Before Formal Training Begins."

For example, let's say you have a dog who chews the rug every time you leave him alone. The dog has been doing this behavior for three years. In order to stop him from chewing the rug, you now crate the dog when you leave the house for periods of up to four hours. (If you must be away for a longer time you must arrange for someone to let the dog out. Failure to do so constitutes misuse of the crate.) By doing this you have found a way to abort the rug-chewing behavior. While in the crate the dog has two options: chew on the toys that you put in the crate with him or curl up and go to sleep. These choices are the new substitute behaviors to take the place of chewing the rug.

Theoretically, it will take three years (equal time) of repeating the new behaviors before you can leave the dog unsupervised without him chewing the rug. But theory is not always reality. The reconditioning process may be shorter or longer than the "equal-time" rule. However, I do not believe it is ever possible to erase completely a learned behavior from the dog's brain. At its best, reconditioning will only diminish the unwanted behavior. Once a habit is formed, the dog may revert back to it at some point. Needless to say, therefore, training is more effective while the dog is young, before you must overcome bad habits.

Brucie is a canine senior citizen who loves learning new tricks. No dog who respects you as the pack leader is too old to train.

Old Age

Different breeds of dogs have different life spans. Veterinarians see toy poodles who are eighteen years old. Great Danes and other giant breeds sometimes live only eight years. The average life span of most dogs is around fourteen years.

As dogs age beyond five years, the changes that occur are more physical than mental. You start to see graying around the muzzle. Older dogs sleep more. Although many dogs enjoy playing throughout most of their lives, the urge to play is less frequent. Puppy crazies occur only rarely.

Older dogs may develop arthritic problems. You will notice the dogs are stiff after a nap. If they are not feeling well, they may not have the same sweet personality they had most of their lives. Some dogs may become grumpy and grouchy as they age. In extreme old age dogs may become senile. I had a friend with a seventeen-year-old poodle who would go out in the backyard to eliminate and forget where she was. My friend would have to go out and show her the way to the back door.

In short, old dogs require the same extra care and understanding that we give to the humans we love when they reach this phase of life.

Five

Canine Personality Types: Their Effects on Trainability

As with humans, canines have many different types of personalities. If you have met more than a few dogs in your life, you may have observed different personality characteristics in the individual dogs. Your approach to training your own dog should be influenced by his personality traits. Your success will depend on interpreting those traits correctly.

Three basic components make up every dog's personality. Think of the components as spectrums. At the opposite ends of each spectrum are the extremes of personality traits. In between are varying degrees of those traits.

The first component has to do with a dog's confidence. The spectrum for this trait ranges from the extroverted, outgoing dog to the shy, fearful creature. An extrovert may greet you by jumping all over you, trying to lick your face, and demanding "Pet me! Pet Me!" A shy dog may run and hide under an end table the instant you enter the house. He may stay there shivering and shaking as if the world were ending. Sometimes this type of dog may growl or bark in distress. These are the extremes. As in any spectrum, dogs exhibit varying degrees of these traits.

The second component has to do with canine dominance. The spectrum ranges from the very dominant dog to the very submissive one. When you meet some dogs you may notice their dominant body posture. They may greet you by confronting you straight on, staring right

Sneakers is an extrovert who greets his friends with great enthusiasm!

Joshua, on the right, uses body motion to communicate his dominance. Bentley submissively greets him.

at you with hackles raised. Their tails will be held high and their ears tipped forward. Other dogs may greet you by urinating submissively. They instantly roll on their backs, belly up. Again, these are the extremes. Different individuals exhibit varying degrees of dominance or submission.

The third personality component has to do with pain tolerance. Some dogs are very insensitive to pain. They may happily swim in the cold Atlantic waters of New England in January. Other dogs are very sensitive to pain and will learn quickly to avoid situations that cause it. They may balk at going outside to relieve themselves on a frosty morning.

As with the other two components, many dogs' pain tolerance falls between these two extremes.

Interestingly, the three personality components are independent of each other. For example, a shy individual does not necessarily have to be submissive and pain sensitive. An outgoing dog is not necessarily dominant and pain *insensitive*. There are as many combinations of these components and their varying degrees as there are rolls of the dice.

Size of the dog is not a factor. I have met great Danes who are shy, dominant, and pain sensitive. I have met Jack Russell terriers who are pain insensitive, outgoing, and submissive. I have also met the opposite combinations in each of these breeds.

If there is any way to predict which combination of traits a dog may have, it is to consider the dog's selective breeding. In my experience it seems as if more Labrador retrievers, for example, have high pain thresholds than not. It appears to me that the majority of greyhounds are pain sensitive. The effects of selective breeding come through in these areas. I have found that huskies appear to be a more dominant breed than golden retrievers. Many of the herding breeds seem to have tendencies toward shyness.

Although many of these traits seem breed specific, there are degrees of these traits within every breed. There are even differences within litters of specific breeds. And there are also complete exceptions to the rule. I have met extremely submissive huskies and pain-insensitive greyhounds.

Personality and Training

When training a dog, it is imperative to determine which combination of personality traits the dog possesses. This is important for a number of reasons. First, it will give you an indication of how your dog will respond to training. Second, it will let you develop and employ the proper attitude and demeanor while carrying out exercises. Third, this knowledge will help you determine what training equipment will enhance your success.

For example, when teaching the dog to lie down and stay (called the "down-stay"), you will get different reactions from dogs with different personalities. A dominant dog will resist this exercise because lying down is a dog's most submissive body posture. A submissive dog will do this exercise much more readily. (This creature spends much of his time on his back in the submissive down position any-way.) The extrovert will want to break the down-stay to greet every person who enters the room. The shy dog may *also* want to break the down-stay when someone enters the room . . . to go hide under the end table.

When the dog does break the down-stay, you may be able to correct the pain-sensitive dog physically with only one shake on the scruff of the neck. This will convince him not to break the stay. You may have to repeat this correction several times to convince the pain-*insensitive* dog that he must not move. If this dog doesn't deem a shake on the scruff of the neck disagreeable, you may have to employ a correction that is—perhaps a bite on the muzzle or a jerk-and-release on the training collar. (See Chapter 9, "Rewards and Corrections.")

During obedience training, your dog's personality should also dictate your demeanor and body posture. A firm, even-toned *"NHAA"* may convince your submissive dog to abort movement and remain in the down-stay. You may be able to deliver this *"NHAA"* while sitting in your easy chair and still get a good response from the dog. On the other hand, you may have to remain standing, hovering over your dominant dog while growling a harsh, threatening *"NHAA"* to convince this guy of what you want. Your voice alone may not do the trick and you may have to accompany your *"NHAA"* with the noise of a shake can.

The personality of the dog you are training should determine the training equipment you choose. For example, when teaching controlled walking you may find that an extremely pain-sensitive and submissive dog will respond to the exercise in order to avoid jerks on a buckle collar. A dog who is moderately pain sensitive but has tendencies toward being dominant may require the jerk and release of a metal training collar to achieve the same results. A highly pain-insensitive dog may require a pinch collar before he will respond to the controlled walking exercise. (See Chapter 8, "Training Tools.")

Before you even begin teaching obedience exercises, stop and think about what type of dog you are dealing with. A shy or submissive dog must never be brutalized with a tough or intimidating approach. Gentle but firm consistency is what is needed to be successful with such a dog. The extrovert requires your constant attention during training. You must be a step ahead of such a dog, or he will be off doing something else very quickly. A dominant dog will test you repeatedly. Be prepared to assert yourself at the first sign of a challenge.

Unfortunately, even some so-called experienced trainers are not

Casey is very willing to please, an ideal trait for trainability.

aware of the three components that make up a dog's personality. Thus they often take the wrong approach when training a particular dog. Dogs are individuals, each with his own special personality and idiosyncrasy, and should be handled and trained accordingly.

What Is the Ideal Trainable Dog?

The ideal dog personality is a subjective concept. A canine personality that is well suited for one situation might be ill suited for another. For example, an aggressive, physically tough dog may not be a good family pet. However, under the right set of circumstances, aggression and physical toughness can be an asset. An individual with these traits may make an ideal military security dog.

The traits required to do various canine jobs—such as guarding, retrieving, or herding—are not necessarily those needed to be a good family pet. This book is written for pet owners. They are typically people who have families, jobs, and live in neighborhoods. They want a happy, responsive, well-behaved canine companion. Although the list is still somewhat subjective, there *are* traits that make some dogs easier to train as a family dog. The ideal family dog is friendly and outgoing (leans toward being an extrovert), willing to please (on the submissive side), and does not require numerous corrections (moderately pain sensitive). If you are reading this book before getting a dog, use these guidelines to select your new puppy.

Six

Pack Leader

In order to train your dog successfully, you must first learn to teach him on a canine level. He cannot learn on a human level. Your dog is first a canine (a group that includes wolves, coyotes, and dingoes), second a domestic dog, third a breed or mix of breeds, and fourth—your lovable pet. By understanding these important distinctions, owners can improve their success in training their dog. What makes a dog capable of following direction from a human being is the instinct to follow a pack leader.

Because your dog is a canine, he has the same instincts, reflexes and behaviors as his wild cousins. In the wild, canines such as wolves live in packs. They interact with each other in a cooperative manner to find food and shelter and to raise their young. This is an extremely successful arrangement that helps each member of the pack survive. Among the pack members is a pack leader and a hierarchy of followers. The most dominate individual in the pack is the leader—usually a large, older male. The rest of the pack's hierarchy is also determined by dominance—and by the submission of individuals lower in the pack order. Each individual holds a particular place in the pack.

To the puppy, your family is his new pack. In fact, it is his second pack experience. His first was with his mother and litter mates where he learned the behaviors necessary to adapt to pack life. In his first pack experience, his mother was the most dominant pack member— the pack leader. Each puppy maintained a position in the hierarchy.

The biggest, toughest, and loudest puppy who did the most growling and biting became "top pup." The more submissive puppy, who accepted being bitten and growled at, assumed a lower rank in the pack. Each puppy's place was determined by how dominant or submissive it was.

When your puppy arrives in your home, he instinctively will seek a position in his new pack. I am not sure if puppies think that they are human or that people are canines, but I am convinced that puppies think people are exactly the same thing they are. If allowed to do whatever he wants, your puppy will naturally assume the role of pack leader. By the time your dog is eighteen months to two years old, he will have developed his full adult personality. If he reaches this age assuming he is the pack leader, you may have behavior problems— and an extremely difficult time training him. He will probably resist training in much the same manner that an old wolf defends his position from a young challenger—by growling and biting. It is *much easier* to convince a puppy or a young dog that you are his leader while he is initially looking for a position in the pack than it is after he has already assumed one.

How large a pack leadership problem you have with your dog is largely determined by two factors: (1) how dominant your dog's personality is and (2) how assertive you are as an individual. If you are naturally an assertive person and your dog is submissive by nature, you may never experience a leadership problem. If you have a dominant dog and you are inconsistent, extremely indulgent, and a nondisciplinarian, you may have a big problem convincing your dog that you are the pack leader. He will by nature assert his dominance and walk all over you.

You can avoid or overcome this problem if you are willing to make a dedicated effort to learn the proper techniques to gain leadership. If you are incapable or unwilling to provide the leadership that the dog needs, do your dog a favor—find him a good home and buy yourself an aquarium! If you learn to be firm and consistent as well as loving and fair, your dog will accept you as his pack leader. No one can undo your leadership role by telling your dog that you are really an old softy and that he does not have to listen to you. The way your dog responds to you correlates directly with the way you interact with him.

From personal experience in training dogs for other people, I have found that many dogs will accept me as their pack leader. This is because I have communicated to the dogs by my voice tones and actions that I am in charge. However, when each dog goes home he will still test his owners to see where he stands with them. Unless the owner has taken the time to learn proper dog-handling techniques, the dog will probably misbehave just as much as he did before training. This is because dogs cannot be programmed like robots or computers! A dog will respond to each person according to how that person presents himself or herself to the dog.

It is for this reason, as I have mentioned, that I believe the best form of obedience training is teaching *owners* to handle and train their own dogs properly. This accomplishes two important objectives: (1) the owner asserts his or her dominance by compelling the dog to carry out behaviors; and at the same time, (2) the dog learns useful obedience exercises and behaviors that make him a more enjoyable part of the family. Through this approach, your dog easily learns to accept *you* as his pack leader.

Your dog will not respond to everyone in your family in the same way. The person who spends the most time training the dog and is the most consistent with him will get the best results. This does not mean, of course, that a six-year-old child can get the same degree of obedience from your dog as the adults in the family do. Small children cannot convince most dogs that they are more dominant members of the pack. (This is also why school-age children should not be given the primary responsibility of training the family's dog. Training is a job for teenagers or adults.)

If you, as the trainer, make a strong effort to be consistent with your dog's training—even though your spouse or children may not—your dog *will* learn to listen to you. He will probably not pay very much attention to commands from others. Once your dog is properly trained, be reassured that no one can undo the training you have achieved.

In order to assert your dominance, you do not need to be mean or cruel. If you hit or kick your dog, he will learn that you are stronger and more dominant than he, but he will also learn to fear and distrust you. Firmness combined with consistency is very important in establishing pack leadership. Canine pack leaders are always consistent, and unless ill or dying, they always defend their leadership position. Pack followers always know what to expect from their leader. Any inconsistency you exhibit is viewed as a sign of weakness by your dog— that you are not firm in your position as pack leader. If you show weakness, your dog *will* test you.

However, obedience training is not all force and dominance. Canine pack leaders also show affection toward their followers. They play with subordinates, groom and lick them, and sleep close to them. This is why it is very important to pet and praise your dog. Once you have convinced him that he must obey you, you also must show him that you love him—and that his obedient behavior is pleasing to you. Praise reinforces good behavior and is an essential part of successful dog training.

Your dog will never resent you for being his pack leader. In fact, he will love and respect you more—just as the pack leader in the wild is the most respected member of the pack. Your dog will clearly understand his place in the pack (your family) and will readily accept your guidance and instruction.

More than anything else, proper obedience training will serve to strengthen the bond between you and your dog. This is because a dog is much happier and more secure when he is treated as a canine rather than as a human. Some of the most confused and unhappy dogs are those who are trained from an anthropomorphic, or human, point of view. (See Chapter 10, "Guilty or Not Guilty.") And their owners are some of the most frustrated people who have ever owned a dog.

DRIFTER

Part Two

Training Fundamentals

Seven

Before Formal Training Begins

The ideal time to begin training your puppy is the first week you bring him home. By training I do not mean formal training or dog obedience class. I mean training your dog to fit in with his new pack (your family) and learning to behave properly in the den (your home). If you adopt a dog over four months old, you should start right in with formal training. However, the advice in this chapter will still be useful.

One behavior that should start the day the pup comes home is housebreaking. You do not want the pup to have accidents in the house for a week before you begin teaching him where he should go to eliminate. Before you even bring your pup home, choose where you want him to go. Then make sure he uses this spot right from day one. (See Chaper 22, "Dealing with Housebreaking and Unwanted Chewing.")

Teach your puppy his name right from the start. Have a name picked out even before you bring him home. Use his name when you want him to come to you. Squat down, clap your hands, and call out his name enthusiastically, followed by lots of praise as he runs to you. This lays the foundation for come-on-command training later.

Be sure never to use your puppy's name as a reprimand. Hearing his name should always have positive associations for the puppy. Otherwise, he will learn to tune out his name and ignore you when you call him.

Introduction to Leash and Collar

You can introduce your puppy to a leash and collar the first week he comes home. This does not mean controlled walking or heeling. It simply means teaching the puppy to be familiar with the feel of the leash and collar. You do not want the dog to be apprehensive or frightened by their feel when you later begin leashwork.

Begin introducing the leash and collar by putting a lightweight nylon or leather buckle collar on your puppy. At first this will feel foreign to him. He may scratch at it with his hindfoot. He may roll around or shake his head. Help your puppy by distracting him. Play with him if he seems bothered by the collar. If he enjoys retrieving, throw a ball or a squeaky toy. Distraction will take his mind off the new feeling of something around his neck. In a few days or a week he will become accustomed to the feel of the collar.

To introduce your pup to the feel of the leash, simply attach a six-foot leash to his collar. While supervising your pup, let him drag the leash around the house. Be sure it does not get stuck around furniture. Watch him closely. After several days of this, pick up the end of the leash. Follow the pup around. As your puppy becomes proficient with this exercise, repeat the procedure outside.

After a week or so, pick a destination in the yard and go to it. If your pup moves along with you, praise him lavishly. When you reach

Do not try to drag your puppy with the leash.

your destination, squat down and pet and praise your pup. Let him know how wonderful he is for learning a new skill.

If your pup does not follow you, do not praise him in an attempt to coax him. If you do so, you will only be praising him for *not* walking on the leash. Do not drag him along at the end of the leash. All that will accomplish is to create apprehension and fear of the leash.

Instead, to get the puppy to walk while on the leash, hold an object of attraction in one of your hands. This can be a piece of dog cookie or a squeaky toy—anything that your pup finds appealing. Coax your pup along by holding the object in front of his nose as you head toward your destination. As he starts to move along with you, praise him. Repeat this exercise a few times each day. Before long your pup will be accustomed to the feel of the leash attached to his collar.

Do not be concerned if your puppy pulls ahead or lunges on the leash at this stage. When he is no longer intimidated by the feel of the leash, you can begin to teach controlled walking, which is an obedience exercise that eliminates pulling.

Use an object of attraction to induce him along. Praise the puppy as he moves.

Socialization is important. Allow your puppy to meet adult dogs who are tolerant of puppies.

Socialization

Socialization is one of the most important things you can do for a young dog. Puppies should meet people! They should see different things and different places. Stable, well-adjusted adult dogs are those who have had lots of socialization.

Be sure a puppy's new experiences are low impact. If your pup is at all shy, do not force new things on him. Take it slow. Let him make the first move.

Make sure that your dog is protected by vaccinations before you expose him to areas where stray dogs may wander. If you take your puppy to an obedience class or other group situation, be sure that all the dogs in it are required to have vaccinations, including one for kennel cough. Get your veterinarian's advice on when it is appropriate to expose your puppy to the big, wide world.

"NHAA!" (Stop Immediately)

Probably the most important training that you should do when you bring your puppy home is extend what mother dog had already begun teaching him. This is the fact that a growl-like *"NHAA!"* means for your pup to stop doing whatever he is doing immediately.

During the weeks before your pup came home with you, mother dog began teaching him this. Whenever he nursed too vigorously or chewed on mom's ear, she would growl at him. Growling was her way of telling him to stop doing whatever he was doing.

Mother dog would escalate her aggression only if the pup ignored her growl. Her more aggressive disciplines might be snapping at the pup, giving him a nip on the muzzle or grabbing him by the scruff of the neck and giving a gentle shake. She would employ one of these tougher corrections so that the next time she growled, her pup would take heed.

I recommend following mother dog's example. If your puppy ignores your growl-like verbal correction, growl a little louder. Give your pup a gentle shake at the scruff of his neck. (Do not lift more than the dog's front feet off the ground.) You can also try biting him. These are all *natural* corrections. I bite puppies all the time. I do not insist that my students bite their pups, although it does work wonders. It's yet another example of "dog talk." Puppies know exactly what you mean by it. (See Chapter 9, "Rewards and Corrections.")

Success in formal obedience training depends on getting your dog to stop immediately when you growl. Puppyhood is the ideal time to teach this to your dog.

Handling Your Puppy

It is important to get your puppy used to being handled as early as possible. Place your puppy on your lap once or twice a day. Gently roll him over on his back with his head on your chest and his tail pointing toward your knees. If he wiggles and kicks and growls, tell

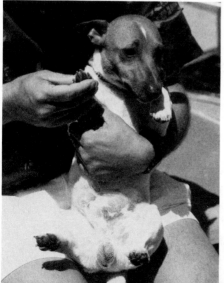

Accustom your puppy to being handled. Touch each toe with a deliberate action. If your puppy wiggles and bites, growl "*NHAA.*" Praise him when he submits.

him *"NHAA"* in a growl-like tone. Be gentle but firm. Do not let him up. Wait until he submits.

Once he settles down, praise him quietly but warmly. After about ten seconds, let him up. Continue to do this every day. Increase the time in which you keep him on his back daily until he will stay there calmly for three minutes.

Once you have accomplished this goal, begin to handle his paws. Handle each toe with deliberate action. Then look into his mouth. Check out his teeth. Gently pull his lips. Look into each ear. If he begins to resist your exam, growl *"NHAA."* It is important that your puppy allow you to do anything that you want with your hands without him biting or having a tantrum. This also teaches him that your hands bring affection and a gentle touch. Never hit your dog.

Accustom your puppy to having things such as rawhide bones or toys taken away from him. If he growls at you when you attempt this, growl back at him, but louder. Periodically take his food dish up and place it back down as he is eating. Do not make him feel threatened or challenged over his food by overdoing this. Do it just once a day during one of his meals for a month or so.

Occasionally take a handful of food from his dish. Let your puppy eat it from your hand. If he growls at you, correct him immediately. There is no excuse for allowing your pup to get away with growling at you. If you allow him to get away with being aggressive toward you at this age, serious behavioral problems will develop by the time he becomes an adult.

Riding in the Car

Some puppies get carsick, just as many small children do. If you depend on a car for most of your transportation, you will want to help your puppy overcome carsickness as quickly and easily as possible.

You can do a number of things to help your puppy avoid or overcome carsickness. From the start, help your puppy form a positive association with the car. Without starting the engine, sit in the car with your puppy on your lap for a few minutes every day. Praise and pet your pup. After a week of this, start the motor. Place your pup on the seat next to you. Pet and praise him, making the experience agreeable.

After a week of repeating this once a day, get a friend or relative to go in the car with you for a daily ride. Be sure that your puppy has an empty stomach and has had the chance to eliminate before getting into the car. Have your helper sit the dog on his or her lap. The helper must not allow the pup to squirm and wiggle around. Take a short ride around the block. Each week increase slightly the distance that you travel. (One-week intervals for each of these steps are not cast in stone. Shorten or lengthen the time depending on your pup's reaction.) Be sure that when you ride with your puppy, you have someone in the car to help control him. If that's not possible, put the puppy in a crate in the car.

Do not let your puppy ride on the driver's lap or crawl under his or her legs. This can become a bad habit and is very dangerous. Once your puppy begins obedience training and understands to lie down and stay, employ this exercise in the car when traveling. Associate trips in the car with fun. Every car ride should not end up at the veterinarian, groomer, or boarding kennel. Use the car to take your dog to the beach, park, or woods.

Most puppies, like most children, outgrow carsickness. In the interim, doing the right things can minimize messes, limit nervousness, and shorten the time it takes for your dog to learn that car rides can be a lot of fun. If none of the above steps seems to help, contact your veterinarian. He or she can provide medical solutions, such as mild tranquilizers, that will help avert sickness when the dog must travel in the car.

Bonding

Bonding is the key to a great relationship with your dog. Bonding means gaining your puppy's love and trust. It's usually easy and is a lot of fun. The formula is simple. Be your pup's buddy. Take him for short romps in the woods or park. Pet him and play with him.

Most puppies are very insecure when they first come home from the breeder. Their entire world has been turned upside down. They are suddenly separated from their mother and their litter mates. You can help overcome some of this insecurity. The ideal place to set up your puppy's crate is in your bedroom. There he will not feel exiled from his pack during the night. In fact, it will help him feel accepted into his new pack. Putting the crate in your bedroom will prevent him crying all night and allow you to hear him whimper if he needs to go outside to eliminate. For the first week plan on getting up at

least once in the middle of the night to take your pup out to eliminate. (See Chapter 22, "Dealing with Housebreaking and Unwanted
Chewing.")

Do not undermine your puppy's growing trust with overly harsh or
badly timed corrections. Trust is essential to bonding and to successful
obedience training. Strive toward convincing your dog that you would
never harm him or put him in a harmful situation. Owners who have
their dog's trust and have formed a close bond with their dog have the
highest potential of training success.

One other very good bonding technique during this period is to
place a piece of kibble or a dog cookie in your mouth. Let the puppy
take it from you. (This is not as bad as it may sound!) This imitates
the regurgitating process that mother dogs do with their puppies.
Remember that mother dog was the ultimate pack leader. Now it's time
for you to assume that role.

Eight

Training Tools

The training tools recommended in this book are designed to make the job of training your dog easier. Without the proper equipment you will have a difficult time mastering the training techniques. Success in training depends on carrying out techniques properly.

The Training Leash

In order to succeed in teaching your dog the exercises in this book, you will need a six-foot-long training leash. The leash should be exactly six feet long. (The only exception would be the very tall handler with a small dog. In this case an eight-foot training leash is acceptable.) Retractable leashes that extend six feet and beyond are *not* acceptable. In training they are cumbersome and ineffective. After your dog fully understands controlled walking and is trained to heel, you can use any kind or length of leash you prefer.

The training leash should be made of cloth or leather. Either will work well. A leather leash is more expensive, but once broken in it is great to work with. For the economy-minded trainer, a cloth leash is fine. Chain leashes should not be used as a training tool. They are not flexible and will hurt your hands when you are doing certain procedures. Nylon leashes are often stiff and do not soften the way a leather

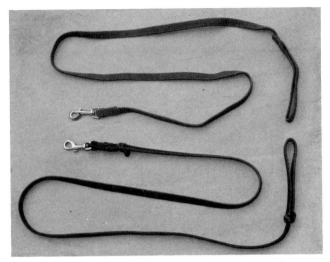

A leather or a cloth six-foot training leash is necessary for training.

or cloth leash will. Nylon leashes also tend to slip and slide when doing the heeling techniques.

The width of the leash you work with is also significant. Proper leash width is subject to two factors. One is the size of the dog. You should not use a wide, heavy leash on a tiny dog. You also should not use a thin, lightweight leash on a large, powerful dog. The other factor to consider is the size of the handler's hands. A person with small hands is not going to feel comfortable with a wide, heavy leash. Someone with large hands will be more at ease with this type of leash.

As with any tool, it is important to keep your leash in top working order. Use saddle soap or leather oil as needed to keep the leather leash from rotting. This will also help soften the leash, making it feel good in your hands. Be careful not to allow a cloth leash to become frayed and worn. It could be dangerous to your dog if the leash snapped when you were near a busy road. Do not allow any type of leash to become knotted, as this will alter its length.

Collars

Three different types of collars are appropriate training tools: a flat or rounded buckle collar, a metal chain training collar, and a small-link pinch collar. Your dog's pain tolerance and how he responds to training will determine which of these collars is best. Some dogs will require all three. Other dogs can become well trained using only one type of collar.

Metal training collars (either medium or heavy gauge), a metal pinch collar, or a buckle collar can be used to train your dog. To succeed you must use the appropriate collar that suits the needs of the dog you are training.

Buckle Collars

I begin all puppies with a buckle collar. It should fit snuggly with just enough room to slide your hand between the collar and the dog's neck. I recommend keeping identification tags off puppies under six months old. Young puppies seem to get into some of the strangest places. A tag could easily get hooked on something. Tags also can prove hazardous in your puppy's crate if they catch on or between the wire bars.

Once your dog is over six months old, use a buckle collar to carry identification and rabies tags. Until then this collar will serve mainly as a device to accustom your puppy to the feel of a collar. (See Chapter 7, "Before Formal Training Begins.") When you begin teaching your dog the exercise called controlled walking, you will be able to determine if the buckle collar will be a sufficient training tool. If your dog is pain sensitive, he will try to avoid corrections while wearing just the buckle collar. You will not need to use a metal training collar on an extremely pain-sensitive dog.

Training Collars

A metal training collar is a straight chain with a ring on each end. There should be no extra hooks or clips attached to it. It should be made from steel, not aluminum. Aluminum training collars have a tendency to bend and also do not release well. Nylon training collars are also not good training tools, as they do not release as smoothly as properly fitted metal collars.

Metal training collars are sold in four different link sizes—fine, medium, heavy, and extra heavy. Use only medium or heavy. The fine links are somewhat sharp-edged and can hurt your dog's neck. The extra-heavy version has thick, wide links that prevent the collar from releasing smoothly. If you have a small or medium-sized dog, go with a medium-link training collar. If you have a large or giant breed, a heavy-link collar is for you.

Training collars are sometimes referred to as choke collars, a name that is incorrect and misleading. A training collar should never be used to choke a dog in an attempt to teach a behavior. No one—animal or human—learns anything when being choked, except to fear and distrust the individual doing the choking. The only time I advocate allowing a training collar to tighten and constrict around the dog's neck is if the dog is attempting a full-fledged, vicious attack on the trainer. In this circumstance, the trainer is using the choking procedure in a self-defense technique called "stringing the dog up." It can—and should—frighten and intimidate a dog into avoiding a future attack.

Personally, I would prefer to humanely euthanize a dog with dangerous aggression problems rather than to subject him to the trauma of being strung up. It is possible to crush a dog's trachea or break his neck with this procedure. I cannot stress strongly enough that this extreme procedure should be employed only by an experienced professional trainer. I have seen this procedure used inappropriately in group training classes by so-called qualified obedience instructors. They have strung up dogs whose only "crime" was to be too distracted in class to concentrate on sitting and staying. Do not subject your dog or yourself to classes when instructors take this approach. (See Chapter 28, "Choosing a Qualified Dog Obedience Instructor.")

When a training collar is used properly, it will jerk and release without any choking effect. Most of the force will hit the dog on the back of the neck. This area and the chest are the strongest parts of a dog's body. The purpose of the jerk and release on the collar is to correct the dog. When performed correctly, it will cause a disagreeable feeling but will not hurt or injure your dog.

The art of jerking and releasing effectively comes with practice. The quick release is the key element. You may want to begin by practicing on something other than your dog. Place the training collar on a doorknob or on your arm. Attach the leash or place your finger through the ring where the leash would go. Jerk and quickly let go. You should hear the collar make a zipping sound. Some elements of dog training are difficult to learn from a book, and this is one of them. Only practical experience will do the job. Practice the quick release with the training collar over your arm until you feel confident you understand the procedure. Be assured that no one is born with dog training skills.

How to Put on the Training Collar Properly

While standing in front of your dog, make a letter *P* with the collar. Place it over your dog's head.

To check the position, run your hand along the leash to the first few inches of the training collar. Make sure that this section of the collar goes across the *back* of your dog's neck.

A training collar must be used properly to ensure a proper correction. First, the collar must be put on the dog correctly. It must not be put on upside down (see photo). If it is, the brunt of the jerk will hit the dog in the trachea, which could damage the dog's throat and create a chronic cough. Also, when the collar is upside down it will not release properly. Rather, it will constrict around the dog's neck, applying pressure on the throat. This can choke the dog.

Second, the collar must fit properly. A training collar should fit around the dog's neck with enough room to slide your hand between your dog's neck and the collar easily. When the collar is on the dog's neck, put your finger through the ring where the leash will attach. Gently pull up on the ring until the collar tightens to fit snugly. (Do not choke your dog.) There should not be more than three inches of excess chain. If the collar is too long, it will not release properly.

When you purchase a training collar, try to find a store that will allow you to take your dog in with you. This will make the job of obtaining a correct fit much easier. Walking into a pet store without your dog and looking at a rack of collars can be baffling. Picking the correct size collar would be like trying to guess how many jellybeans are in a jar.

The Pinch Collar

Pinch collars are made up of a series of metal links that pop on and off from each other, allowing you to determine the length of the collar. Between these links is a small chain with a swivel ring to which you attach the leash.

The pinch collar comes in three different link sizes: small, medium, and large. I recommend using a small-link collar on all dogs. The medium and large collars are cumbersome and weigh too much. They allow the dog to know when he is wearing the pinch collar. In addition, the transition from a small-link pinch collar to a training collar or buckle collar is easier.

Pinch collars are sometimes referred to as prong collars. Though either name is correct, I call them pinch collars because they work by pinching. When the trainer jerks and releases on this type of collar, the links close together, causing a pinch of the skin. Despite the pinch collar's somewhat shocking appearance, I have never seen it cause irritations or abrasions. Even though the correction it gives is more intense, it will not cause injury as sometimes occurs with the training collar. Used incorrectly, a training collar could become a lethal device. A pinch collar is not designed to tighten like a noose around a dog's neck, and it cannot choke a dog. Interestingly, the correction this collar delivers is a more natural sensation to the dog than that of a training collar because it is bitelike.

There is a good reason that pinch collars are not more widely used. Dogs who are not highly pain-insensitive would react adversely to the correction of a pinch collar. They would cry out in pain and become frightened. Any training procedure that causes a dog to cry out in pain is improper. It indicates that the dog is being overcorrected. When this happens the dog loses emotional control and his ability to concentrate. Dogs cannot learn when they cannot concentrate.

The pinch collar should be used as a training tool on only the most stoic, pain-insensitive dogs. It is a very useful, humane training tool when used on the appropriate individual. I recommend that the decision to use a pinch collar be made with the approval of a professional trainer who has experience using this tool. If you do use a pinch collar on your dog, you will get many different reactions from people. People who see the collar for the first time often say, "Oh my God, a spiked collar!" The pinch collar is *not* a spiked collar. It does not stick into the dog's neck.

You will also hear, "Isn't that cruel to use?" The answer is no. It is much crueler to subject the pain-insensitive dog to repeated corrections on a collar that has no effect. The dog learns nothing and you risk injuring the dog with rough, ineffective corrections borne out of frustration.

Some obedience instructors have no experience using pinch collars. They refuse to allow the use of this so-called cruel collar on dogs that may benefit from it. The dogs that could have succeeded in training with a pinch collar ultimately become class dropouts. Training class dropouts often end up on doggie death row—because they are uncontrolled and eventually unwanted.

Another reaction you will hear when a person sees a pinch collar on your dog is "Oh, is he mean?" This collar is not designed to train the mean, aggressive dog. As a matter of fact, the pinch collar should *not* be used on dominant dogs who think they can get away with biting their trainer. Before you can think about training a dog with a pinch collar, he must first be taught that biting is not acceptable.

You may tire of answering questions about the pinch collar. If so, place a bandana around your dog's neck to cover the collar.

Long Line

A long line is a piece of rope twenty-five to fifty feet in length. It can be made of cloth or synthetic fibers. It has a leash clip at one end, which attaches to the dog's collar. Long lines can be purchased ready-made, or you can make your own with rope and a clip from a hardware store.

Handlers use the long line to gain the upper hand in situations where

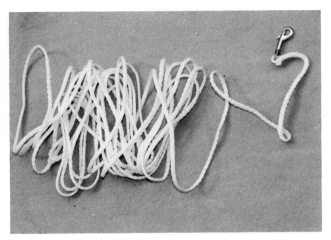

A twenty-five- to fifty-foot-long line is mandatory equipment to teach your dog to come on command.

the dog is running free. It is effective on the dog who stays in the handler's general vicinity but does not respond to the command *"Come."* It is ineffective on the dog who is oblivious to the handler and heads for the next county when the leash is unclipped. Such dogs must stay on the leash until fully trained to come on command.

Unlike the dog's training leash, you do not hold the long line. The dog drags it behind him. To get your dog back to you, step on the line, pick it up, and move in the opposite direction from the dog. It is not necessary to reel the dog into you. Once you are moving, you will see that the dog will follow in your direction. (See Chapter 19, "Come on Command.")

Always step on the long line to stop the dog before picking it up. Never pick the line up with your bare hands when the dog is running. This will result in a rope burn. Wearing gloves is a good safety precaution.

A long line should be attached *only* to the dog's buckle collar. Never use it with a training collar or a pinch collar. Be careful that the line does not get stuck in the woods or on a rock wall. Watch that the line does not wrap around anyone's ankles—your own or those of people nearby. If the line is attached to a large dog, a person tangled in the line could easily be knocked down. Even a line attached to a small dog could result in a nasty rope burn. Small children should never be present when you train your dog with a long line. Although the long line is a very effective training tool, it must be used with caution.

If your dog does not respond to the sound *"NHAA"* or to other natural corrections, use a shake can or a squirt bottle. They should be used in conjunction with the sound *"NHAA"* to teach your dog to stop immediately when you growl.

Plastic Squirt Bottle

A plastic squirt bottle is a refillable plastic bottle with a squirt top and an adjustable nozzle. It is the type often used to spray houseplants. The squirt bottle can be an effective training tool. If your dog does not stop what he is doing when you growl *"NHAA,"* a squirt of water from the bottle may do the trick. You should squirt water at your dog's face *simultaneously* as you say *"NHAA!"* Many dogs are intimidated by this, and it can be especially effective in squelching dog fights.

Water will not physically harm your dog. *Do not* use anything other than water in the bottle. Do not use vinegar, lime juice, lemon juice, what have you! These items will irritate or burn your dog's eyes.

Some dogs are not the least bit bothered by the squirt bottle, and some actually enjoy a squirt in the face. Obviously, if this is the case with the dog you are training, the squirt bottle will not be an effective training tool.

Shake Can

A shake can is an empty soda can with ten pennies in it. The opening of the can is sealed closed with a piece of tape. The shake can is used for the same reason as a squirt bottle. Shake the can if your dog does not stop whatever he is doing when you growl *"NHAA."* Most dogs do not like the sound of the shake can.

If the noise of the can intimidates your dog, he may learn to respect the sound *"NHAA."* The can must be shaken *simultaneously* as you verbally growl *"NHAA!"* The dog will eventually associate *"NHAA"* with the sound of the can. Again, the shake can will be an ineffective training tool if your dog is not bothered by the sound.

Your Voice

Your voice is another important training tool, although you will have to learn to use it correctly. You must use your voice in three distinct tones.

One tone is for commands. You should give commands in a clear, pleasant but firm voice. You do not have to shout commands at your dog. Do not sound like a drill sergeant! On the other hand, you should not give commands in a pleading tone. Give a command as if you are telling the dog what you want him to do. Do not give the command as if you are asking him to "please do it."

Another voice tone is for praise. You should praise enthusiastically using a high-pitched, happy sound. Men with deep voices may have a difficult time with this at first. With lots of practice they will succeed. The praise tone should be used generously—whenever your dog does what you tell him. The words you use should vary. Keep it fun and interesting for the dog. If the dog is not looking at you and wagging his tail, you are not praising effectively.

A third voice tone is for correction. The sound is *"NHAA."* This tone must be throaty and guttural. From now on, your *"NO"* should be *"NHAA."* Loud is not as important as deep and tough-sounding. The tone should sound like a growl. You are imitating dog language. When a dog tells another dog to stop doing whatever he is doing, he growls. He does not say "Bad dog" or "Stop it." He growls.

I have heard trainers use the word "Fooey." Think of how ridiculous this is. Have you ever heard a dog tell another dog "Fooey"? Learn to use "dog talk" if you want to succeed in training. Your corrective tone will be effective only if it convinces the dog that if he does not stop, you will bite him.

Rolled-up Newspaper

A rolled-up newspaper can be an effective training tool when used properly. For example, use the rolled-up newspaper if your dog chews something or has a housebreaking accident. It should be employed only when you cannot correct the dog with proper timing . . . because *you* were not supervising him.

Take the rolled-up newspaper and hit *yourself* on the head six times, as you repeat the phrase "I forgot to watch my dog. I forgot to watch my dog." Be consistent with this technique. After several corrections you will become conditioned to watch your dog! This is the *only* time a rolled-up newspaper should be used in training. If your dog laughs at you when you do this, praise him.

Nine

Rewards and Corrections

Dog training is based on communication between trainers and their dogs. Even though we can't talk to canines in the same way we talk with other people, we certainly can communicate with our canine companions. One of the most effective ways to communicate with dogs is through rewards and corrections. Both are needed to shape a dog's behavior and to succeed with obedience training.

Rewards

Rewards are essential if your dog is to understand that behaviors he is doing please you. Because rewards are agreeable, they will encourage him to repeat behaviors in the future. Rewards are meaningful to dogs if they satisfy certain needs. Two basic canine needs are social interaction and food.

Social acceptance and interaction are vital to dogs. Wild canines, such as wolves, groom, play, sleep, and eat as a pack. Our domestic dogs, descendants of wolves, instinctively seek out social interaction with fellow pack members. Your dog views the humans and canines in your household as his pack.

Trainers can capitalize on canine social behavior when rewarding their dogs. Three very effective "social" rewards are petting, playing, and verbal praise. Dogs love to be touched. A gentle rub behind the ears or a vigorous massage down the back feels great to dogs. Receiving such treatment after completing an obedience exercise will be viewed as a reward. The dog will know that his performance pleased you. Dogs do not seem to appreciate being patted on the head like a bongo drum. Each individual canine seems to have his own favorite spot to be petted.

Playing is another form of enjoyable social interaction. Most dogs enjoy playing. Select an object that your dog seems to love, such as a squeaky toy or a ball. Play with your dog after he successfully completes an obedience exercise. When I was training my golden retriever, Woody, for A.K.C. obedience trials, I always carried a tennis ball in my jacket pocket. I would do a two-minute heeling pattern, then Woody and I would play toss and retrieve with the tennis ball for two minutes. Woody loved tennis balls and soon came to associate heeling with an anticipated game of fetch.

Your dog will also interpret verbal praise as a reward. Dogs are attracted to enthusiastic, high-pitched sounds. A dull "Good dog, good dog" will not do the job. Be vivacious. Make the praise interesting to your dog. Get his tail wagging and him looking at you. Keep in mind that all dogs have different levels of excitability. Some individuals may require less enthusiasm to elicit the same response. Tailor your verbal praise to suit the dog you are training.

Food is another basic canine desire. Eating is a very agreeable experience. Dog trainers have different opinions on the use of food as a training reward. Some feel it will interfere with the dog's ability to concentrate on the behavior it is learning. I disagree. The thought of dinner certainly does not disrupt a young wolf's concentration when he is learning to hunt rabbits. On the contrary—it enhances his concentration.

Other trainers feel that if food is used in training, the dog will respond to a behavior only for food. In this book I do recommend using food as one way to reward your dog. If used properly, food as a reward will not cause a problem in training the family dog. It becomes a problem only in the obedience ring where you lose a point if your dog sniffs your hand looking for a treat. As discussed in Chapter 1, "The *Dog Talk* Approach," this book is not concerned with the artificial world of the obedience competition ring. It is concerned with developing a responsive canine family member who will live his life with you safely and obediently.

Corrections

Love, praise, and reward are vital aspects of a successful dog training program. Unfortunately, they are not enough. Corrections are also necessary if handlers are to succeed in communicating with their dogs. As described earlier, training through a canine point of view is essential. A wolf maintains order in his pack through the use of verbal and physical interaction. However, a wolf does not punish his pack followers. Likewise, I recommend that you refrain from punishing your dog.

There is a great difference between punishment and a well-timed correction. Punishment comes after the individual has committed an unwanted deed. A correction, or what behaviorists call a negative reinforcement, happens precisely as the individual is doing the unwanted behavior. Better yet in the case of dog training, it happens as the dog is *thinking* about doing the unwanted behavior.

Punishment also is designed to make an individual pay for a crime. Negative reinforcement, on the other hand, is designed to shape the subject's behavior. Canines are incapable of understanding that "the reason I am being punished now is because I did a certain action two hours before." (See Chapter 10, "Guilty or Not Guilty.") The way to provide negative reinforcement most effectively is through natural corrections.

Natural Corrections

A canine pack leader does not kick, punch, or choke pack followers in order to communicate to them what he desires. I strongly recommend that you avoid these abusive techniques. Instead, use natural corrections when training your dog.

Your voice is one natural way in which you can emulate canine behavior and communicate with your dog. Canines growl. When a feisty pup nurses too vigorously, the mother dog growls. She is saying with her growl "Stop what you are doing immediately." Whenever you want to tell your dog to stop what he is doing, say "**NHAA**" in a deep, throaty growl-like tone. Loud is not as effective as guttural.

Dogs also bite each other. You may witness a dog chewing a bone. Along comes another dog and tries to take the bone. The dog with the bone may first warn the intruder with a growl. If this does not work he may snap and bite the potential thief.

I bit my first puppy many years ago. I was visiting Captiva Island

If your dog does not stop when you say *"NHAA,"* growl louder and give a shake on the scruff of the dog's neck.

If a shake on the scruff of the neck does not work, you may want to bite the dog's muzzle.

in Florida with my girlfriend. During a shopping trip, my friend went into a store while I waited outside. Tied in front of the store was a small, German shepherd–like, mixed-breed pup. He looked to be about nine or ten weeks old. Naturally, I was interested in him, so I picked him up. It was like picking up a baby alligator! He growled and snapped like a wild animal. I growled *"NHAA"* at him, but to no avail as he tried to bite my wrist. I growled louder, held his mouth closed, and bit him lightly right on the muzzle between his nose and eyes. He let out a yip. I turned his face to mine and looked him in the eye. He licked me frantically all over my face, as if I were his long-lost father.

As this was happening, his owner appeared. He said, "What the hell did you do to my dog? I've never seen him kiss anyone! He bites everyone who comes near him. In fact, I think there's something wrong with him."

"He did try to bite me," I said, "but I held his muzzle closed and I bit *him*."

With a bewildered look on his face, the puppy's owner replied, "You bit my dog?" Before I could respond he added, "I'm going to have to try that. When I hit him with my hands, he bites worse. This morning I hit him with a rolled-up newspaper and he attacked the newspaper."

Clearly this dog's owner had never effectively corrected his puppy for unwanted biting behavior. The puppy's last effective correction probably came from his canine mother before he left the litter. The minute I communicated to the puppy using "dog talk," he knew exactly what I was saying: "Stop that immediately!"

If you are going to try this technique, be careful that the dog does not bite you in the face. Hold his mouth closed before you bite. *Never* bite a dog you do not know well. I do bite my students' puppies, but only if they are under five months old. I bite my own adult dogs, although they rarely need it, because I know they would not dare bite me back. Pack followers don't bite the undisputed pack leader. (I know this sounds macho, but it is quite true.)

Another natural correction is a shake on the scruff of the dog's neck. The scruff is the loose skin at the back of the neck between the head and shoulders. Shaking by the scruff is a procedure mother dogs use to correct their puppies. I also have witnessed adult dogs grab each other by the scruff when trying to assert dominance. If you are not inclined to bite your dog, you may feel more comfortable with this correction. Both procedures speak to dogs in their own language. The more you communicate with your dog in canine language, the quicker he will understand what you want.

At times you will have to train your dog using techniques that may not be natural. Canines certainly do not use training collars and leashes. They do not squirt each other with water bottles to break up fights or to teach noisy pack members to be quiet on command. What makes one technique acceptable as opposed to another is quite simple. If the procedure is humane and it works, then use it.

What Is Humane?

Any procedure or training tool that causes a dog to yelp in pain, causes injury, or that mentally terrorizes a dog is unacceptable. Humane techniques are those that help a dog to learn something in a constructive, nonviolent way. Well-timed praise teaches the dog that a behavior should be repeated. Well-timed corrections for unwanted behavior teach the dog to avoid that behavior the next time.

Poorly timed corrections, no matter how mild, could be considered inhumane, or at least unfair. Scolding the dog hours after you find a chewed bed pillow is nothing more than random anger from the dog's point of view. He's getting yelled at for what?—sleeping there by the fireplace? Why is that bad? Should he stop sleeping? The next time he's sleeping by the fireplace he'll probably feel apprehensive when you walk into the room. That's not as fair as a tough-sounding *"NHAA!"* would be when the dog first reaches for the bed pillow. With well-timed natural corrections, the dog will quickly and efficiently learn to avoid unwanted behaviors without any confusion or stress.

Humane training does not destroy the trust that exists between the handler and the dog. On the other hand, an extremely harsh or brutal correction, no matter how well timed, can frighten or intimidate a dog. Although you may be successful in getting him to avoid unwanted behaviors, you will have lost his trust and confidence. If you own a dog for the reasons that I advocate—companionship, affection, and fun—you will have no chance of achieving these things without your dog's trust. Don't be *afraid* to use corrections. Just be sure that when you make them they are appropriate to the dog. They should be strong enough to get the dog to stop a behavior but not to cause him to cower in fear.

With the guidelines I've just presented, the concept of humane treatment may seem easy to grasp. However, I have observed that in some ways, "humane" is a highly subjective term. Consider this story:

I lived with a standard poodle for twelve years. I got Joslyn when she was approximately eighteen months old from the veterinarian hospital where I worked. She had been brought in to be put to sleep because her owners had tired of her behavior. Jossie urinated, defecated, and chewed whenever left alone. She snapped at the family's three small children. As soon as a door was opened, she bolted outside. She refused to come when called. She had a long list of undesirable behaviors. Quite simply, Jossie was not trained.

I felt that Jossie basically had a good temperament and thought that in the right environment and with proper training, she could be "salvaged." The owners were thrilled that I wanted her and relieved that they did not have to destroy her. After I developed her trust and eventually bonded with her, Jossie was ready for training. During this period in my career, I was training dogs for obedience competitions. After about a year and a half, my curly canine friend was ready to go into the ring for her A.K.C. Companion Dog obedience title. Before long this once-unwanted castoff was an obedience-titled, wonderful companion.

One day I was practicing a down-stay with Jossie on the grounds of the local state college. She was doing pretty well with this exercise but was not quite ready for competition. When a passing jogger distracted her and she stood up, I corrected her with a firm *"NHAA."* Jossie looked at me. I did not have to touch her. She lay back down. Suddenly I was approached by a woman who verbally blasted me.

"You shoud be arrested," she said. "I should call the humane society on you. This is so *mean* making that poor thing lie there like that. You should be ashamed of yourself." This went on for ten minutes.

I tried to explain that I had saved this dog's life. Jossie was going to be put to death simply because she was untrained. To me that was the ultimate cruelty! But I could not get a word in edgewise. This woman's interpretation of "cruel" and inhumane was training a dog to lie down and stay.

Consider this next story: When I was working for a veterinarian, an elderly woman brought her little dog in. Its toenails had grown so long that some of them were growing back into the poor dog's feet. When asked why she did not clip them or bring the dog to us sooner so that we could clip them, her reply was "Because she doesn't like having her nails clipped, and I think it's mean to make her." Again, I couldn't believe the irony. This dog needed an anesthetic and surgery—and treatment for sore feet for two weeks. Certainly the mild stress of periodic nail clippings would have paled in comparison to the trauma this dog was put through.

The point here is that you need to use common sense when evaluating humane treatment. Go with your sensibilities. Do not use techniques that you feel uncomfortable with. Be sure to consider any ramifications to your dog. Humane obedience training and regular medical care may not always be convenient or easy or affordable, but they enhance the dog's life and, in the long run, the owner's life as well.

Ten

Guilty or Not Guilty: Don't Judge Your Dog by the Look on His Face!

Anthropomorphism: (n.) ascribing human form or attributes to a being or thing not human.

For years Hollywood has portrayed motion-picture canines as animals whose motivations are based on human perceptions and values. Lassie saves a rabbit from death, for example, or Benji solves a crime, or Rin Tin Tin protects the fort from outlaws. These animal films are very entertaining, and the canine actors are extremely well trained, but they tend to give the viewer a distorted, unrealistic picture of a dog's ability to think and reason.

This misrepresentation of canine behavior is the downfall of many dog owners and their unfortunate pets. A person who has never taken a dog training course or read a good training manual containing information on canine behavior very often expects from his or her dog things that canines are unable to do. Such a person may teach even those behaviors that the dog *is* capable of carrying out in a confusing and haphazard manner. The unfortunate end results are slow learning and unreliable responses on the part of the dog. Many poor dogs are then unjustly labled spiteful, stupid, stubborn, and sometimes just plain bad. The proper label is ignorant, and it belongs to the owner, not the dog. Whenever you try to evaluate canine behaviors through a human point of view, you will misinterpret them.

All but the very worst anthropomorphic dog owners can be helped if they make a valid effort to understand their dogs. It is not a crime to be anthropomorphic, but it *should* be a crime if you own a dog and make no effort to understand him. As a dog trainer, I do not ask my students *never* to be anthropomorphic with their dogs. I do ask them, however, always to be aware of when they are.

Some aspects of anthropomorphism are harmless to the dog—and can even be enjoyable. For example, giving your dog a special dinner on his birthday or filling a Christmas stocking with dog toys and treats is not detrimental. What I want owners to learn about anthropomorphism concerns the dog's training, especially when it comes to good timing and fair corrections. For example, owners often correct their dog based on a "guilty look" on the dog's face, assuming he "knows" he was wrong. The dog *doesn't* know, any more than he knows it is his birthday or Christmas.

Here is another good example of anthropomorphism. Many dog owners—especially owners of younger dogs—experience a chewing problem at some point. I get phone calls on a regular basis from frustrated owners who say that their dogs chew furniture, rugs, shoes, and the like when left alone in the house. They say that they have tried *everything*. "He knows he has done wrong," they say. When asked what they have done to correct the dog, they say, "I holler at him and show him what he chewed. I tell him he is bad, and I smack him with the newspaper."

This procedure is usually repeated many times while the dog continues to destroy the house. Eventually the time arrives when the owner comes home and the dog runs and hides. Some dogs may even stand and shiver with a terribly "guilty look" on their face. Then, periodically, the owner will come home and *not* find a mess. The owner will be happy and will praise and pet the dog. The dog will respond to the happy sound and good-feeling rubs with a wagging tail and a happy appearance.

This cheerful behavior, unfortunately, reinforces in the owner's mind that the dog *knows* that avoiding chewing is "right" and that chewing up the house is "wrong." "He's just a bad dog," the owner thinks or "He's really spiteful. He wants to *get even* with me for leaving him home." These statements are all based strictly on human emotions and a human perspective. Owners such as these are being anthropocentric. They view everything in terms of human experience and human values.

So what is an example of a *canine* perspective? Here is the tale of one of my dogs, Carrousel's Jason U.D.

Jason, my Irish setter, holder of the American Kennel Club's Utility Dog obedience title, may have been one of the all-time greatest garbage dogs. He was also one of my best teachers.

Jason was two years old and had earned his first obedience title (Companion Dog) when I became aware of the anthropomorphism syndrome. By almost all other counts, Jason was a "good dog." A dog-training friend and I attended an obedience demonstration given by a well-known professional dog trainer from New York State. This trainer demonstrated some obedience exercises and some fun tricks with his dog. We were all impressed.

After the demonstration, the trainer held a question-and-answer session. Many people asked questions: "How do I get my dog to come when I call her?" "How do I housebreak my new puppy?" "How do I keep my dog from jumping on people?" Finally, my turn: "How do I keep my Irish setter out of the garbage?"

"Catch him in the garbage bin and correct him as he is making the mess," responded the trainer.

"I've done that a couple of times," I replied, "so now he will not go near the garbage bin if I am home. It's only when I'm not home that he gets into the garbage. And believe me, he *knows* he shouldn't be doing it."

"Why do you think he *knows* he has done wrong?" the trainer asked.

"When he first started getting into the garbage," I replied, "I would come home and find garbage all over the kitchen floor. I would immediately get the dog wherever he was and drag him to the mess. I would tell him 'Bad dog!' and push his nose into the mess. Jason would be very upset and shake and look very sorry. But he has continued to get into the garbage most of the time!

"Sometimes he doesn't get into the garbage, and then I always praise him. I now know that he *knows* he shouldn't get into the garbage, because when I get home, Jason takes off and hides only if he has been in the garbage and there is a mess on the floor. When he has not been in the garbage, he is at the front door wagging his tail, happy to see me. He *knows*. He is just very stubborn when he wants to be."

"I don't believe he knows he is doing anything wrong when he goes into the garbage bin," the trainer said. I looked at him skeptically.

"Try a little experiment," he suggested. "Bring your dog into the kitchen and let him watch *you* dump garbage on the floor. Do not say anything to your dog. Leave the house and come back in five minutes. When you return, evaluate the dog's behavior. Do not praise or correct your dog."

I did this, and as soon as I dumped garbage on the floor, Jason acted scared and nervous. I did not say a word to him as I left. When I returned, Jason acted really nervous and looked guilty. I was sure he had not spent much time nosing around in what I had spilled on the floor, because there was not anything that would appeal to him in the bin. When I approached him, he ran upstairs and hid. I called the trainer and told him what happened.

"If your dog *knows* when he is wrong," he asked, "why did he act guilty and run away when he saw *you* spill the garbage?" I had no idea.

"Because you taught him to act apprehensive—and have misinterpreted apprehension for guilt. Your dog knows that if there is garbage on the floor when you come home, it results in bad news for him. Unfortunately, what your dog cannot understand while he is creating the mess with the garbage is that at some point in the future, you will come home and be angry.

"Dogs do not project thought into the future. They do have great memories, though. That's why Jason quickly figured out that garbage on the floor plus your coming home meant trouble. He does not understand that *putting* the garbage on the floor is bad. As a matter of fact, while your dog is in the garbage enjoying tasty food scraps, he considers this behavior great. Because it is enjoyable and nothing ever happens to make it disagreeable *while he is doing it,* he will continue to do it every chance he gets."

I saw the light. What had to be done in order to teach my dog to avoid the garbage bin (when no one was around to correct him) was to create a disagreeable experience as he went into the bin.

The trainer made a few suggestions. Place a mousetrap in the bin. When the dog sticks his nose in the bin—wham! Disagreeable experience. He will probably avoid the bin. (Although this technique may work, I felt my dog could be injured and so did not feel comfortable using it. I do not advocate others using it either.)

Another suggestion was to place hot pepper sauce in the food scraps. When the dog eats the food, it will taste bad. Again—disagreeable to the dog *as he is performing* the behavior you want him to avoid. I tried that. However, Jason quickly learned to visit the garbage bin only when there was no hot pepper sauce. He could smell hot pepper sauce from at least three feet away.

This type of training is called behavior modification. An alternative to this is controlling the environment. In the case of Jason and the garbage, it meant that I must be sure to put the garbage bin where the dog could not get into it when I was not home. This would not teach the dog to avoid the garbage while he was alone, but it would effectively terminate my problem.

No behavior will ever be considered good or bad, right or wrong by your dog. If a behavior is agreeable to your dog and you allow him to continue the behavior, it will at some point become a habit, or conditioned response. If a behavior is made disagreeable to the dog, the more he experiences it the more he will want to avoid it. With enough repetitions, the dog will develop a conditioned avoidance.

Remember, though, that just one experience rarely transforms a behavior into a habit or an avoidance. Behaviors often take many repetitions to become reliable. So even though your dog performs a certain behavior once or twice, it does not mean that the behavior has become a habit. You should be certain that the dog has performed the behavior many, many times the way you want him to. Only then should you test him and expect a "good" response.

Keep all these points in mind the next time you see a basset hound, for example, with those big sad eyes and droopy ears. Before you say "Oh, the poor dog, he seems so sad!" remember that if you had that expression on your face, you would be sad. But the basset hound just looks that way from a human point of view. From his own canine point of view, he may be the most happy and contented dog in the world.

JENA

Part Three

The *Dog Talk* Training Program

Eleven

A Step-by-Step Training Program for Your Dog

When you train your dog, it is extremely important that you do not train haphazardly. Instead, you must develop a workable, systematic training program. For the novice handler, this can be a difficult task.

A recommended ten-level training program follows. This program includes all of the obedience exercises described in detail in Chapters 13 through 19. As you read these chapters, you will see that the exercises are broken down into simple steps. Each new step builds on the previous step, working toward an end result.

You do not have to read all of the steps of all of the exercises before you begin training. Read step 1 of each exercise—then get your dog and try it. Practice it tomorrow and again the next day. There, you have begun training your dog!

All of the steps in Level One are the beginning steps of each exercise. Level Two has the next group of steps, Level Three the next, and so on. Don't skip steps. Reliable results depend on sticking with the program. However, you many have to alter this program slightly to use with the dog you are training. This is because trainers should not try to force all dogs to adhere to one specific program. One specific program will not work for *every* dog. Good trainers design a program for each individual dog they train.

When Barbara and I train our dogs, we use the training techniques taught in this book. We also introduce the steps in the sequence shown. However, we disregard time. If a dog is not ready for step 2 of a certain exercise, we continue to practice step 1 until the dog does it perfectly. When you read the training chapters, you will see instructions that say, for example, "Practice step 1 every day for a week before going on to step 2." These time frames are not cast in stone. With the individual dog you are training, you may have to practice a particular step for three weeks—or more!

Work on each step until your dog does it perfectly. Then go on to the next step. Like humans, all dogs learn at different rates of speed. If you adapt this training program to *your* dog, you will have a better chance of success.

In addition, do not feel compelled to spend an hour every day going through the entire list of exercises for each level. In fact, that is not the best way to train. Work on a few exercises in the morning, a few others in the afternoon or after work, and a few in the evening. You will be more inspired to keep practicing if you must commit only fifteen minutes here and there throughout your day. Chances are better that you will approach training with a happy, positive attitude. Your dog will pick up on your demeanor, and you both will be on the road to success. (For additional tips on training sessions, see Chapter 12, "General Training Suggestions.")

Level One

- Sit on Command
    - Step 1: Compelling the Dog (see page 92)
- Down on Command
    - Step 1: Compelling the Dog (see page 103)
- Sit-Stay
    - Step 1: Sitting at Your Side (see page 113)
- Stand-Stay
    - Step 1: Hands on the Dog (see page 131)
- Down-Stay
    - Step 1: The Imaginary Circle (10 minutes) (see page 142)
- Controlled Walking and Controlled Standing
    - Minimal Distractions (see page 150)

 ## *Level Two*

- Sit on Command
    Step 2: Inducing the Dog (see page 93)
- Down on Command
    Step 2: Inducing the Dog (see page 104)
- Sit-Stay
    Step 2: Stay from in Front (see page 114)
- Stand-Stay
    Step 2: Removing Your Hands (see page 133)
- Down-Stay
    Step 2: Increasing the Time (20 minutes) (see page 144)
- Come on Command
    Step 1: Chase Reflex (see page 172)
- Controlled Walking
    Review (see page 150)

 ## *Level Three*

- Sit on Command
    Review Steps 1 and 2 (compulsive and inducive
        techniques) (see pages 92 and 93)
- Down on Command
    Review Steps 1 and 2 (compulsive and inducive
        techniques) (see pages 103 and 104)
- Sit-Stay
    Step 3: Adding Distractions (two steps away)
        (see page 116)
- Stand-Stay
    Review Step 2 (removing your hands) (see page 133)
    Add distractions
- Down-Stay
    Step 3: Increasing the Distractions (30 minutes)
        (see page 145)

Level Three *(cont.)*

- Come on Command
    Step 2: Chase Reflex from Six Feet Away (see page 173)
    Continue to review Step 1 (chase reflex)
- Controlled Walking
    Add distractions to the training environment
        (see page 152)

Level Four

- Sit on Command
    Step 3: A Controlled Test (see page 96)
- Sit on Command from a Down Position
- Down on Command
    Step 3: A Controlled Test (see page 105)
- Sit-Stay
    Step 4: Increasing the Distance (to six feet) (see page 118)
- Stand-Stay
    Step 3: Stay from in Front (see page 134)
- Down-Stay
    Step 4: Away from Home (see page 145)
- Come on Command
    Step 3: Chase Reflex from Controlled Walking
        (see page 175)
    Continue to review Steps 1 and 2 (chase reflexes)
- Controlled Walking
    Practice in new areas

Level Five

- Sit on Command
  - Step 4: A Controlled Test from in Front (see page 97)
- Down on Command
  - Step 4: A Controlled Test from in Front (see page 106)
- Sit-Stay
  - Step 5: Beyond the End of the Leash (see page 119)
  - Increase distractions
- Greeting People Without Jumping (see page 126)
- Stand-Stay
  - Step 4: Increasing the Distance (three feet away)
    - (see page 136)
- Down-Stay
  - Review Step 4 (away from home) (see page 145)
  - Add more distractions
- Come on Command
  - Step 4: Chase Reflex with Distractions (see page 177)
- Controlled Walking
  - Review (see page 150)
  - Add more distractions
- Heeling: In a straight line (see page 156)

Level Six

- Sit on Command
  - Review Steps 3 and 4 (a controlled test from side
    - and front) (see pages 96 and 97)
- Down on Command
  - Step 5: Hand off the Shoulder (see page 107)
- Sit-Stay
  - Review Step 5 (beyond the end of the leash)
    - (see page 119)

Level Six *(cont.)*

- Greeting People Without Jumping
    Review (see page 126)
- Stand-Stay
    Review Step 4 (three feet away) (see page 136)
- Down-Stay
    Review Step 4 (away from home) (see page 145)
    Add more distractions
- Come on Command
    Step 5: Recall (the testing stage) (see page 180)
- Controlled Walking
    Review (see page 150)
- Heeling: About-Turn, Slow Pace, Fast Pace (see page 160)

Level Seven

- Sit on Command
    Step 5: Random Sits (see page 98)
- Down on Command
    Step 6: Standing Straight (see page 108)
- Sit-Stay
    Step 6: Stay from Twenty Feet Away (see page 120)
- Greeting People Without Jumping
    Review (see page 126)
- Stand-Stay
    Step 5: Stay During Handler Exam (see page 137)
- Down-Stay
    Review Step 4 (away from home) (see page 145)
- Come on Command
    Step 6: Recall with a Sit (see page 181)
- Controlled Walking
    Review (see page 150)
- Heeling: Right Turn, Left Turn (see page 161)

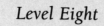

Level Eight

- Sit on Command
    - Step 6: Off Leash (see page 98)
- Down on Command
    - Step 7: Down from a Standing Position (see page 109)
- Sit-Stay
    - Step 7: Stay Without a Leash (see page 121)
- Greeting People Without Jumping
    - Review (see page 126)
- Stand-Stay
    - Review Step 5 (handler exam) (see page 137)
- Down-Stay
    - Out of Sight (see page 146)
- Come on Command
    - Step 7: Recall with a Stand (see page 182)
- Controlled Walking
    - Review (see page 150)
- Heeling: Automatic Sit While Heeling (see page 162)

Level Nine

- Sit on Command
    - Review Step 6 (off leash) (see page 98)
- Down on Command
    - Step 8: Random Drops (see page 110)
- Sit-Stay
    - Out of Sight (see page 122)
- Greeting People Without Jumping
    - Review (see page 126)
- Stand-Stay
    - Step 6: Stand for Examination (see page 138)
- Down-Stay
    - Review Out of Sight (see page 146)

Level Nine *(cont.)*

- Come on Command
  Step 8: Recall from a Standing Position (see page 182)
- Come-on-Command Hand Signal
  Part A: Teaching the Hand Signal (see page 187)
- Controlled Walking
  Review (see page 150)
- Heeling:
  Review all Heeling Variations (see pages 160–163)

 Level Ten

- Sit on Command
  Review Step 6 (off leash) (see page 98)
- Down on Command
  Review Step 8 (random drops) (see page 110)
- Sit-Stay
  Review Out of Sight (see page 122)
- Greeting People Without Jumping
  Review (see page 126)
- Stand-Stay
  Review Step 6 (stand for examination) (see page 138)
- Down-Stay
  Review Out of Sight (see page 146)
- Come on Command
  Step 9: Come While Running Free (see page 184)
- Come-on-Command Hand Signal
  Part B: Eliminating the Verbal Command (see page 188)
- Controlled Walking
  Review (see page 150)
- Heeling: Off Leash (see page 162)

Twelve

General Training Suggestions

When using the training exercises in this book, be careful to follow each step precisely. To ensure good results, keep in mind these basic tips whenever you are training your dog.

When you begin to teach your dog a new behavior, choose a training environment that is conducive to learning.

People are sometimes under the mistaken impression that they must train their dog in an environment with distractions. They feel this is necessary so that their dog will respond to commands when distracted. This is comparable to trying to learn a foreign language with loud music blaring in your ear. Such an approach will *not* teach you to understand the foreign language when loud music is playing. It will only distract and confuse you.

A more logical approach is to study in a quiet environment where you can concentrate. When you start to become proficient in the foreign language, you can study with quiet music playing in the background. After you become fluent in the language, you can blast music as loud as you please and still understand what you are reading.

The same philosophy applies to your dog. Begin teaching new behaviors in an environment where your dog can pay attention. As your dog progresses, gradually incorporate distractions into the training area. When your dog totally understands a new behavior, you can practice in a chaotic environment.

Practice obedience exercises every day.

Dogs form habits through repetition. It is the trainer's job to repeat behaviors with the dog consistently. This takes perseverance. Some exercises may require hundreds of repetitions before the dog develops a habit, or conditioned response. Inconsistency on the part of the trainer will confuse the dog and slow down the learning process.

It is not necessary, nor for that matter advisable, to set aside one designated time every day to practice. The most effective approach is to do a little training before you leave for work in the morning, a few minutes when you get home, and a few minutes later in the evening. However, the most important point is to be consistent with your dog in between practice sessions. Whenever you interact with your dog, perpetuate your training.

Do not pattern train your dog.

Although it is important to be consistent when you train your dog, it is also important to avoid pattern training. Pattern training means teaching obedience exercises in the same sequence, at the same time, and in exactly the same place.

For example, let's say you are teaching your dog four exercises. These exercises could be sit, down, heel, and come. Pattern training would be practicing every afternoon in your driveway, precisely at three o'clock, and always going through the exercises in the same order.

The drawback to pattern training is the fact that dogs are very routine-oriented creatures. If you pattern train, your dog will soon anticipate what you are going to do next. Pattern training is also boring to dogs. A dog's brain needs to be stimulated to keep him interested and working with enthusiasm and a wagging tail. It is also very likely that your dog will become conditioned to perform these exercises by rote. He will perform the exercises only in your driveway at three o'clock in the order that you taught them.

It is easy to avoid pattern training if you are aware of it. Train your dog in different parts of the yard or house. For a change of pace, take him to a quiet park or schoolyard to practice. Train at different times of the day or night. Vary the sequence of the exercises that you are working on. Keep the training interesting, and your dog will enjoy learning and will respond more reliably.

Break exercises into the simplest components.

A dog is perfectly capable of learning more than one behavior in the same day, as long as the behaviors are clear-cut and simple. It is difficult, if not impossible, for a dog to understand a complex obedience exercise immediately. If you expect too much too soon, you are setting up yourself and your dog for failure.

You must first analyze any behavior that you decide you want to teach your dog. Try to determine what its simplest component is. Practice this step with your dog first and then add simple steps. Build a behavior chain toward the end result. This is exactly what the *Dog Talk* training program provides. If your dog has a problem with any specific component, backtrack to a simpler step. This approach, hand in hand with repetition and patience, will guarantee success.

Always think and act as a pack leader.

Your dog is going to follow direction only from a pack leader. Pack leaders are never wishy-washy! However, as pack leader you do not have to be a tyrant.

In the pack, the leader is the "dominant" animal. But "dominant" does not mean macho or bullying—either in regard to the canine pack leader or to you, as the pack leader in your home.

A word that is more accurate and to which owners relate better is "assertive." You do not have to be mean or overbearing to your dog, simply assertive. You have to take charge and be the leader. Imagine taking a five-year-old child to the mall. Either you are in charge or the five-year-old is in charge. If it is the latter, you will be in for one heck of a day. But you do *not* need to be a child abuser and beat the kid up! You simply have to lay the ground rules and be consistent. Be assertive and you *will* be a pack leader.

Never lose your temper while training your dog.

Patience is a virtue. Fortunately, it is an acquired virtue. Most people are not born saints. Many new trainers lose their tempers to some degree while training their dogs. This is usually the result of the trainer's frustration.

Unfortunately, losing your temper is always detrimental to training. Every time it happens you lose ground. If you happen to have a bad day and start losing your temper, end the training session immediately. If you have the type of personality in which you cannot help losing your temper, get an aquarium. A dog is the wrong animal for you.

If you want to own and train a dog, you must stop and think about what is happening when things are not going smoothly. Try to analyze the situation. Is it something you are doing wrong? Are you carrying out the technique correctly? Are you presenting the exercise to your dog clearly?

Is the dog having a physical problem? Do his ears, hips, or feet bother him? Does he have to urinate or defecate? Is your dog under emotional control? Has he had enough exercise this week? Is he frightened or nervous about something in the training area?

These are just some of the things that can create problems during training. Your job as the trainer is to keep your cool and think things through. Losing your temper will not speed up learning on your dog's part. It will only undermine your dog's trust in you. If your dog does not trust you completely, all is lost.

Keep training fun and lively.

Along with training your dog to do specific behaviors, you can also shape his attitude toward training. Your demeanor during training will greatly influence your dog's state of mind. If you act bored, your dog will become bored. If you move around like a sloth, your dog will be sluggish.

On the other hand, if you move quickly during motion exercises, your dog will become conditioned to react quickly. If you praise your dog enthusiastically, his tail will wag and he will look at you. If your neighbors don't think you have lost your mind, you are doing it wrong! It is your job to make training fun.

Use your dog's name effectively.

Use your dog's name to get his attention. Use it in the same way that humans use names for each other. For example, if Barbara were on the other side of a crowded room, I would call her name: "Barbara!" Using her name would get her attention. Then I could communicate my request: "Please come here."

The same is true with a dog. If Drifter is sniffing a tree in a park, I must get his attention by calling his name: "Drifter!" When the dog looks at me, I can give the command: *"Come!"*

To condition the dog to pay attention when you call his name, use his name *prior* to giving any command that will require the dog to move. "Drifter, *come*," "Byron, *sit*," "Bentley, *heel*" are examples of using the name prior to a command that initiates a motion exercise.

Do not use the dog's name *after* giving the command. There is no point. For example, *"Down*, Cork" puts the "attention-getter" at the end. Commands given in this manner can be confusing to the dog, especially if there is more than one dog in the household.

I never use the dog's name prior to a stay command, only prior to a motion command. This is because I do not want him ready to move before I tell him to stay. Besides, I already have the dog's attention before telling him to stay. I have just told him, "Drifter, *sit*" or *"stand"* or *"down."*

In addition, do not use your dog's name as a substitute for *"NHAA"* when you must correct him. A dog learns to tune out his name when it is used constantly in this manner. Your dog should associate his name with positive things as much as possible. You want him conditioned to look up at you when you call his name—not look the other way.

Give one command, one command only!

It is very important in the early stages of training to condition your dog to respond to the first command you give. If you associate five commands with a behavior, your dog will never respond immediately. He will learn to wait for five commands.

To make matters worse, handlers who repeat commands never repeat them the same number of times. They sometimes give the command twice, sometimes five times, sometimes ten times. Their dogs never know *when* to respond! In fact, these dogs become conditioned to ignore commands altogether.

Dogs are perfectly capable of being trained to respond to one command. It is up to you to teach them to do so. Remember when you train to give *one command only*.

Thirteen

Sit and Down on Command

You do not have to train a dog to sit or lie down. Dogs do these behaviors naturally. However, you do have to train a dog to sit or lie down *on command*. This means conditioning the dog to sit or lie down in response to a specific signal.

Teaching a Dog to Respond on Command

There are two reasons a dog will respond to any command. The first is that the dog clearly understands what we want from him when we give a command. If the dog only partially understands what we want, we *will not* get a reliable response. Almost every time a person tells me that his or her dog is stupid or stubborn, the proper word is "confused."

The second reason that a dog will respond to a command is that he knows he *has* to respond. The dog may understand very well what we want, but if he has learned through the trainer's inconsistency that he does not have to respond, he may choose not to.

Imagine visiting a foreign country where you do not speak the language. A woman walks up to you and in her native tongue tells you to open a door. You look at her with a confused look on your face because you have no idea what she is saying.

It does not matter how many times this person repeats the request. You do not understand. You would not understand any clearer if she screamed the request at you. You would become even more confused if she beat you on the head with a rolled-up newspaper and screamed "Open the door!" in a language you did not understand.

But imagine that this woman gently led you by the arm and said the phrase—as she helped you open the door. With enough repetition, you would eventually understand what the phrase meant.

After several weeks of repeating this process, the woman could then test you. She could say to you in the foreign language, "Open the door." If you did not respond, she would be justified in correcting you. By this time you would understand why you were being corrected. If you wanted to avoid future reprimands, you would open the door when told to do so.

This same philosophy of teaching applies to dogs. You should not correct a dog for not responding to a command that he has never learned. You have to first teach the dog what the command means.

In order to accomplish this, you must go through three steps. The first step is to find a way to get the dog to do the behavior that you would like to teach. Simultaneously as he does the behavior, the dog must hear a sound, which becomes the command. This is essential. The dog will never respond reliably if he does not understand what his body is supposed to do when he hears the command.

The second step is to form an association between the command and the behavior. This means repetition. Make sure the dog repeats the behavior every single time he hears the sound. You do not have to designate fifteen minutes every day for boring, military-style drills. Practice randomly throughout the day. Whenever you encounter your dog, cause him to do the behavior and associate the command.

Be sure to give only one command each time you have your dog do the behavior. If you repeat commands, it will not be clear to your dog exactly *when* he should respond.

At this stage in training you are not testing the dog. He does not have to respond on his own to the command. Your dog's only response should be to allow you to handle him. The only thing the dog can do wrong is fight, bite, and resist. If he will not allow you to handle him, then you have a pack leadership problem. (See Chapter 6, "Pack Leader.")

After several weeks of associating the sound, or command, with the behavior, your dog will be ready for the third step, testing. By testing I mean giving the command without doing any technique that will cause the dog to react. If the dog responds promptly, praise him enthusiastically. If he does not respond, quickly correct the dog. The dog will understand what the correction was for because you have spent weeks showing him what he is supposed to do with his body when he hears the command. If you had not shown the dog what to do, the correction would be unfair and confusing.

Sit on Command

When I begin to teach the sit exercise, 95 percent of my students say to me, "My dog already knows sit." They are usually right. Sit on command is the one obedience command that most dogs in the world respond to—even if they never had formal training. Why?

There is an interesting phenomenon with dogs, particularly attentive young puppies. If you take any word, repeat it enough times, the dog will look at you and eventually sit. It does not matter what the word is. You could say "down" or "roll" or "bone" or even "pizza." They are all equally meaningless sounds to the untrained dog. Let's use *"Sit"* for the purpose of this exercise.

Owners look down at their dogs and say, *"Sit. Sit. Sit. Sit. Sit."* Eventually the puppy puts his rear end on the ground. The owner then praises the dog for sitting. As a result, the dog has inadvertently learned to sit on command.

Sitting (and sometimes giving the paw) are the only automatic responses you can elicit from a dog by bombarding him with meaningless sounds. One drawback to teaching the dog to sit using this "method" is that you have to repeat the sit command at least five times. Another drawback is that most dogs who have been trained this way respond only when they feel like it. The objective of the sit-on-command exercise is to condition the dog to sit reliably and promptly with one command.

How to Teach Sit on Command

Step 1: Compelling the Dog

- Start with your dog standing at your left side.
- Place your *right* hand, palm up, through your dog's training collar. Your fingers should be pointing toward your dog's tail.
- Place your *left* hand at the back of your dog's neck.
- Say your dog's name and give the dog the command *"Sit."* At the

Step 1: Place your right hand through your dog's collar, palm up. Run your left hand along your dog's spine.

Pull up gently on the collar and tuck your dog into a sit with your left hand.

same time pull up and back with your *right* hand on the training collar. Simultaneously slide your *left* hand down your dog's back along his spine and over his tail, tucking him into a sit.

- As soon as he sits, praise him enthusiastically. Be sure to give *one* command only.

Practice many sits throughout the day. Be sure *not* to test your dog at this stage by throwing a meaningless sound at him and waiting to see what he will do. Make sure every time you give the command you are in a position to make your dog comply immediately. Your job is to form an association between the sound *"Sit"* and what your dog is supposed to do with his body when he hears this sound. Your dog's job is simply to comply—to allow you to sit him. The only thing your dog can do wrong is fight, bite, and resist. If you encounter this problem, refer to Chapter 24, "Preventing Biting Problems."

This beginning step is called a *compulsive method* of training. You are showing, or compelling, the dog to do a behavior as you associate a command. In addition, by manipulating your dog's body, you are asserting your authority as pack leader. This helps your dog understand that he must take direction from you—and not the other way around.

Step 2: Inducing the Dog

This exercise is called an *inducive method* of training. You will be luring, or inducing, your dog into a sit instead of compelling him. The inducive method adds spirit and animation to the dog's response. It also seems

Step 2: Use the object of attraction as a lure above your dog's head to induce him into a sitting position.

to quicken the association process between hearing the command and doing the behavior.

If this exercise works with your dog, it will speed up learning to sit on command. If your dog does not respond to this inducive training method, rely exclusively on the compulsive technique. If your dog *does* respond to inducive methods, alternate between inducing and compelling your dog into the sit position. The goal of both these steps is to show your dog what you expect him to do with his body when he hears the word *"Sit."*

For step 2 you will need an "object of attraction." An object of attraction is simply something that your dog likes and that will hold his attention. It may be a tennis ball, squeaky toy, dog biscuit, and so on. (Do not use the family cat!) If your dog likes many things, select an object that you can easily hold in one hand and can slide into a pocket when not in use.

• Put the leash on your dog and hold it in your *left* hand. Hold the object of attraction in your *right* hand.

• Attract your dog's attention with the object by waving it in front of his nose until he becomes interested in it.

• When you have your dog's attention on the object, move the object above and behind his head. This will cause him to sit. Say your dog's name and give the command *"Sit"* as you induce him into the sitting position.

• Give *one* command only. If your dog does not follow the object into a sitting position, do not repeat the command. Do not stand there waving the object in his face saying *"Sit. Sit. Sit."* Instead, quickly bend over and compel him to sit using the step 1 technique.

• If your dog does follow the object into a sitting position, praise him enthusiastically.

Alternate between the step 1 compulsive technique and the step 2 inducive exercise. Do *not* test your dog on these exercises at this point by merely using the command *"Sit"* without showing him what you want him to do. This would slow down the association process.

Dogs fall into four distinct categories in responding to the object of attraction in the step 2 procedure:

1. The first category are dogs who get so excited by the object of attraction that they get out of control. These individuals leap, flip, and fly when they see something they like. If your dog gets overly excited and cannot concentrate on the object, you will not be able to induce him into a sitting position. Do not despair. Instead use the step 1 compulsive technique to cause your dog to sit. Often the type of dog who has problems with the sit version of inducive training responds fine to the down version.

2. The second category consists of dogs who could care less about any object of attraction. They turn their noses up at food, toys, and anything else you can think of. If dogs are not interested in the object, it will be impossible to use it to induce them. Rely on the step 1 compulsive technique to show this type of dog what you want.

3. The third category contains selective individuals. These dogs may show little or no interest in most objects, but they love a certain type of doggie cookie or one particular squeaky toy.

I once gave an obedience lesson to a woman whose great Dane appeared to be in category 2. The dog did not like *anything* we tried. I recommended that the owner rely on the compulsive method. Two days later the woman called to tell me that she had found an old squeaky toy under a piece of furniture that her dog had played with as a puppy. She tried inducing her dog to sit with this object and the dog responded perfectly. Experiment. You may find something your dog loves.

4. The fourth category is the best one. Dogs of this type love everything—biscuits, balls, squeaky toys, and so on. Alternate objects of attraction with these individuals to keep them interested.

The compulsive and inducive techniques on their own will not teach a dog to sit on command. Use them primarily to form an association between the sound and the action.

After several weeks of consistently practicing these techniques, your dog will have a good idea of what you want him to do when he hears the sound *"Sit."* This next exercise will train your dog to respond promptly to the command.

Step 3: A Controlled Test

This step of training is the testing stage. At this point you will simply give the dog the command *"Sit"* without using either step 1 or step 2 training techniques.

If your dog responds to the command by sitting promptly, praise him lavishly. If he does not respond to the command by sitting quickly, correct your dog with a jerk and release on the training collar. Do not give the correction simultaneously with the command. Be sure to give your dog a few seconds to respond to the command before you give a correction. Do not repeat the command. Give one command only.

Your dog will understand what you expect him to do when he hears the command because you have shown him many, many times what you want. Unfortunately, knowing what you want may not be enough to get him to respond reliably. Most dogs also must understand that they *have* to respond. If your dog learns that a correction will follow if he does not respond immediately, his response will be more reliable. In addition, your dog will be more motivated to respond if his correct response is promptly rewarded with lavish praise.

Although this step is a testing stage, it is a controlled test. When you test your dog at this point you must always be in a position to correct him if he does not respond. This means he should be wearing his leash and collar. Do not test haphazardly by giving the command to sit when your dog is across the room and you are in no position to make him comply.

Step 3: Hold the leash gathered up in your right hand. Grasp the leash in your left hand, palm down. Be ready to jerk and release if your dog does not respond to the command *"Sit."*

- Start with your dog standing at your left side.
- Gather up the leash into your right hand. Your left hand should be holding the leash, palm down, halfway between you and the dog.
- Call your dog's name and give the command *"Sit."* If he sits quickly on his own, praise him lavishly!
- If he does not respond within a few seconds, give a series of gentle jerks and releases. Do not repeat the command *"Sit."* Give one command and one command only. The jerks that follow should be in a direction toward the dog's tail. This will cause him to sit.
- Be sure to give effective jerks and releases to get your dog to sit, but do not overcorrect your dog.
- When your dog sits, stop jerking immediately and praise him lavishly.

Practice many sits throughout the day with your dog. Ideally, you should do this every day for two weeks. Be consistent! Do not test your dog by giving the command without being prepared to follow through with the correction.

Step 4: A Controlled Test from in Front

After practicing step 3 with your dog at your left side, try the procedure from a new position. Your dog should be doing the "stand-stay," step 3, before you are ready for this sit on command step (see page 96).

- Start with your dog standing at your left side.
- Tell him to stay and pivot out in front of your dog. There should be only a few inches between his nose and your knees (or ankles).
- Hold the leash gathered in your left hand. Your right hand should be holding the leash, palm up, between your left hand and the dog. (Reverse your hands if you are left-handed.)
- Give your dog the command *"Sit."* Allow him a few seconds to respond. If he sits, praise him lavishly.
- If he does not sit, give a series of gentle jerks and releases on the training collar. The jerks should be given in a direction that is up and back toward your dog's tail.
- As soon as your dog sits, praise him lavishly.

Work on sit on command by alternating between step 3 and step 4. Continue to practice until your dog sits quickly, avoiding the correction that will come if he does not respond. Be sure your collar

Step 4: Practice the testing phase from a knees-to-nose position.

corrections are given in the proper direction. You must jerk back toward your dog's tail. If you are jerking forward or straight up, your dog will not be able to sit.

When your dog sits reliably from the step 3 and step 4 positions, move farther away from him, toward the end of the leash. (Increase the distance *only* when you are having success closer in.) Progress away from the dog in two-foot intervals until you are six feet away. Be sure to step toward your dog to give a collar correction. Stepping toward him will help you correct in the proper direction.

Step 5: Random Sits

Once your dog is sitting reliably on command from six feet away, you are ready to incorporate random sits into your training program.

- Walk your dog in any direction.
- As you are walking along, give your dog the command *"Sit."* If he responds by sitting, praise him enthusiastically.
- If your dog does not sit quickly, give a jerk and release on the training collar up and back toward his tail. Do not give the correction simultaneously with the command. Give your dog a few seconds to respond.

Work on the random sit exercise two or three times a day for one minute per session. Tell your dog to sit when he is in front, behind, or on either side of you. Practice until your dog sits quickly when he hears the command.

Step 6: Off Leash

Once your dog is sitting reliably on command, it is time to test him off the leash. Give your dog the command to sit. If he responds by sitting, praise him enthusiastically. If he does not sit, quickly bend over and push his backside into a sitting position. Do not repeat the sit command. If your dog persists in not responding to the command, go back to practicing on-leash.

Keep in mind that learned behaviors or conditioned responses need reinforcement. Even after your dog is responding reliably to commands off the leash, the day will come when his response will not be as quick.

When a long enough time has passed, you will give your dog a command and he will stand there looking at you as if he never heard the sound before. To prevent this from happening or to rectify this when it does, practice regularly with your dog. Even when he is well trained, go back to the basics once in a while. Use the training techniques that taught him the behavior in the first place. This will keep your dog sharp.

Sit on Command from a Down Position

A dog who has learned to sit on command from a standing position will not understand how to sit on command from a lying-down position. Although the end result of the sit command is the same, sitting from a lying-down position has to be taught to the dog as a separate exercise. In order to accomplish this, you must use a specific technique designed to teach the dog to sit from a down position.

As mentioned, the emphasis in this book is not on obedience for the show ring. It is on obedience for real life. Sit from a down position is the only behavior in this book (not counting the exercises in the chapter on fun tricks) that most owners may not find useful in everyday life. The exercise is included because it is useful when practicing the testing stages of down on command. Your dog is ready to learn it when he knows the down-stay exercise.

Two techniques are used to teach sit from a down position. With small to medium-size dogs, I prefer method 1. With large to giant-size dogs or any size dogs who prefer to lie down on their backs, I use method 2.

Method 1: Stepping Toward the Dog

• Start with your dog sitting at your left side. Give the command *"Down"* and down your dog at your side.
• Give the command *"Stay."* Pivot out directly in front of your dog, toes to toes.

Method 1: Give the command *"Sit"* and then step toward your dog. Give a gentle jerk and release up on the training collar. These actions will cause your dog to sit from a down position.

• Hold the leash gathered up in your *left* hand. Your *right* hand should be holding the leash, palm up, between your left hand and your dog.

• Give the command *"Sit."* At the same time, give a jerk and release as you step toward your dog. Stepping toward your dog will crowd his space and cause him to sit up. This greatly reduces the force of the jerk needed to get your dog up. Be sure not to step on your dog's toes. Do *not* allow the training collar to tighten for more than a second around his neck.

• As soon as your dog is sitting, praise him enthusiastically.

• Keep your dog in the sitting position. Tell him *"Stay"* and return around him so that he is at your left side.

• Keep your dog sitting at your left side for several seconds. Then release and praise him.

Method 2: Stepping Away from the Dog

• Start with your dog in a down position at your left side.

• Tell him to stay and pivot directly in front of your dog, toes to toes.

• Hold the leash gathered up in your left hand. Grasp the leash in your right hand, palm up, between your dog and your left hand.

• Give your dog the command *"Sit."*

• As you give the command, give a gentle jerk and release on the training collar. Simultaneously walk backward away from your dog.

• The jerk and release on the collar and backing up will cause your dog to get up. As he starts to get up, step *toward* your dog.

Method 2: Tell your dog to "*Sit*" and take two steps back, away from the dog. Simultaneously give a jerk and release on the collar.

Quickly step toward your dog.

Push your dog's backside down into a sitting position.

• Once you have stepped back to your dog, be prepared to prevent him from standing. If he starts to stand, give a gentle jerk and release back toward his tail to cause him to sit.
• Tell your dog to stay as you pivot back or return around him. Stop when he is at your left side.

Practice this exercise every day until your dog will sit from a down position without a correction.

Sit-on-Command Hand Signal

To give the sit hand signal, start with your right arm at your side. Sweep your arm upward with the palm of your hand open facing your dog. As your arm comes up, bend your elbow so that the palm of your hand faces your shoulder. After giving the hand signal, lower your arm back to your right side.

When your dog will respond reliably to the verbal sit command from the standing and down positions, incorporate the hand signal into your practice sessions. Give the hand signal simultaneously with the verbal command. Practice for several weeks to associate the hand signal with the verbal command. Eventually eliminate the verbal command and see if your dog will respond to just the hand signal. If he does respond, praise him warmly. If your dog does *not* respond, quickly give the appropriate collar correction. After correcting be sure to praise lavishly.

Some trainers feel that it is advantageous to give the sit hand signal with the opposite arm that you give the down hand signal (see pages 186–188). There may be some advantage to this in the obedience ring. I do not think it matters in real life, but teaching it this way certainly will cause no harm.

Down on Command

Some dogs resist down-on-command training more than any other exercise. This is because lying down is the most submissive position a dog can be in. If the dog has the slightest ambition to be pack leader, he may resist your efforts to cause him to lie down. Perseverance on the part of the trainer is imperative when working on this exercise. If you allow the dog to resist being handled, you are telling him, in "dog talk," that he is the pack leader.

Although throwing meaningless sounds at a dog will often elicit a sit response, this is not true of down. Regardless of how many times you arbitrarily repeat the *"Down"* command, an untrained dog will not respond. Down on command is an exercise that must be taught to the dog in order to get a reliable response.

The objective of this exercise is to train the dog to drop to the ground in response to one verbal command. Some dogs will learn to go down by following the owner's hand as he or she points to the ground.

However, if your dog is racing toward a busy street, pointing to the ground will be useless. If the dog will drop instantly at your verbal command *"Down,"* you can save his life. It *can* be useful to have your dog trained to go down in accordance to a hand signal, although pointing to the ground is not the ideal one. (See pages 110–111.)

How to Teach Down on Command

Step 1: Compelling the Dog

- Start with your dog sitting at your left side.
- Hook the thumb of your *left* hand through the training collar. Place your open palm on your dog's back with your fingers pointing toward his tail.
- Slide your right arm under your dog's right leg. Lift his left leg off the ground until both legs are in the air.
- Pull back with your *left* hand on the collar as you lift both legs up. Pulling back will keep your dog's backside on the ground and prevent him from standing up. Be sure to pull back gently.
- Say your dog's name, give the command *"Down,"* and lower your dog's body to the ground.
- Keep your dog in the down position for a few seconds. (You are not teaching him to *"Stay"* with this exercise.) Praise him and then let him get up.

Step 1: Hook the thumb of your left hand through your dog's collar. Open your hand, palm down, with your fingers pointing toward the dog's tail. Reach under your dog's right leg and gently take hold of his left leg. Lift both legs off the ground. Give the command *"Down"* as you gently lower your dog into a down position.

Practice many downs throughout the day. Be sure *not* to test your dog at this stage by throwing a meaningless command at him. Make sure that every time you give the command, your hands are on the dog and you are in a position to make him comply immediately. Your job is to make an association between the sound *"Down"* and what your dog is supposed to do with his body when he hears this sound. Your dog's job is simply to comply—to allow you to down him. The only thing your dog can do wrong at this stage is to fight, bite, and resist. Show him what you want him to do each and every time he hears the command *"Down."*

Step 2: Inducing the Dog

- Start with your dog sitting at your left side.
- Hook the thumb of your *left* hand through the training collar. Place your open palm on your dog's back with your fingers pointing toward his tail. Pull back slightly on the collar.
- Get your dog's attention with an object of attraction held in your *right* hand. When you have his attention on the object, say his name, give the command *"Down,"* and lower the object straight down from his nose to the ground.
- As your dog lowers his body into the down position, extend the object along the ground in front of him so that he must reach for it.

Step 2: Hook the thumb of your left hand through the collar, as you did in step 1. Get your dog's attention with the object of attraction.

Lower your right hand with the object straight to the ground.

• When your dog is in the down position, praise him and let him have the object.

• Give one command only. If your dog does not go down by following the object of attraction, cause him to go down right away by using the step 1 compulsive method.

Alternate between the step 1 compulsive technique and the step 2 inducive exercise. Do *not* test your dog on these exercises at this point by merely using the command *"Down"* without showing him what you want him to do. This would slow down the association process.

Keep in mind that the compulsive and inducive techniques on their own will not teach a dog to lie down on command. They are used primarily to form an association between the sound and the action.

After several weeks of consistently practicing these techniques, your dog will have a good idea of what you want him to do when he hears the sound *"Down."* This next exercise will train your dog to respond promptly to the command.

Step 3: A Controlled Test

• Start with your dog sitting at your left side.

• Gather the leash into your *right* hand so that you have leverage, but do not make the leash tight.

• Place your open *left* hand, palm down, on your dog's shoulders to prevent him from standing up.

• Call your dog's name and give the command *"Down."* If the dog

Step 3: Gather the leash into your right hand, close to where the clip is sewn. Place your left hand on your dog's midback.

does not go down, give a series of gentle jerks and releases toward the ground. Be sure to jerk in the direction that the dog's body is leaning.

• Give one command only, regardless of how many jerks and releases are needed to get your dog to go down.

• Make sure you give an effective correction, but do not overcorrect your dog. Jerk and release just hard enough to get him to go down. *Do not pull on the leash.* Pulling will create resistance on your dog's part.

• When your dog goes down, stop jerking and praise him lavishly.

Practice many downs throughout the day with your dog. Be consistent! Do *not* test your dog by giving the command without following through with the correction if he does not respond. When you are not doing the step 3 procedure, continue to compel or induce him down using the step 1 and step 2 procedures.

Step 4: A Controlled Test from in Front

Continue to practice the step 3 training technique when giving the down command. You may also incorporate into your training program this variation of the exercise.

• Start with your dog sitting at your left side.

• Using both the verbal command and the stay hand signal (open palm flashed in front of the dog's face), tell your dog to "*Stay.*" Pivot out in front of your dog, nose to knees.

Step 4: Practice this exercise from both your left side and the knees-to-nose position.

Give the command *"Down."* If your dog does not respond, give a series of gentle jerks and releases. Do *not* pull.

- Gather your leash into your *right* hand. The leash should be loose, but be sure that you have enough leverage to jerk and release. Place your *left* hand on your dog's shoulder to prevent him from standing up.
- Give your dog the command *"Down."* If your dog does not go down immediately, give a series of gentle jerks and releases toward the ground. Continue to jerk and release until your dog goes down.
- Give only one *"Down"* command. Do not repeat the command regardless of how many jerks and releases it takes to get your dog down. As soon as your dog is down, stop jerking and praise him lavishly.
- After your dog is in a down position and you have finished praising him, tell him to *"Stay"* and return around him so that he is at your left side.
- Keep him in this position for ten seconds. Release and praise him.

Alternate between downing your dog from your left side and from the knees-to-nose position. The object of this exercise is to condition your dog to drop at the command *"Down"* to avoid the correction.

It is important to keep your hand on your dog's shoulder when using the step 3 and step 4 testing techniques. Do so until your dog is going down on command without having to be corrected. If you do not keep your hand on his shoulder, your dog will stand up when you give the collar corrections.

Step 5: Hand off the Shoulder

When your dog is doing steps 3 and 4 reliably, it is time to wean away your left hand from his shoulder. At this stage in training, your dog is receiving three cues telling him to go down. One cue is your verbal command *"Down."* The other two cues are your left hand on his shoulder and the body motion of leaning over him. It is important gradually to eliminate the last two cues so that your dog goes down exclusively in response to the verbal command.

- Start with your dog sitting at your left side.
- Gather the leash into your right hand. Be sure that the leash is loose but that you have leverage to jerk and release.
- Hold your left hand, palm down, about six inches above your dog's shoulder.

• Give your dog the command *"Down."* If he goes down, praise him exuberantly.

• If he does not go down immediately, give a series of gentle jerks and releases toward the ground. Do not overcorrect your dog. Be sure to jerk in the direction that his body is leaning.

• If your dog starts to stand up as you give the jerks and releases, quickly place your left hand on his shoulder. This will prevent him from standing up.

• Do not repeat the *"Down"* command. Give one command only.

• As soon as your dog goes down, stop jerking and praise enthusiastically.

Also practice this step from the knees-to-nose position. Continue to do this step until your dog will go down quickly on command with your left hand off his shoulder.

Step 6: Standing Straight

When your dog is going down on command with your left hand off his shoulder, it is time to eliminate excessive body motion.

• Start with your dog sitting at your left side.

• Hold the leash in your right hand. Your left hand should be palm down, grasping the leash in the middle, between your right hand and your dog.

• Stand straight but relaxed. Do not be rigid.

Step 6: Give the command *"Down."* If your dog does not respond, bend at the knees and give a series of gentle jerks and releases until the dog lies down.

- Give your dog the command *"Down."* If he responds by going down, praise him enthusiastically.
- If he does not go down immediately, quickly bend at the knees and give a series of gentle jerks and releases with the leash. Be sure that you do not repeat the command.
- As soon as your dog goes down, stop jerking and praise enthusiastically.

Practice this step with your dog sitting at your left side and from the knees-to-nose position. When practicing from the latter position, you must reverse the position of your hands on the leash.

As your dog becomes proficient with this exercise, practice with more distance between yourself and the dog. Move the leash down and away from your dog, in two-foot intervals. If you give your dog the down command from farther away and he does not drop, quickly step toward him to give the collar corrections. Continue to practice until your dog will lie down on command from six feet away.

Step 7: Down from a Standing Position

When your dog will lie down on command from six feet away, you are ready to introduce down from a standing position.

- Start with your dog standing at your left side. You should stand straight but relaxed. Turn your body slightly toward your dog.
- Hold the leash in your right hand. Your left hand should be palm down on the leash between your right hand and your dog.
- Give the command *"Down."* If your dog lies down, praise him enthusiastically.
- If he does not lie down immediately, give a series of gentle jerk-and-release collar corrections. Be sure to jerk toward the ground. Do not repeat the command.
- The instant your dog lies down, stop jerking and praise exuberantly.

Practice this step with your dog at your left side and from the knees-to-nose position. When your dog is dropping reliably into the down position, move away from him toward the end of your leash. Increase the distance away from your dog in two-foot intervals. Practice until your dog will lie down on command from a standing position when you are six feet away.

Step 8: Random Drops

Besides being a useful exercise around the house, a fast, reliable down on command can save your dog's life—particularly if he will drop while in motion. When your dog will lie down on command while in a standing position from six feet away, you are ready to train him to do random drops when he is in motion.

• Start walking in any direction with your dog doing controlled walking (see pages 150–152).
• Turn toward your dog and give him the command *"Down."*
• If he drops to the ground, praise him lavishly.
• If he does not drop instantly to the ground, quickly give a series of gentle jerks and releases with the leash on his training collar. Remember not to pull. Do not repeat the *"Down"* command.
• The instant your dog's body hits the ground, praise enthusiastically.

Practice random drops with your dog every day. Vary the direction that your dog is moving when you give the *"Down"* command. Get your dog responding quickly enough so that his body hits the ground before you can jerk the collar. Remember that a quick drop can be a life saver!

Down-on-Command Hand Signal

When your dog will lie down on command without your having to use any body motion, you are ready to associate a hand signal with the command. The down hand signal is very useful when you need your dog to drop quickly.

I have found that my dogs go down the fastest when I give the verbal command and the hand signal simultaneously. In the A.K.C. obedience ring, you are allowed to give only one of the two commands. However, in the real world such restrictions do not apply. If a double signal will cause your dog to react quicker, by all means use them both. Quick response can keep your dog safe.

The down hand signal is given with your right arm held straight up over your head. The palm of your right hand should be open, facing your dog. You *can* create any signal you wish and associate it with the

When your dog responds reliably to the "Down" command, introduce the "down" hand signal.

down command. However, I feel this is the best signal because it is visible to the dog from a distance.

- Start with your dog sitting at your left side.
- Tell him to *"Stay."* Go three feet away from your dog and turn to face him.
- Hold the leash in your left hand. The leash should be almost tight.
- Give your dog the verbal command *"Down."* Simultaneously give the down hand signal. If your dog quickly goes down, praise him lavishly.
- If your dog does not lie down immediately, step toward him with your right leg. Give a series of gentle jerks and releases with the leash in your left hand. (Keep your right hand in the air.) Be sure to jerk *down*, toward the ground. As soon as your dog is down, stop jerking and praise lavishly.
- When your dog is down, pivot back to your dog (or circle around him) so that he is at your left side. Praise your dog!

Practice the down signal with your dog every day for several weeks. You can dictate how fast your dog lies down in response to the hand signal by quickly correcting him if he does not drop immediately. The longer you hold your arm in the air without correcting, the slower your dog's response will be.

When your dog will go down quickly in response to the verbal command and the hand signal, eliminate the verbal command. If your dog does not respond to the hand signal, be sure to quickly step toward him and give collar corrections. The instant his body hits the ground, stop jerking and begin praising. As your dog becomes proficient with his response to the hand signal, increase the distance away from him toward the end of the leash.

Fourteen

Sit-Stay

Sit-stay means to keep your dog staying in a sitting position until he is released with a specific signal. The dog's head can move and his tail can wag, but his front feet and his backside must remain on the floor. Sit-stay is useful in many situations. I use it to prevent my dogs from running out an open front door. The dogs have learned to sit and stay at the open door instead of charging through it. More than once this has proven to be a life-saving behavior.

Sit-stay also can be used to keep your dog under control when getting in and out of the car. For example, if I need to get organized before letting the dogs in the car, I have them sit and stay until I give the release word. Sit-stay also prevents the dogs from jumping out of the car the instant the door is opened. Again, this can save a dog's life. Sit-stay is useful on walks, too. Whenever my dogs and I come to a curb, I have the dogs sit and stay. When traffic is clear I give the release word to cross the street. If a jogger or a person with a dog goes by, I have the dogs sit and stay to keep them under control.

You can use sit-stay when you are having fun with your dog. I use the command when my dogs and I are playing "retrieve the stick" at the lake. I have the dogs sit and stay, throw the stick, and make them wait. Then I tell them *"Get it!"* Sit-stay also prevents the dogs from jumping on me when they return the stick. They hold the stick until I say *"Let go."* Only then do I release the dogs. I stay dry, and this becomes a fun way to practice sit-stay.

Besides having practical uses, the sit-stay exercise is necessary for dogs to learn other behaviors. For example, a dog needs to understand sit and stay before you can teach him to come when called. He must know sit-stay to learn to greet people without jumping on them and to do controlled walking and heeling.

How to Teach Sit-Stay

Step 1: Sitting at Your Side

• Start with your dog sitting at your *left* side. Place the rings of your dog's training collar on the right side of his neck.

• Give him the command "*Stay.*" (Do not use your dog's name when giving the "*Stay*" command).

• Watch your dog closely. If he starts to move, tell him "*NHAA*" and place him back into a sitting position. Use your hands to push down gently on his rump if he stands up. Remind him again to "*Stay.*"

• While you are keeping the dog staying at your side, gather the leash up in your right hand. Your left hand should be palm down on the leash between your right hand and the leash's clip.

• If your dog starts to get up, tell him "*NHAA.*" At the same time give a jerk and release back on the training collar toward the dog's tail. The best time to correct your dog is when you think he's *thinking* about getting up. The next best time is when your dog starts to get up. And

Step 1: Begin practicing this exercise with the dog sitting at your left side.

Step 2: Place the rings of your dog's training collar between his ears. Hold the leash in your left hand, above your shoulder. Reach across your body with your right hand, palm up.

the worst time is when you look down and he's gone. Watch your dog closely!

• Start practicing for short periods of time. The first practice session should be fifteen seconds long. The second practice session should be thirty seconds long. Increase each successful session by fifteen seconds, until your dog will stay without moving for three full minutes.

• At the end of the designated time, use a release word such as *"Okay"* as you take a step forward. This word releases your dog from the stay. Do not release your dog with praise. Release him, *then* praise lavishly.

If your dog does well with the sit-stay exercise, you may increase the time beyond three minutes. Do *not* increase the distance away from your dog. Stay right next to him where you can correct as soon as he starts to move. *Timing your corrections properly is essential to help your dog understand what you want from him.* Practice at least three sit-stays a day with your dog.

Step 2: Stay from in Front

• Start with your dog sitting at your *left* side. Place the rings of the training collar between his ears at the back of his neck.

• Slide the leash up through your left hand until your hand is slightly above your left shoulder. Gather up the dangling end of the leash into your left hand. Pull back slightly on the leash to keep your dog sitting.

• Reach across your body with your right arm and grasp the leash with your right hand, palm facing upward.

After telling your dog to *"Stay,"* pivot in front of the dog, knees-to-nose.

- Tell your dog to *"Stay."* (Do not use your dog's name when giving the *"Stay"* command.) After telling the dog to stay, pivot out in front of him knees to nose. Relax the leash so there is no pressure on the dog's neck.
- Watch your dog closely. If he starts to move, tell him *"NHAA."* Simultaneously give a jerk and release in the direction your dog is sitting (up and back toward his tail). Use your hands to push down on his rump if he stands up and you can't get him into a sitting position using the leash and collar.
- Start practicing for short periods of time. The first practice session should be fifteen seconds long, the second practice session should be thirty seconds long, and so on. Increase each successful session by fifteen seconds, until your dog will stay without moving for three full minutes.
- At the end of the designated time, pivot back so that your dog is at your left side.
- Keep your dog sitting in heel position for an additional ten seconds, then use your release word. Release and praise him lavishly.

If your dog does well with the sit-stay exercise, you may increase the time in front of him beyond three minutes. Do *not* increase the distance. Stay right in front of your dog where you can correct him as he starts to move.

Most beginning trainers want to work on distance first. However, when you begin to teach this exercise, chances are the dog will break the stay. To correct this, you must associate the sound *"NHAA"* with a jerk and release on the collar—*as the dog moves*. This is the only way the dog will understand that he should *not* move. When trainers are too far away, they cannot make a timely correction.

Stay close to your dog at this stage. If you follow the steps described here, you will build a chain of reliable sit-stays at increasingly greater distances. Eventually you will be able to go as far away as you wish and have a dependable stay.

Practice at least three sit-stays a day with your dog.

Step 3: Adding Distractions

- Start with your dog sitting at your *left* side.
- Place the rings of the training collar under your dog's neck. Hold the leash in your *left* hand by the handle.
- Tell your dog to *"Stay"* using both the verbal command and the hand signal. The hand signal for all "stay" exercises is an open palm held for a moment in front of the dog's face.
- After you tell your dog to *"Stay,"* take two steps forward, turn, and face your dog.
- Tell your dog *"NHAA"* if he starts to move. Step toward him with your right foot and give a jerk-and-release correction. Be sure to jerk and release in a direction that will keep your dog sitting.
- You are now ready to add distractions to the training environment. It is important that your dog learn to stay even with distractions. Shuffle your feet, pat your leg, stoop down on the dog's level, and so on. If these distractions cause the dog to break the stay, correct him immediately.
- Keep your dog staying in this position for at least five minutes.
- At the end of the designated time, return so that the dog is sitting at your left side. Keep him sitting for ten additional seconds.
- Use your release word to release him from the stay. Praise him lavishly.

Systematically adding distractions to your training environment is called proofing. Proofing is imperative in order to have a well-trained dog. A stay is useless if distractions cause the dog to break.

Introduce mild distractions at first. When your dog will stay successfully, move to moderate distractions. When you are successful with moderate distractions, go to chaotic distractions. Your goal is a dog who will stay under any circumstances.

Step 3: Practice the stay halfway to the end of your leash. Incorporate proofing into your training program.

Any distraction is fine *except* using the word "Come."

Every dog handles distractions differently. What is a mild distraction to one dog may be a moderate distraction to another dog. The very same thing may be a chaotic distraction to a third dog. You will have to figure out what distractions are appropriate for your own dog. The guideline is this: The distraction should be just enough to get your dog to begin getting up. If you are struggling to keep your dog under control, the distraction is too intense. Back down to a moderate or mild level.

Here are some examples of distractions. Be creative in thinking of others.

Distractions for Your Dog

Shuffle your feet
Whistle
Jingle your car keys
Stoop down to the dog's level
Have someone knock on the door
Have someone ring the doorbell
Turn on the radio or TV
Have children walk by

Bounce a tennis ball
Hold a dog cookie
Drop a dog cookie on the floor
Let the cat in the room
Clap your hands
Sing
Eat a sandwich

There is one taboo. *Never* call your dog to you and then correct him for coming. Doing so would undo all your come-on-command training.

Step 4: Increasing the Distance

• Start with your dog sitting at your left side. Tell him to *"Stay"* using both the verbal command and the hand signal.

• After telling your dog to stay, walk to the end of the leash and turn and face him. Do not back away from your dog after telling him to stay. Walk with your back to him but watch him over your shoulder.

• If your dog starts to move, tell him *"NHAA"* and step toward him with your right leg. Give a jerk and release with the leash at an angle that will keep your dog sitting. Remind him to *"Stay"* in a normal command tone.

• While your dog is sitting, pull lightly on the leash and at the same time tell him to *"Stay."* Do *not* jerk and release. This would force your dog to break the stay. A light, steady pull on the leash will cause your dog to resist getting up. This will reinforce the stay. Do not pull too hard, just hard enough to feel your dog's body resist.

• Keep your dog in a stay at this distance for at least five minutes. Return so that the dog is at your left side.

• Keep him sitting at your side for at least ten seconds, then release your dog. Praise him lavishly.

Continue to proof your dog. If your dog is staying with mild dis-

Step 4: Practice sit-stay six feet away, at the end of your leash.

It is important to associate the sound *"NHAA"* and a jerk on the collar with the dog's movement.

tractions, increase to moderate distractions. If you need to make a correction, be sure to step toward your dog first. Do not jerk and release from six feet away—doing so would pull the dog out of his sitting position. Remind the dog to *"Stay"* if you think he is thinking about moving.

When you leave the dog to walk toward the end of the leash, be sure to walk facing forward—with your back to the dog. Turn your head so that you can watch the dog over your shoulder and verbally correct him if he starts to follow you. Do *not* walk backward so that you face the dog as you move away. Dogs are very aware of body language. You always face the dog when teaching him to come on command. Using the body language for *"Come"* and the verbal command for *"Stay"* will confuse him. Do not correct your dog for coming when your mixing of signals is the problem. Doing so would undermine all your work in teaching him the come-on-command exercise.

The next step in sit-stay training is to go beyond the end of the leash. You are not ready for this step until your dog stops dead in his tracks when you growl *"NHAA."* Until you have reached that point, keep the leash in your hand so you can associate *"NHAA"* with a jerk on the collar if your dog gets up.

Step 5: Beyond the End of the Leash

• Sit your dog at your left side. Tell him to *"Stay"* using both the verbal command and the hand signal.

• Leave your dog. Be sure to watch him over your shoulder as

Step 5: If you must correct your dog when you are beyond the end of the leash, use your voice. Do *not* charge back to the dog.

you walk away. If he starts to move, growl *"NHAA."* When you reach the end of the leash, drop it and continue on for another four feet. Then turn and face your dog.

• Watch your dog closely. Again, if he starts to move, growl *"NHAA."* Without the leash in your hand, perfect timing of your verbal correction is essential. You must correlate the sound *"NHAA"* with his initial movement. If your *"NHAA"* comes late, your dog will not understand what you want.

• If your *"NHAA"* does not stop your dog from breaking the stay, walk calmly back to him. Do not run. (This will trigger the flight instinct.) Bring him back to the spot where he broke the stay and re-sit him. In a normal command tone tell him *"Stay."*

• Keep your dog in a sit-stay for at least five minutes. Then return to him so that he is at your left side. Wait ten additional seconds, then release and praise your dog.

If your dog does not stop reliably when you say *"NHAA,"* you are not ready for this step. Go back to the previous step at six feet away with the leash in your hands.

Step 6: Stay from Twenty Feet Away

• Begin with your dog sitting at your left side.

• Give the command *"Stay"* using both the verbal command and the hand signal.

• After giving the command, leave your dog. Be sure to watch him over your shoulder as you walk away. When you reach the end of the leash, drop it and continue on until you are *twenty feet* from your dog. When you reach your destination, turn and face your dog.

• Watch him carefully from this position. If he starts to move, tell him *"NHAA."* Timing is essential.

• If *"NHAA"* does not stop your dog from breaking the stay, return calmly to him. Bring him back to the spot where he broke the stay and re-sit him. In a normal command tone tell him to *"Stay."*

• Keep your dog in a sit-stay for a least five minutes from this position. Then return so that he is at your left side. Keep him sitting for an additional ten seconds, then release and praise your dog.

As your dog becomes proficient with this step, increase the distraction level. You should also change the training environment. Practice in a new place every day. Work in the basement, the yard, a neighbor's yard, and so on. If you advance to practicing in busy public places,

Step 6: Invite all your dog's friends over to practice sit-stay together. Sit-stay is a useful exercise for all breeds of dogs.

be sure your dog's safety is guaranteed. Do *not* go beyond the end of the leash—if your dog breaks the stay, he might end up in a busy road. Use your long line in such situations. (See Chapter 8, "Training Tools.") Then you can still go beyond six feet and have control over the dog. Stand on the long line if you do not want the dog to see you holding it.

Step 7: Stay Without a Leash

• Start with your dog sitting at your left side. Remove his leash, but hold onto it.

• Give him the command *"Stay"* using both the hand signal and the verbal command.

• After you give the command to *"Stay,"* walk away with your back to the dog, watching him over your shoulder. Go three feet and turn and face your dog.

• Watch your dog carefully from this position. If he starts to move, tell him *"NHAA."* If he does not sit back down in response to your *"NHAA,"* return to him, snap the leash on, and correct him. Put him back in the spot from which he broke. Minimize hand contact. Use the leash and collar to correct your dog.

• If your dog does not move, stay three feet away with the leash off for at least five minutes.

• At the end of the designated time, return so that the dog is at your left side.

• Keep your dog sitting at your left side for at least ten seconds. Release and praise him.

As your dog becomes proficient with this step, increase the time of the off-leash sit-stay by small increments. When the dog will stay for five full minutes, start adding a few mild distractions, just as you did with on-leash training. Then advance to moderate distractions. Only when your dog will stay with distractions should you increase the distance away from him. Go six feet away and practice for a short time. Increase the time. Then add distractions. Then increase the distractions. Then start the routine all over again at ten feet away.

If you are careful to keep the priorities of time first, distractions second, and distance last, you can build an invisible chain of reliable sit-stays and go as far away as you wish. Then when you leave your dog for a stay, you know you will succeed.

Out-of-Sight Sit-Stay

Eventually you may want to try the sit-stay out of sight. To do so you must find a place where your dog cannot see you—but where you can see him. You cannot go out of sight and *assume* your dog is still staying. When you first go out of sight of your dog, go only for a few seconds. If and when he makes a mistake, you should step into the room and correct your dog with a firm *"NHAA."* Your dog should think that you could pop out from anywhere to make a correction. See the section on out-of-sight stays at the end of Chapter 17 for more details on how to teach this.

Watch Me

Dogs who are attentive are easier to train. Some dogs are naturally attentive. Other dogs must be trained to pay attention. Teaching a dog to look at you on command takes patience and perseverance on the part of the trainer.

I do not put a strong emphasis on this exercise, especially for beginners. You will find that the obedience exercises in this book will build up your dog's attentiveness on their own.

Step 1

- Start with your dog sitting at your left side. Tell him to *"Stay."*
- Hold your leash in your left hand. In your right hand hold a dog

Get your dog's attention by holding a piece of food near your face. Give the command *"Watch"* as your dog looks at you.

biscuit. (If your dog is not interested in food, use his favorite object of attraction.)

• Get your dog's attention with the food by waving it in front of his nose.

• Bring the food up to your face. As your dog looks at the food, say *"Watch."*

• Keep the food near your face, holding your dog's attention. Praise your dog soothingly as he looks up. Continue to praise him while he watches you.

• If your dog looks away, regain his attention with the food, as you did at the beginning.

• After ten seconds tell your dog *"Okay!"* to release him from the exercise. Pet and praise him.

Practice this exercise every day. Increase the time your dog watches you in ten-second intervals. Remember to praise him warmly the entire time he is looking at you. Practice step 1 until your dog will watch you for thirty seconds.

Step 2

When your dog will watch you for thirty seconds, you are ready for step 2.

• Start with your dog sitting at your left side. Tell him to *"Stay."*

• Hold the leash in your right hand so that it crosses in front of your body. Your left arm should be held at your side.

• Give your dog the command *"Watch."* If your dog looks up at you and holds your gaze, praise him warmly as he watches you.

• If your dog does not look at you after the command *"Watch,"* reach over his head with your left hand and *gently* scoop his face up toward yours. Repeat the command *"Watch"* as you do so. As soon as he looks at you, praise him warmly.

• After your dog has looked at you for a few seconds, tell him *"Okay!"* and break eye contact. Pet and praise your dog.

Continue to increase the amount of time that your dog watches you in short increments. When your dog will watch you on command for thirty seconds, try step 3.

Step 3

• Start with your dog sitting at your left side. Place the rings of his training collar under his chin.

• Hold the leash in your left hand. The loop of the leash should almost be touching the ground.

• With your voice and the hand signal, tell your dog to *"Stay."* Take two steps away from your dog and turn to face him.

• With your right hand, grasp the leash palm up, as you did for the sit-stay exercise. You should be holding the leash halfway between your left hand and your dog. Do not pull the leash tight.

• Practice the sit-stay exercise from this position. When your dog turns his head to look at something behind him, step toward him with your right leg. Your foot should be even with his toes.

• Give a *gentle* jerk and release on the training collar in the direction of your dog's tail. As you give the jerk and release, repeat the command *"Watch."*

• As soon as your dog looks at you, praise him lavishly. Do *not* stop praising until your dog breaks eye contact on his own.

Settle for a few seconds of eye contact from this position at first. As you practice, you will find that your dog will watch you for longer periods of time. Do *not* nag your dog with this exercise. Do it just two or three times when you practice a sit-stay. It may take several months before your dog will watch you for a full minute.

Fifteen

Greeting People Without Jumping

A friendly dog greeting you at the front door is one of life's small but wonderful pleasures. A muddy, eighty-pound mutt bouncing against your best suit is one of life's miserable annoyances. Is it possible to teach dogs to say hello in a controlled manner? Yes. It is accomplished with a simple obedience exercise called "greeting people without jumping."

Dogs jump on people they greet for one reason: They want attention. This is precisely why a training method such as kneeing the dog in the chest does not work. Kneeing the dog is a form of attention, even though it is negative. The dog is getting exactly what he craves. Dogs will settle for negative attention over no attention at all.

Not only is kneeing dogs ineffective, it is also dangerous. If you knee a dog *hard* enough, you may discourage him from jumping on you, but you may also cause a severe injury. Over the years veterinarians have shown me X rays of several dogs hurt by people trying to discourage unwanted jumping. The X rays revealed injuries ranging from broken jaws to fractured shoulders.

No training method should cause injury or pain! Avoid any physically abusive training methods that attempt to eliminate unwanted jumping. Such techniques are ineffective at best and harmful to the dog at worst. The best way to train your dog to greet people without jumping is to capitalize on your dog's motivation. Attention is what the dog wants. He must become conditioned to seek attention from a sitting position.

Dogs jump on people for one reason and one reason only:
They want attention!

For this training procedure to work, your dog must known the sit-stay exercise. (See Chapter 14, "Sit-Stay.")

- Start with your dog sitting at your left side. You should be near an entrance where visitors come in. Tell your dog to "*Stay.*"
- Hold the leash gathered up in your right hand. Your left hand should be gripping the leash palm down, between the dog and your right hand.
- Have a friend ring the doorbell or knock on the door. Make your dog stay sitting at your left side. Invite your friend to come in.
- If your dog gets excited and tries to break the stay, correct him with a tough-sounding "*NHAA*" and a jerk and release on the collar. Tell him again to "*Stay.*"
- When your dog is under control sitting and staying at your left side, have your friend say hello to the dog from a few feet away. The greeting should not be so exuberant that it sets your dog into a frenzy. A pleasant, calm, verbal greeting will do.
- Have the friend approach your dog. If the dog starts to break the stay or jump, correct him *as your visitor backs away.* Put the dog back into a sitting position. Remind the dog again to "*Stay.*"
- Have your friend repeatedly approach your dog until the dog keeps his front feet on the ground and does not break the stay. During this time you can remind your dog to stay by repeating the command "*Stay.*"
- When your dog is under control, have your friend reach down and pet and praise your dog. Again, if your dog breaks the stay, have your visitor back up as you correct the dog.

Teach your dog that his desire for attention will be fulfilled if he keeps his front feet on the ground.

As the visitor approaches, give your dog a jerk and release on the collar—if he starts to jump up.

Practice this exercise five or six times in a row. Always start by having the visitor knock on the door or ring the doorbell. Even though the person was in the house only a moment before, your dog will still attempt to go through his wild greeting ritual. This is good because it allows you many repetitions per training session.

This procedure will *not* be effective if you employ it only occasionally when an unexpected visitor shows up. You must simulate visits every day. A good time to practice this exercise is when your wife or husband comes home from work at night. Also use the exercise when the kids come home from school.

Remember, to train a dog all that is needed is to first find a way to get the dog to do a behavior. Then repeat the behavior until a habit is formed. For example, if the dog jumps on your wife every evening when she comes home from work, you are practicing jumping. Before long this unwanted behavior will become a habit.

Instead, clip the leash on the dog every evening when you hear your wife pull into the driveway. Have your dog in a sitting position when he greets her. Eventually the dog will become conditioned to sit to be greeted when she comes home. The more you repeat this behavior—

When your dog keeps his front feet and backside on the ground, the visitor should provide *lots* of attention.

and the earlier you introduce it into your dog's life—the quicker it will become a habit.

You can continue to condition your dog to greet people without jumping even when the leash is not clipped on. If you are greeting the dog without a second handler present, be sure to bend down quickly and push the dog's backside into a sitting position. Do this *before* the dog jumps on you. If your dog beats you to the punch and jumps on you, tell him *"NHAA"* and quickly sit him.

Keep in mind that telling the dog *"NHAA"* after he already has his front feet on you does *not* teach the dog to avoid jumping. It simply tells him to stop jumping once he has already begun. You want the dog conditioned not to jump in the first place. It is your responsibility to react quickly and push his backside down *before* he jumps on you.

As I've mentioned, if dog training was easy, everyone would have well-trained dogs. It takes perseverance and hard work to shape a dog's behavior—especially jumping up to greet people, which so many dogs love to do.

Sixteen

Stand-Stay

The stand-stay exercise is designed to keep your dog staying in a standing position. The dog's head can move and the tail can wag, but his feet must stay in place. In obedience competitions a slightly moved foot means lost points, but that is not a catastrophe for our purposes. Our goal is simply to keep the dog standing calmly in one spot.

Stand-stay is a practical control mechanism with many uses in everyday life. You can use stand-stay when you brush your dog. It is handy when drying wet, muddy dog feet on rainy days. Veterinarians and groomers love to see dogs who know stand-stay walk through their doors. They know that the dogs will be easy to deal with, making their jobs easier.

Stand-stay can help you maintain your pet's good health. Use this exercise to thoroughly examine your dog, something you should do at least once a week for your dog's entire life. The consequences of not doing so can be distressing.

For a number of years, I worked in veterinary hospitals. Often people would bring their dogs in for routine procedures, such as vaccinations or a heartworm test. During the visit the veterinarian would find something on the dog that the owner was completely unaware of—a lump or bump, a broken tooth or toenail, a scratched cornea. Sometimes he would discover that the dog had an infected mouth where a piece of broken stick had wedged into the palate.

We would take the dog back into the treatment room for care. I recall asking the veterinarian on several of these occasions "Why didn't the owners know about this problem?"

The veterinarian's response usually would be "They haven't looked at this dog in months!"

Often the condition that we discovered required extensive medical care. The dog would have to be put under a general anesthetic, and the owner would receive an unexpectedly high veterinary bill. A simple office visit became a stressful event for everyone involved—particularly the dog.

As a responsible dog owner, you should check your dog thoroughly once a week at the very least. Put the dog in a stand-stay in a quiet room with good light. Start at the muzzle. Lift up the gums and open the mouth, checking for broken or chipped teeth. Check the roof of the mouth. Look into both of your dog's eyes. Run your hands down both front legs. Check between each toe. Go over your dog's back and under his belly. Feel along the tail, hips, and back legs. Check for discharges from the rectum, vagina, or penis.

Be familiar with what is normal anatomy on your dog. I remember one woman hysterically upset calling the veterinary hospital where I worked. She was sure her dog was dying from some dreadful form of mouth cancer. Why? One day she happened to lift the lips of her six-year-old Irish setter and discovered black spots on her dog's gums. Had she known what she was looking at, she would have realized that many dogs have black pigmentation in their mouths.

How to Teach Stand-Stay

Step 1: Hands on the Dog

The dog who is trained to stand-stay will stay in a standing position without moving his feet, although his head and tail can move. This dog will stand and stay while being brushed, bathed, or examined, either by the owner or another person.

• Start with your dog sitting at your *left* side. Kneel down next to your dog so that you are facing him.
• Slide your *right* hand through your dog's training collar, fingers pointing toward the tail.
• Give the command *"Stand."* At the same time lift your dog into a standing position with your *left* hand under his belly.

Step 1: After standing your dog from a sitting position, tell him to *"Stay."*

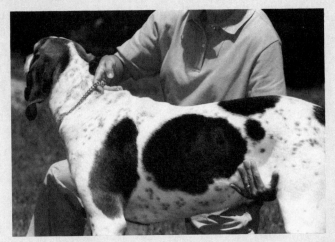

Keep your hands on your dog! Minimize heavy restraint while your dog stands calmly.

- Tell him to *"Stay."* KEEP YOUR HANDS ON YOUR DOG.
- Use your hands on his collar and under his belly to keep him from moving. If he tries to move or walk away, tell him *"NHAA"* and pull up with your right hand on his training collar. If he tries to sit, tell him *"NHAA"* and use your left hand under his belly to stop him. After either correction, tell him *"Stay"* in a normal command tone. Your dog may move his head or wag his tail while standing and staying.
- After your dog has been standing without moving for ten seconds, release him with a specific release word, such as *"Okay!"* This signals the dog to move. Remove your hands and praise him enthusiastically.

132

At each practice session increase the time slightly so that by step 2 you can keep your dog standing without moving for two full minutes. Do not take your hands off the dog at all during step 1. Do not pet or praise your dog until you have used your release word. Petting or praising before the release word may cause the dog to move during this stage in training. Practice at least three stand-stays a day.

Step 2: Removing Your Hands

• Place your dog in a stand using the step 1 technique. Tell him to *"Stay."*

• When you feel that your dog is relaxed and is not going to move, remove your left hand from under his belly. At the same time tell him to *"Stay."* Next remove your right hand from his collar. Again at the same time tell him to *"Stay."*

• Watch him closely. If he starts to move, firmly tell him *"NHAA."* As you say *"NHAA,"* quickly put your hands back into position under his belly and through his collar. Remember that it is okay for his head to move and his tail to wag.

• When he feels steady, tell him to *"Stay"* and remove your hands again. Be sure that every time you remove your hands from your dog, you correlate the word *"Stay"* with this action.

• If he does not move after you remove your hands, keep him staying for ten seconds. Then use a word such as *"Okay!"* to release him.

• Praise your dog enthusiastically.

***Step* 2:** Practice stand-stay with your hands off your dog.

Continue to increase the time that your dog stands with your hands off by fifteen-second intervals. Do this until your dog will stand without moving for two full minutes. Be sure that your dog will stand and stay for two full minutes with your hands *on* him before you attempt to remove your hands. Remember to tell your dog *"Stay"* as you remove your hands from him. If he moves, remember to tell him *"NHAA"* firmly as you place your hands back on him.

Your dog may respond best to this step if you first remove your collar hand and then the belly hand. If not, try removing the belly hand first. Some dogs respond best if you remove both hands at the same time. All dogs are different, so experiment. However, no matter which hand you remove first, the key element is to say *"Stay" as you remove your hands.* This is one of the many training steps that requires good timing—the most basic ingredient to all good dog training.

Step 3: Stay from in Front

If your dog has been successful standing and staying for two full minutes with your hands off him, you are ready for step 3. If you have not been successful, continue to practice steps 1 and 2.

- Start with your dog sitting at your *left* side.
- Do not kneel down as you did in step 1. Instead, bend over and stand your dog. As you do this, give the command *"Stand."*
- After your dog is in a standing position, tell him to *"Stay."* Re-

Step 3: Practice stand-stay from a knees-to-nose position.

move your hands and stand upright. Face in the same direction as your dog. Your dog should be standing at your left side.

- Watch your dog closely. If he starts to move, tell him *"NHAA."* Bend over and get your hands back into position.
- When you feel he is steady, repeat the command *"Stay."* Remove your hands and stand up as before.
- Using the verbal command and the hand signal (an open palm flashed in front of the dog's face), tell your dog to *"Stay."* Pivot directly out in front of him, knees to nose.
- Watch your dog closely from this position. If he starts to move, tell him *"NHAA."* Stay in front of the dog but get your hands back into position (*right* hand through the collar, *left* hand under his belly). As you remove your hands from your dog, remind him again to *"Stay"* as you stand erect.
- At the end of the designated time, pivot back so that the dog is at your left side. Keep your dog standing for a few additional seconds. Use your release word and let him go.
- Praise your dog enthusiastically!

Stay in front of your dog for short periods at first. Increase the time until you can keep him standing without moving for two full minutes. Do not hold the leash during this exercise. Keep the leash on your dog and let it hang to the floor. You *cannot* jerk a dog to correct him during a stand-stay. Jerking him would make him move and would be counter-productive.

If your dog moves, tell him *"NHAA."* Reach over and gently restand him.

Often people find that their dogs will stand and stay successfully at this point in training. However, sometimes dogs have a "dejected" look on their faces while doing so. This may be hard for owners to understand because they were never rough or abusive in training. I believe the reason for the dejected look is simple: The stand-stay exercise, while very useful to humans, is not very natural to dogs. In the wild, canines frequently sit or lie down without moving. Rarely, however, do they stand without moving for long periods of time. I believe that this exercise seems a bit strange to the dog.

You can compensate for this by praising your dog *during* the stand-stay. Don't make him go wild, but get his ears up and his tail wagging. Tell him what a good stand-stay he is doing. Remember to keep control of the dog as needed by interjecting the command *"Stay"* as you praise. Your praise will reassure your dog if he is feeling uncertain. It will also improve his appearance during the stand-stay. With a little practice he will stand and stay confidently, with ears held high and tail wagging.

Step 4: *Increasing the Distance*

- Start with your dog sitting at your left side.
- Place your dog into a stand using the step 3 technique.
- As you tell your dog to stay, remove your hands from him and stand up straight. Your dog should be standing at your left side. Do not hold the leash. Leave it on your dog but let it lay on the ground.
- Tell your dog to *"Stay"* using the verbal command and hand signal. Take two steps away from him. Turn and face your dog. The distance between you and your dog should be only about three feet.
- If your dog starts to move, firmly tell him *"NHAA."* Return to him. Put your hands back into position, and restand your dog. Tell him *"Stay"* again in a normal command tone.
- After your dog has stood without moving for thirty seconds, return to your dog so that he is at your left side.
- Keep your dog standing for an additional ten seconds. Then give the release word, and praise your dog lavishly.

Keep your dog in a stand-stay at this distance for thirty seconds at first. As he becomes more proficient staying in this position, increase the time away from him. Your goal is to keep your dog standing and staying for two full minutes. If you have trouble keeping your dog in a stand-stay from this position, backtrack to a step in which you will be successful.

Step 5: Stay During Handler Exam

- Stand your dog. Tell him to *"Stay."*
- If you were successful with stand-stay step 4, you are ready to go six feet away from your dog. Walk to the end of the leash and drop it on the ground. Turn and face your dog. The leash should be attached to your dog but laying on the ground.
- Watch your dog carefully. If he moves, firmly tell him *"NHAA"* and return to him. Do *not* run back to your dog. Walk calmly and place him back into a stand. In a normal command tone repeat *"Stay."* Leave the dog again, going to the end of the leash.
- When your dog is standing and seems steady, walk back to him so that you are facing the dog, knees to nose. From this position examine your dog. Look at his teeth. Check both of his eyes and look into both of his ears. Run your hands down both front legs, along his back, and down his hind legs. Also examine his tail. If your dog starts to move, tell him *"NHAA"* and reposition him. Work with your dog until you can give him a thorough examination without him moving.
- After examining your dog, circle him and then return back to the end of your leash. Keep your dog standing from this position for at least two minutes.
- After two minutes return so that the dog is at your left side. Release and praise your dog.

Some dogs are very distracted by the stimulation of the handler's touch during the examination. If this is the case with your dog, start with a superficial examination. Lightly touch the top of the dog's

Step 5: Get your dog used to being examined while in a stand-stay.

head, the shoulders, and the rump—then return back to the end of the leash. Remind the dog to stay while you touch him. If he starts to move, quickly say *"NHAA"* and restand him if necessary. Tell him again to *"Stay."* Praise your dog when you finish the exam, no matter how brief it was.

When your dog will stay during a superficial examination, begin to examine him more thoroughly. Touch him a little more each time you practice. Be sure to use a gentle touch. If one day you find that your dog cannot tolerate your touching a certain body part, you probably have found a medical problem. If necessary, take your dog to the veterinarian for professional care. With practice you can get the dog used to lots of touching and examining. Even the most excitable dog will learn to like (or at least tolerate) a thorough checkup.

Step 6: *Stand for Examination*

- Start with your dog sitting at your left side. Remove the leash.
- Give your dog the command *"Stand,"* then place him into a standing position.
- Give your dog the command *"Stay"* using both the verbal command and the hand signal.
- After you have told him to stay, walk six feet away. Turn and face your dog.
- Have a friend or family member approach your dog from the front. Let the dog sniff the person's hand. Have the person examine your dog in the same manner in which you did in the previous step.
- Watch your dog carefully. If he starts to move, tell him *"NHAA."* Return calmly to your dog and restand him. Remember, never run back to your dog during a stay exercise.
- If your dog does not move and accepts being examined, keep him standing at this distance for at least two minutes.
- At the end of two minutes, return around your dog so that he is at your left side.
- Release and praise your dog.

Remember to use stand-stay in everyday life. Have your dog stand and stay while you brush him. Keep a towel by the door on rainy days—your dog can stand and stay while you dry his feet. Use stand-stay when your dog is on the veterinarian's examining table. The more you put this exercise to use, the better your dog will become at staying.

Seventeen

Down-Stay

To be well trained, a dog must be able to perform the down-stay. If I could teach my dogs only one thing, it would be this exercise.

Down-stay means for your dog to lie down where you indicate and not move from that spot until he is given a release word. His tail can wag and his head can move. He may shift positions to make himself comfortable as long as he does not move from the designated area.

Down-stay was the saving grace of Topbrass WoodDrift C.D., an all-time great dog. Woody was my beloved, exuberant, Frisbee-catching golden retriever. When I trained Woody for obedience trials, we usually practiced in busy, public areas for the benefit of the distractions. I chose areas such as shopping centers, supermarkets, the local college campus, and the town park.

People often would stop to watch us. Many times while Woody was in a down-stay, I would get comments like this: "Oh, what a beautiful golden! He's so nice and calm. I wish our dog was like that. Our dog is such a nut. She has *so* much energy." I would simply smile and give Woody his release word. Hearing his cue, Woody would leap up from his down-stay and bounce around like the energetic, fun-loving creature he was. The people watching us would then exclaim, "He's just like ours!"

"I'm sure he is," I would reply. "A lot of dogs have exuberant personalities. But I can control my dog." I also would slip in, "Have you ever considered obedience training *your* dog?" As I stated earlier, down-stay was Woody's saving grace. I could take this eighty-pound bundle of energy anywhere and keep him under complete control.

As your dog's trainer, you will find three important benefits in teaching the down-stay. The most immediate benefit is that down-stay allows you to control your dog in any situation. For example, I may own the meanest dog in town, but if Killer is doing a down-stay, he cannot bite a guest entering my home. The two behaviors—lying down and staying, and simultaneously running to the door to bite someone—are not possible. A dog cannot be doing both at the same time.

You may own the biggest beggar in town, but while doing a down-stay on the other side of the room, Chow-Hound would find it impossible to beg at the table. My neighbor may own Snuggles, the sweetest, friendliest, seventy-five-pound lapdog anyone has ever met. Snuggles can't drive her owner's house guests crazy with "Pet me, pet me, pet me," if she's doing a down-stay. I could probably fill two pages with examples of how down-stay can be useful in controlling your dog in everyday life. The three examples should give you the idea.

The second benefit of down-stay is that this exercise eliminates having to isolate your dog socially. Social isolation is extremely unnatural to canines. Canines are pack animals who normally spend most of their time with fellow pack members. You and your family are your dog's fellow pack members. Your dog instinctively needs and wants to be with you as much as possible.

When guests come to visit, social isolation is generally what happens to Killer, the meanest dog in town, and to Snuggles, the seventy-five-pound lapdog. These canine family members are sent to the basement, to the bedroom or the garage, or are locked away in a crate for the evening.

Canines who are exiled from the pack will experience tremendous stress and frustration. Unlike humans, canines do not have nervous breakdowns. Canines have built-in frustration releases. They bark, dig, chew, urinate, and/or defecate in order to release their stress and frustration. That is exactly what Killer or Snuggles may end up doing in your basement, bedroom, garage, or crate.

Every time you put Snuggles in the bedroom to avoid having her bother your guests—and each time frustrated Snuggles chews the bedspread—you are practicing chewing the bedspread. As discussed, dogs eventually form habits by consistently repeating behaviors. Before long you may have a dog who chews the bedspread every time you put her "out of the way" in the bedroom.

However, if your dog knows down-stay, she can say hello to your guests, go to whatever spot you choose, and lie down and stay. Your guests will spend a pleasant evening not being bothered by your dog. Your dog will be under control. In addition, she will be emotionally content, not exiled from the pack.

The third benefit of teaching down-stay is that this exercise is a great way to convince your dog that *you* are the pack leader. (See Chapter 6, "Pack Leader.") Down-stay allows you to convince your dog of this without having to hit, knee, choke, or do any other abusive behaviors that are not natural to canines. A dog first demonstrated this to me many years ago.

I once taught obedience classes and trained dogs at a boarding and breeding kennel. The kennel owner bred collies. At one point the kennel had a collie "mom" with three eleven-week-old puppies. The six other puppies in the litter had been placed in homes when they were seven weeks old. The last three were being held for a few more weeks until the breeder could determine which puppy she would keep for herself.

Several times a day the pups and their mom would be let out into a small fenced yard to play and enjoy the sunshine. The breeder, the kennel staff, and I often would watch mom and her puppy pack interact and play.

One day the three pups were romping around mom. They were getting wild, jumping up to nip at her face and ears. The pups darted about, being careful to avoid her quick disciplinary snaps. Suddenly mother dog became much more assertive than we had ever observed. She quickly ran down each pup, showing her teeth and growling. Each pup rolled on its back and stayed there. Mom then patrolled the yard a short distance away from her pack. Every time a puppy attempted to get up and run, mom quickly moved in and pinned him back down. This behavior went on for close to twenty minutes. Finally mom let each puppy individually slink over to her and lick her mouth.

My first reaction when I saw this was "She's teaching them down-stay, almost like I do in dog obedience class!" A second later it occurred to me that mother dog could care less about dinner guests. She was simply saying to her pups, in "dog talk," *"I'm pack leader."*

The obedience exercise down-stay accomplishes the very same thing. It is a natural way to let your dog know that you are the pack leader.

An interesting side note on *human* behavior must accompany any discussion of down-stay. On various occasions, Woody, my energetic golden retriever, would be in a down-stay on my living-room floor. I would have guests say, "Oh, the poor thing! Does he really have to stay there? That's so mean!" Of course the alternative was a big furry dog trying to climb in their laps, sample the hors d'oeuvres, and so on. The guests wouldn't approve of *that* either. Locking a dog away is unkind and unnecessary. It also can create serious social-isolation problems, as we have discussed, such as nonstop barking, indoor urinating, or destructive chewing.

The moral of this story is that with some people you'll never win. So *you* set the canine rules in your home. Don't let Aunt Tootsie talk you into locking the dog upstairs. Don't let Uncle Bill go through any foolish antics to try to cause your dog to get up from the down-stay. And don't let their kids convince you that it would be fun for the dog to run wild through the house.

It's up to you to make sure your dog is well trained, well adjusted, and pleasant to be around. When you've accomplished this with consistent training, you'll realize that Aunt Tootsie and Uncle Bill wish *their* dog could be as terrific as yours.

How to Teach Down-Stay

Step 1: The Imaginary Circle

Down-stay is a major control exercise. To successfully obedience-train your dog, you *must* be successful with this exercise. Being successful means being persistent. If your dog gets up 10,000 times, you must put him back 10,001 times. If you give up and do not do the exercise, your dog will not perceive you as his pack leader. Giving up is being unsuccessful.

• Pick a spot where you would like your dog to lie down and stay. Put the training collar and leash on your dog.
• Give the command *"Down"* as you down your dog. Use the step 1 down-on-command technique (see page 103).
• In your mind draw an imaginary circle around your dog. Tell him to *"Stay"* using both the verbal command and the hand signal (an open palm held for a moment in front of the dog's face). Give your dog a toy to chew on while he is doing the down-stay. This will enhance your success.

Step 1: After placing your dog in the down position, tell him to *"Stay"* using your voice and the hand signal, shown in a close up above.

- Make sure your dog is not upright on his haunches. If he is, roll his hip over to one side. With a hip rolled to one side, the dog must first right himself to stand up. This gives you an extra cue to indicate that the dog is about to break the stay.
- Go no more than two feet away from your dog. You may stand or sit in a chair, but do *not* sit on the floor with your dog. Watch him closely.
- Keep your dog in a down position within the imaginary circle for a full ten minutes. It does not matter if he lies on his chest, side, or back. He may shift positions as long as he does not roll or crawl out of the imaginary circle.
- Watch your dog closely. If he starts to move out of the imaginary circle, correct him with a firm *"NHAA."* Put him back in the circle and down him quickly using minimal hand contact as you correct him. Repeat the command *"Stay"* after you have corrected him.
- The best time to correct your dog is when he is thinking about getting up. If you *think* he is thinking about getting up, tell him *"NHAA."* Don't wait until he has taken off down the hall to correct him.
- Keep the leash on your dog, stretched out in front of him. Step on the leash if he attempts to run away. Do not allow your dog to chew on his leash. If he does, tell him *"NHAA"* and take it out of his mouth. Give him a chew toy instead.
- If your dog falls asleep during the down-stay, this is fine. You don't mind if he curls up and goes to sleep when you have dinner guests over.

• At the end of the designated time, return to your dog so that he is at your left side. Do not release him from any other position or he will anticipate the release. Wake your dog up if he has fallen asleep. Wait ten seconds, then use the release word and release your dog. Praise him enthusiastically.

Practice this exercise for a full ten minutes *every day*. Most dogs respond well to down-stay when their owners start with a ten-minute goal. However, some dogs respond better if you start with shorter periods. You can go from one minute to two minutes to three minutes and then beyond.

If you have a busy day, you may not have time for a ten-minute down-stay. Even a short down-stay is better than none at all.

Step 2: Increasing the Time

Continue to practice the down-stay. As your dog becomes proficient with this exercise, increase the length of time to twenty minutes (only if you have been successful for ten minutes).

If your dog stays without moving for the designated time, add mild distractions to the training area. You may try to induce your dog to get up. However, *never* call your dog to you using the command

Step 2: If your dog starts to get up, tell him *"NHAA"* and push him back into a down position. Do not get into a wrestling match with your dog.

"Come," and then correct him for breaking the stay. Doing so will undo all your hard work of teaching him to come on command.

Step 3: Increasing the Distractions

Continue to practice the down-stay every day. Increase the time to a full half hour if you have been successful at twenty minutes. Be sure to use this exercise in practical situations. If your dog is doing really well, add many distractions to see if you can induce him to get up. Every time he breaks the stay and you correct him, you will be reinforcing what "stay" means. You may distract him any way you wish, but be sure *never* to use the command *"Come"* and then correct him for breaking the stay.

Step 4: Away from Home

Practice the half-hour down-stay exercise every day. Add unusual distractions to the training environment as your dog becomes more proficient at this exercise. Throw a tennis ball back and forth. Clap your hands. If your dog breaks the stay, tell him *"NHAA"* and correct him immediately. Do not allow your dog to break the stay even if the earth quakes!

If your dog has been doing the half-hour down-stay successfully at home with distractions, it is time to practice in a new environment.

- Take your dog to a softball game or similar activity.
- Put him in a down-stay (with the training collar and leash on), and go two to ten feet away. Watch him carefully so that you can time your verbal corrections perfectly.
- If he starts to move, tell him *"NHAA."* At this point your verbal correction should cause the dog to lie back down. If it does not, calmly return to your dog and place him in a down position.
- At the end of the designated time, return to your dog so that he is at your left side.
- Release and praise him.

Remember, down-stay is a major control exercise. The more you practice, the better your dog will become at staying. Once your dog learns this exercise, you can take him anywhere and have complete control over him.

Out-of-Sight Stay

When your dog is doing a reliable stay with major distractions, you are ready to begin training for an out-of-sight stay. This variation on the stay exercise is optional. You certainly can have a well-trained dog without teaching him out-of-sight stays.

However, an out-of-sight stay can be very practical. I frequently use this exercise when I have guests over or when my dogs and I visit our friends. I can move around the house, prepare food, carry items from the car, and so on, while my dogs stay calmly where I put them. The routines of your own life will determine if out-of-sight stays are something you want to teach your dog.

I use two techniques to teach the out-of-sight stay. In the first technique you and your dog work alone. In the second technique, you need a helper. When teaching your dog this exercise, do not simply disappear, hoping your dog will be there when you return. If you do try this approach, no harm will be done . . . if when you return your dog is staying where you left him. However, problems will arise if your dog is *not* where you left him when you return. You will be teaching your dog that when you are not watching him, he does not have to stay. It is too late to correct the dog after he has broken the stay. You must correct him as he is about to get up.

A more dependable approach to teaching out-of-sight stays is to practice the stay in an environment where you can walk out of sight in one direction and then quickly circle around and watch your dog from another direction. As soon as your dog begins to get up, tell him "NHAA." Convince your dog that you can come out of the woodwork at any time! Make him believe that even when he cannot see you, you can see him.

Your dog may lie back down or sit on his own after your verbal correction. If he does not, calmly return to him. *Never* run back to the dog. Gently down or sit your dog, remind him to stay, then go out of sight again and watch him.

Leave your dog for short periods of time at first. Slowly increase the time as the dog becomes more dependable. Return to your dog unexpectedly and praise him while he is staying. If he gets up when you do this, be sure to correct him with a tough "NHAA." At the end of your designated time, return so that the dog is at your left side. Wait several seconds. Release your dog and praise enthusiastically. Find many different environments where you can practice this technique.

You should alternate another technique with the one just described. Place your dog in the down position, tell him to *"Stay,"* and leave the room. Have a friend or family member sit in the same room with your dog. This person should act as if he or she is watching TV or reading. Have the person discreetly keep an eye on the dog. As soon as the dog starts to break the stay, this person should correct your dog with a firm *"NHAA."* This will convince your dog that even when you are not there, other people in the area will correct him if he attempts to break the stay.

Enter the room periodically and praise your dog while he is staying. Then leave the room again. At the end of the designated time, return to your dog, release him, and praise enthusiastically. Get many different people to help you with this procedure. The more you practice, the more dependable the dog's out-of-sight stay will become.

Once your dog is responding well to the two previous techniques, you can start to leave him unsupervised for short periods of time. Place the dog in a down position and tell him to *"Stay."* Step out of the room for ten seconds. Step back into the room, go to your dog, and praise him. Reward him with a small tidbit of food. Do not release him. Praise him while he is staying. Do this several times. As your dog becomes proficient with this exercise, slowly increase the time out of sight. Eventually your dog will become dependable staying for long periods of time when he cannot see you.

Be sure to use this exercise fairly. Don't ask your dog to stay and then head off to work. Staying under such circumstances is unrealistic and only sets your dog up to fail. Common sense should dictate when an out-of-sight stay is appropriate.

Eighteen

Walking on the Leash: Controlled Walking and Heeling

How many times have you tried to walk your dog around the block and been dragged down the street? Has a cat ever run across your path causing your dog to lunge forward, nearly pulling your arm out of the socket? Maybe you have tried walking your dog on a busy city street and had him wandering all over the sidewalk, tangling up pedestrians with his leash. If you ever had any of these experiences, you and your dog need some skills with leash work.

This chapter covers two forms of leash work: controlled walking and heeling. It also covers biting at the leash, a common leash-walking problem.

Many people know what heeling is. This is where the dog walks directly at the handler's left side. But what is "controlled walking"? It is one of the most useful obedience exercises you and your dog will ever learn. Unfortunately, not many trainers know what it is or how to teach it. Neither did I, until a certain autumn day early in my dog training career.

When I was active in A.K.C. obedience trials, my dogs usually did quite well in the ring. One afternoon my German short-haired pointer, Jena, performed the on-leash and off-leash heeling exercises almost perfectly. A fellow trainer and I were standing ringside, watching the next competitor also do a beautiful job heeling with her dog. I commented how amazing it was that many competition dogs, mine included, could heel perfectly. But *without* the heel command, these same dogs would drag the handler down the street. I felt that it was highly impractical always to keep the dog at my left side. The choices were frustrating: Either the dog had to be glued to my left side or he dragged me down the street. Too bad there wasn't something in the middle. That was when my friend enlightened me. He told me about controlled walking.

Controlled walking requires the dog to be aware of the handler at the other end of the leash at all times. When performing this exercise, the dog does not pull on the leash. He walks on a loose leash, always staying in the handler's immediate vicinity. To accomplish this, the dog does not have to look at the handler constantly. He stays attuned to the handler by using peripheral vision and his senses of smell and hearing.

Unlike heeling, controlled walking does not require the dog to walk on the handler's left side. It does not matter where the dog is as long as he is not pulling on the leash and is mentally focused on the handler. No verbal command or hand signal tells the dog to perform controlled walking. The dog will become conditioned to begin controlled walking as soon as the leash is clipped on.

In this chapter I will be teaching you both controlled walking and heeling. Although the end results of the two exercises are different, I have found that teaching controlled walking to the dog first enhances heeling. Controlled walking teaches the dog to pay attention to the handler. And paying attention improves the dog's heeling ability.

A dog learns controlled walking by learning the consequences of his actions. Controlled walking is one of the few obedience exercises that cannot first be shown to the dog. When the dog is not paying attention to the handler and is about to pull on the leash, he receives a jerk and release on the collar. He learns to avoid the collar correction by staying attuned to the handler and not pulling on the leash.

It is especially important to employ proper collar corrections when teaching this exercise. The guideline for finding the proper collar correction for each individual dog is simple. Start off by giving gentle jerks on the collar. If your dog does not respond, jerk a little harder. Continue to jerk a little harder until the dog responds. If you jerk the dog with the collar and he yips in pain, then you overcorrected him. Do not jerk as hard the next time.

Overcorrections will frighten the dog and form a bad association to walking on the leash. Dogs should never be crying out in pain during training. If they are, they are either being overcorrected or the technique being used is cruel. There are no exceptions to this guideline.

You also do not want to undercorrect your dog by not jerking hard enough on the collar. Undercorrections only nag the dog. They will not teach him to avoid future corrections. As a result, the dog will never learn controlled walking. Only collar corrections given with just the right amount of force will teach the dog controlled walking without frightening or hurting him.

How to Teach Controlled Walking

To be successful with controlled walking, you must develop the skill of jerking and releasing the training collar. As already mentioned, a training collar becomes a choke collar only when it is used incorrectly. Pulling on the collar will choke your dog. It will cause him to resist and pull in the opposite direction. To learn to jerk and release properly, you must practice.

The dog who has mastered controlled walking will not want to pull on the leash and will learn to be attentive to the handler at the end of the leash.

Start with your dog sitting at your left side. Keep your leash loose, with both hands together.

- Start in an area with minimal distractions.
- Hold the leash in your *right* hand, with your *left* hand directly below it. KEEP BOTH HANDS TOGETHER throughout the entire exercise. Allow the leash to be as loose as possible without it touching the ground or wrapping around your dog's legs.
- Pick a destination about twenty feet away. Look at your dog and step off toward that destination. Walk at a normal, brisk pace.
- As you are walking forward, back up in your tracks. Do *not* turn your body. Do not run backward. Merely back up at the same speed you were moving forward. Keep your eyes on your dog at all times so that you do not trip over him.
- If your dog keeps moving forward as you back up, give a jerk and release on the training collar with your leash. Do *not* pull.
- After you have given a jerk and release, your dog will turn to look at you. As soon as he looks at you, praise him enthusiastically. Continue praising while you move backward until you reach your original starting spot. When your dog reaches you, pet and praise him. He does not have to be at your left side.
- If your dog turns to look at you as soon as you back up, do *not* jerk him. Praise him enthusiastically as you both move back to your original starting spot.
- Step off again in the same direction. Repeat the process.
- Practice until your dog turns and looks at you without having to be jerked. Your goal is four successful repetitions.

As you are walking along, back up in the opposite direction. If your dog continues straight ahead, give a jerk and release on the training collar.

As soon as your dog turns to look at you, praise him enthusiastically. Keep praising and moving backward to your starting position.

As your dog becomes proficient with controlled walking, practice with major distractions.

If you are consistent with your handling, your dog will learn to be focused mentally on you at all times. The key to success is: *Never* let your dog pull on the leash. You must keep the leash loose at all times. If your dog pulls on the leash, back away in the opposite direction from which he is pulling—and jerk and release.

As your dog becomes more attentive to you, slowly increase the distractions in his training environment. Remember that attentiveness and good leash behavior are not achieved overnight.

Situations will arise in your daily life that are well beyond the distraction level you and your dog are working on. For example, a cat running across your dog's path is an intense distraction for most canines. If and when your dog tries pulling (or even lunging) in such situations, *don't* stand there yelling *"NO"* while trying to pull your dog toward you. Grip the leash firmly with both hands. Give repeated jerks and releases on the dog's collar and *back up*. The momentum of your movement plus the jerks and releases will give your dog no choice but to turn and follow you. Remember to praise your dog when he does turn toward you. With repeated experiences like this, your dog will learn a new response to a cat running across his path. He will first turn and look at you! That's the kind of attentiveness that controlled walking can teach.

Controlled Standing

If you stop during a walk to greet a neighbor or to look in a shop window, your dog should not be straining or lunging on the leash. To keep control, you should not try to restrain your dog on a short, tight leash. The principles of controlled walking hold true even when you are standing still. Keep the leash loose and do not allow the dog to pull.

The way to teach this is similar to controlled walking. First, draw an imaginary circle around your body. This is the area in which the dog is expected to remain while you are standing still. The edge of the circle should be about three feet away from you. Your dog should be kept in this circle on a loose leash at all times.

When the dog attempts to move out of the circle, give a jerk and release on the collar. The correction should be directed toward your body. Do *not* pull. Give additional jerks and releases until your dog is back inside your imaginary circle. When he is, stop jerking immediately and praise your dog.

The dog will quickly learn that it is agreeable to stay comfortably by your side on a loose leash. He will realize that it is disagreeable to pull or lunge away from you, because it always results in a correction. With practice you will be able to stand still in any environment and have your dog under control at the end of the leash.

If you enroll in a group dog obedience class, you will find controlled standing especially helpful. Dogs in a group setting are usually fascinated with each other. However, their handlers are usually trying to listen to the instructor and watch training demonstrations. A dog pulling and lunging on a leash becomes an intense distraction—to the handler, to other students, and to the instructor. Use controlled standing to get your dog under control.

There is never any point in trying to restrain a dog on a tight leash. *Restraint teaches dogs nothing.* With controlled walking and controlled standing, dogs learn how to keep themselves under control, and their owners can take them anywhere without a struggle.

Biting the Leash

When walking your dog on a leash, the leash becomes an extension of you, the handler. Allowing the dog to bite or chew on the leash is the same as allowing him to chew on your shirt sleeve. The dog is testing you. If you allow this behavior to continue, you are saying to your dog—in "dog talk"—"You are the pack leader." (See Chapter 24, "Preventing Biting Problems.")

Leash biting should be eliminated as soon as possible. However, with puppies who are eight to sixteen weeks old, I do not make a

Never allow your dog to chew on the leash. It may seem like play, but he is really testing your authority.

major issue out of jumping up and biting at the leash. I want the puppies' first association to the leash to be positive. Depending on a pup's personality, I might discourage it somewhat with a growl-like "NHAA." If the pup is insecure about the leash, however, I don't discourage leash biting at all at this point.

At around four months old, the puppy should be corrected more vigorously for leash biting. Watch the pup very closely. As soon as he thinks about putting his mouth on the leash, firmly growl "NHAA." If he aborts his attempt, praise the puppy.

If the puppy ignores the growl and takes the leash in his mouth, growl again and give the leash an abrupt jerk upward. This correction is difficult to describe in writing. It should not be a violent correction. Do not jerk the puppy off the ground! Just give an abrupt jerk, straight up, that pops the leash out of the dog's mouth. Dogs do not like this.

Between the ages of four-and-a-half and six months old, your puppy will lose his milk teeth. Do not be alarmed if a loose, dangling tooth comes out when you do this procedure. Once the dog's adult teeth are in, this technique will not affect his teeth.

After you jerk the leash up and the dog releases it, bait the dog by waving the leash around in front of his mouth. If he starts to go for the leash, growl "NHAA." If he ignores your growl and grabs the leash, repeat the correction.

After a while when you wave the leash in front of the dog, he will simply look at you, as if to say "Yeah, right! I'm not going to bite that leash." Praise the dog when he does this! You are on the road to overcoming leash biting.

Remember that dogs rarely form habits with just one or two experiences. However, many dogs stop biting the leash with three or four corrections. With other dogs you may have to do this several times a day for a couple of weeks. If you are consistent, your dog will soon have a solid habit of *not* biting at the leash. Also, never leave the leash on an unsupervised dog where he can develop a habit of chewing on it.

Chemical products are available to spray on the leash to help overcome leash biting. Some dogs do not like the taste or smell of these products and will avoid biting a leash that is sprayed with them. However, in my experience most dogs are not fazed by the chemicals. Most dogs have to be taught with training techniques that biting and chewing on the leash are not acceptable.

Heeling

The heeling exercise that I will be teaching in this book is not precision competition heeling. Precision heeling is designed for the artificial world of the obedience ring. You will not need to be concerned with the things that lose points in the obedience ring, such as stopping the dog from occasionally brushing against your leg. You will not need to nag your dog to sit perfectly straight at your side when coming to a stop.

I teach heeling for the pet dog for two reasons. One reason is to give handlers a means of moving, with their dogs under complete control, from one place to another. This can be accomplished either on or off a leash. The other reason is that, mentally, heeling is a great exercise for the dog. It allows handlers to create a situation where they are working with their dogs as a team. Not only that, it allows the handler to be the captain of the team. In canine language the synonym for "captain of the team" is "pack leader." If you were a wolf pack leader, you would be the captain of the team on a caribou hunt. The followers in the pack would hunt as a team following your direction. Of course, you are not about to lead your dog on a caribou hunt. However, you can simulate situations in which you and your dog work together as a team. The heeling exercise is one of these simulated situations.

"*Heel*" means for the dog to walk on the handler's left side, adapting to whatever pace or direction the handler may go. While heeling, the dog's right shoulder should be even with the handler's left leg. Whenever the handler comes to a halt, the dog should sit automatically. Unlike controlled walking, a command is necessary when heeling a dog.

Situations and living environment will dictate whether heeling or controlled walking is the more practical exercise for you. In a park while your dog searches for a place to eliminate, you certainly do not want to be dragged from tree to tree. But you would not want your dog heeling, glued to your left side. He may urinate on your leg! You will find controlled walking more practical. If you live in the middle of a busy city and walk your dog along crowded streets, you probably will want your dog to heel. Imagine going to the veterinarian with your dog. When you arrive, you realize that you have forgotten your leash. Faced with the dilemma of getting your dog from the car to the office, your dog's ability to heel off-leash is a real problem-solver.

How to Teach Heeling

It is not difficult for your dog to learn how to heel. However, you must practice to perfect your technique. Always practice a few minutes of controlled walking prior to heeling training. This ensures that your dog is paying attention to you and is not pulling on the leash.

How to Begin

• Start with your dog sitting at your left side. Line up his right shoulder with your left leg. This is called the "heel position." Tell your dog to stay while you prepare yourself.

• Place the leash over your shoulders (see photo). *Remove your left hand from the leash.* Hold the leash by the handle with your right hand.

• Pick a destination about twenty yards away.

• Call your dog's name and give the command *"Heel."* Using your left hand, give a jerk and release with the leash in a forward direction. At the same time, step off at a brisk pace toward your destination. Quickly remove your left hand from the leash.

• Move briskly in a straight line toward your destination. Do not hesitate regardless of what your dog may do. If you hesitate, you will be adapting to your dog's pace. Your dog should be adapting to you.

• While your dog is in heel position, praise him enthusiastically, Keep your left hand *completely* free of the leash so that there is no pressure on his neck.

• When your dog strays from heel position, give him the command *"Heel."* Simultaneously as you give the command, give a jerk and release with the leash to bring the dog back into heel position. Once your dog is back in heel position, quickly REMOVE YOUR LEFT HAND FROM

Start with your dog sitting at your left side. Place the leash over your shoulder. Hold the leash in your right hand and keep your left hand free.

As you step forward, give your dog the command *"Heel"* and give a gentle jerk forward on the leash.

When your dog is in heel position, praise him and keep your left hand *completely* free from the leash.

THE LEASH and praise him enthusiastically. *Keep walking.* Do not hesitate.

• As you approach your destination, prepare to sit your dog at your left side. While you are still moving, reach over with your *right* hand and grab the leash close to the clip. Take a few more steps. When you stop, tell your dog to sit. Pull up and back on the leash with your *right* hand and use your free *left* hand to tuck your dog into a sit. This begins to teach your dog to sit whenever you stop moving. To avoid pattern training, incorporate the sit at random while heeling, not just when you reach your destination.

The training technique of placing the leash over your shoulders provides two benefits. One, it forces you to jerk and release instead of pulling on the leash. The key to a proper correction is a quick jerk and release. This technique also stops you from training with a tight leash. Leaving the leash loose prevents the dog from becoming leash dependent and makes the transition to off-leash heeling easier.

Directing Your Collar Corrections

A dog can be out of heel position in four directions. You must give a jerk and release in the correct direction in order to bring the dog back into heel position. Always accompany the jerk and release with the command *"Heel"* followed by enthusiastic praise.

Forging ahead, where the dog attempts to be in front of you, is the most common heeling mistake. You should jerk and release straight back on the leash to correct this problem. Another improper position is for the dog to heel wide of you. In this case the dog is at your left side but is too far away. To correct this, jerk and release toward you. Dogs sometimes crowd their handlers. When this happens, your dog pushes his body into your left leg. In this case, the corrective jerk and release should be away from you. The fourth improper heel position is for the dog to lag behind you. Dogs lag while heeling for one of two

When your dog strays from heel position, give the command *"Heel"* as you grab the leash and give a jerk and release, bringing the dog back to your left side.

reasons. They are either nervous and intimidated or they are bored and lazy. The dog who is just beginning to learn heeling may lag if nervous and intimidated. The dog who has been heeling fine for a long time and suddenly becomes a lagger is probably bored and lazy.

If the dog lags due to nervousness or intimidation, induce him back to heel position by showing him an object of attraction. Use the object of attraction in the same manner it is used for introduction to off-leash heeling. (See pages 162–163.) While you show the object, give the command *"Heel"* and a gentle forward jerk on the leash. Praise the dog enthusiastically as soon as he is back in heel position.

If the dog lags because of laziness, the proper correction is the command *"Heel"* and a slightly firmer forward jerk on the leash. This correction should be followed immediately by extremely enthusiastic praise. When a dog becomes bored with heeling, chances are the handler is the cause. It is the handler's responsibility to make heeling routines lively, fun, and interesting.

Agreeable versus Disagreeable

Successful heeling takes practice. Be consistent with the training techniques. Good results depend on carrying techniques out precisely.

Think of heeling in terms of agreeable versus disagreeable. Agreeable is when the dog is in heel position and your left hand is completely free from the leash. You are praising the dog enthusiastically.

Disagreeable is when the dog strays out of heel position. When this

As you come to a halt, reach across your body with your right hand and grab the leash. Gently place your dog into a sitting position with your left hand.

happens, you give the command *"Heel."* At the same time you grab the leash with the left hand and give a jerk and release. The jerk is given in a direction that brings the dog back to heel position. As soon as the dog is back in heel position, you completely remove your left hand from the leash and begin praising.

If you keep heeling training agreeable versus disagreeable, your dog will quickly learn to choose agreeable, which is proper heel position. He will learn to avoid disagreeable, which is being out of heel position.

You will confuse the dog if you introduce intermediate areas. For example, an intermediate area is the dog walking in heel position when you still are holding the leash in your left hand. Another intermediate area would be when the dog is in heel position but you are not praising. A third area is when the dog strays out of heel position but you forget to say *"Heel"* and jerk the leash. As the handler, it is your responsibility to perfect the training technique so as not to confuse your dog.

Heeling Variations

If you have been successful heeling in a straight line with minimal corrections, you are ready to incorporate some heeling variations. Be sure to always practice controlled walking prior to heeling. This will get your dog's attention and eliminate pulling, which will in turn enhance heeling.

About-Turn While Heeling

• While you are heeling, do an about-turn to the right, *away* from your dog. As you turn, give a jerk and release on the training collar.

• Step off in the opposite direction. As you do so, give a *second* jerk and release to bring your dog into heel position.

• Be sure to praise your dog enthusiastically as you apply the collar corrections.

Be sure your dog is in heel position before you make an about-turn. Always give the two jerks and releases when making an about-turn. In some cases you may need a third jerk and release to bring the dog into heel position. If your dog remains in heel position as you make the turn, he will not feel the jerks. If he is out of heel position, he will be corrected with proper timing.

Slow Pace While Heeling

• While heeling in a straight line, slow your pace significantly. As you slow down, jerk and release *back* on your leash to keep your dog with you. Quickly remove your left hand from the leash.

• Take slow, evenly paced steps, not choppy, erratic ones.

• Be sure to keep your dog's attention by praising enthusiastically while heeling at a slow pace. Although your pace slows down, your praise should not.

• As you return to a normal pace, give a forward jerk and release on the leash. After the jerk and release, remove your left hand from the leash. Praise your dog when he is in heel position.

Fast Pace While Heeling

• While heeling in a straight line, break into a high-stepping jog. (You do not have to sprint like a track star.) Simultaneously, give a *forward* jerk and release on the leash. Quickly remove your left hand.

• Keep your dog in heel position. Do *not* let your dog get wild while doing the fast pace. If he does get wild, change your voice from the praise tone to a firm-sounding *"NHAA"* and continue on. Praise your dog when he is in heel position.

• Jerk and release back on the leash as you slow down and return to a normal pace.

Right Turn While Heeling

• While heeling in a straight line, make a right turn away from your dog. (First be sure your dog is in heel position.) Then continue straight ahead.

• As you make the right turn, grasp the leash and give a jerk and release toward your body, across your waistline.

• Praise your dog enthusiastically as you give the correction.

Be sure not to be late with your jerk and release. Give the collar correction and praise your dog *as* you make the right turn.

Left Turn While Heeling

• While heeling in a straight line, make a left turn into your dog. (Be sure your dog is in heel position before you make the turn.) Then continue straight ahead.

- Give a jerk and release correction *away* from you, across your dog's shoulders as you turn into him.
- Praise your dog enthusiastically as you give the correction.

Automatic Sit While Heeling

- Be sure your dog is in heel position before coming to a halt.
- Plan the halt ahead of time. When you are ready, stop *abruptly*. Give a jerk and release straight up and back toward your dog's tail. This will cause your dog to sit. As you do this, give the command "*Sit.*"
- Praise your dog enthusiastically when he sits. Don't worry if he does not sit straight. Your objective is to condition your dog to watch your body and sit when you stop.

It is very important that you praise your dog enthusiastically when teaching heeling variations to compensate for the collar corrections. Whenever you are heeling in a straight line, give the command "*Heel*" every time you jerk and release. Praise your dog as soon as he returns to heel position. When changing directions during the about-turn, right turn, and left turn, do not say "*Heel.*" Simply accompany the collar correction with more exuberant praise.

You have now learned all of the heeling variations. Be sure not to pattern train by doing the same routine in the same place, at the same time of day, every time you practice. Vary your heeling patterns with each practice session. Isolate heeling variations that are difficult for your dog and practice these individually.

Off-Leash Heeling

There are no magic tricks to teach the dog to heel off the leash. Good off-leash heeling is simply an extension of good on-leash heeling. Most dogs have a problem heeling off the leash if they are leash dependent. Leash dependency is caused by being guided around on a tight leash. Leash-dependent dogs have not learned where proper heel position is and that it is agreeable to be there.

Do not attempt to heel without a leash until your dog can do a complete heeling pattern with no more than two corrections. Even if your dog is ready for off-leash heeling, you should practice heeling using a leash 98 percent of the time. Without a leash you will not be

If your dog learns the heel position correctly, off-leash heeling will be easy to master.

able to correct your dog if he makes a mistake. When your dog is ready, test him once or twice a week without the leash.

Begin off-leash heeling by walking in a straight line, just as you did with on-leash heeling. Introduce heeling variations gradually as your dog becomes proficient working without a leash. When you first try heeling without a leash, hold an object of attraction in your right hand at your belt buckle. Your dog may begin to stray from your left side while heeling off leash. If this happens, give the command *"Heel."* Put the object in front of the dog's nose, using it to induce him back to heel position. When the dog returns to heel position, put the object back at your belt buckle and praise your dog.

If your dog makes repeated off-leash heeling mistakes, immediately clip the leash back on and continue to practice on-leash heeling. This is a good indicator that your dog is not quite ready for off-leash work. Do not let your heeling success start to break down by forcing your dog through a long, unsuccessful off-leash heeling session. There are no timetables for learning this exercise. Try it again in the future.

Nineteen

Come on Command

Does this scene seem familiar to you?

"Rover, come." Rover looks away.

"Rover, come!" Rover sniffs a bush.

"Rover, come!" Rover heads toward the neighbor's yard.

"Rover, COME!" You guessed it. Rover doesn't come when called.

But don't feel too badly. You and Rover certainly aren't alone.

Getting a dog to respond to the command *"Come!"* appears to be one of the biggest problems people have with their dogs. Ironically, it is one of the exercises dogs learn most quickly and seem to enjoy learning the most in my training programs. To be successful teaching the dog this exercise, the trainer must use techniques specifically designed to teach the dog *how* to respond to the command *"Come!"* Equally important is the trainer's need to be fully aware of the many, many factors that can influence a successful response.

Dogs do not learn to come on command on their own. They must be taught, or conditioned, to do so. In general, dogs fall into three categories in their response to the command *"Come!"*

In the first category is the dog who has no real relationship with his owners. He is the dog who has been exiled permanently to the basement or to the backyard pen. His relationship with his owners may consist of nothing more than a dish of food thrown at him once a day. In addition, the owners probably did all the wrong things in trying to get the dog to come. This dog will *never* come when called. In fact, he's probably looking for the first opportunity to escape. When he is called, he acts as if he were deaf. He'll come home at dinnertime or maybe the next day—whenever he is inclined. He certainly will not come when his owners want him to. The dog who roams free also falls into this category. (See Chapter 27, "Roaming Free.")

Category 2 consists of the dog who has a close relationship with his owners and is part of the family. However, this dog has never been trained to come. Possibly the owners tried to train him, but they made mistakes. When called, this dog comes when he feels like it. He comes occasionally because he likes his owners. They feed him, play with him, take him for walks, and so on. When this dog has something more interesting to do—say sniff a bush, look at the neighbor's cat, or visit the kids getting off the school bus—he won't come.

Owners with dogs in this category will often say, "He *knows* what 'Come' means, but he comes only when he wants to." This is only partially true. These dogs have learned from experience that they do not *have* to come. Also, just because dogs do a behavior periodically, that behavior is not necessarily a habit, or conditioned response.

In category 3 is the dog who, when he hears his name and the command *"Come!"* stops what he is doing and runs to his owner as fast as he can 99 percent of the time. This is a dog who has been conditioned, or trained, to come on command. (I used "99 percent" because any learned behavior—in canines or in humans—is not infallible. Even a well-trained dog can make a mistake. For this reason, never put your dog in a dangerous situation where you must rely on his coming on command.)

Most people would like their dog to be in category 3. But very few dogs are. Why? The reason is that so many factors influence coming on command. It is easy to do a lot of wrong things. However, with a little understanding of canine behavior and an effective training plan, you can teach most dogs to come dependably. This chapter teaches you how to train your dog to come on command. It also helps you understand the many factors that influence exactly how a dog will behave when he hears the magic word *"Come!"*

Factors that Influence Coming on Command

The ideal time to begin teaching a dog to come on command is during the instinctive learning period (seven to sixteen weeks of age). Dogs respond very well to coming when called at this young age because they are dependent on staying close to adult pack members for survival. For best results it is important to get an early pattern formed of coming

Do *not* charge after your dog to get him to come.

on command before they reach their independence phase (four months to one year). Unfortunately, many owners are not aware of potential come-on-command problems that may arise when the pup stops feeling so dependent on them.

A major factor that can significantly influence the dog's response to coming when called happens in the first few weeks after the dog enters the new home. Does the following scenario sound familiar? You take your puppy into the yard to eliminate. After he does so, you praise him. Then you want him back, so you call him: *"Come!"* If he does not respond, you try again: "Puppy, I said *come!"* Still no response. Feeling that you should be the boss, you try it a little louder. "Puppy, *come!* Get over here!" Still nothing. Puppy just looks at you. So louder still: "GET OVER HERE! *COME! I SAID COME!" And you go after the pup.*

Your puppy does not know what *"Come"* or "Get over here" means. All he knows is that you are big and tall, and he is little and small— and that the big creature (you) is emitting harsh sounds while charging toward him. Try to imagine what that looks like from a puppy's point of view!

When you do this your pup feels threatened, and a defense reaction is triggered. When a canine defense reaction is triggered, a dog has only three options. One is to submit, which for a canine is to roll over on its back and give up. When this happens, the owner simply goes and picks up the pup. Option 2 is to attack. I have never heard of a puppy choosing this option under this set of circumstances. But, theoretically, this is a choice.

The third option is what happens to most puppies: flight instinct takes over. That is, they have the urge to split, leave town, run away. Now consider this fact: Training a dog is basically a simple process.

166

You find a way to get the dog to do a behavior and repeat it until you have a habit. Okay, you found a way to get the dog to run away. Yell *"Come!"* and chase after him. Now repeat this scenario every day. Eventually your dog will develop a habit. He will be thoroughly trained to *run away on command.*

Getting the Response You Want

So what should you as an owner do to get your dog to come on command? To start, do not appear threatening to your dog. Use a pleasant tone of voice when you call him. Squat down on the dog's level, which takes away your dominant body posture. Wave an object of attraction (dog treat, favorite toy, tennis ball, and so on) in the dog's face. Make a big, appealing fuss by clapping your hands and making lots of pleasant, happy noise to attract his attention. Most dogs, especially puppies, find this irresistible and will run to you. Now *that's* the response you want.

If all of this fails and your dog just looks at you, try this: Stand up and run in the opposite direction away from the dog. This will trigger the dog's chase reflex, something all dogs have that makes them chase things that move quickly. (This is what makes cats such doggone fun.) The motion will cause your puppy to come running after you. When you see him running after you, wave the object of attraction in his face, squat down on his level, and praise him as he comes to you. When he reaches you, praise the daylights out of him! Make him think this is the greatest thing he has ever done in his dog life.

Using the object of attraction can make the difference between suc-

Make coming to you agreeable. Get down on your dog's level and call him with a pleasant tone of voice. Follow your command with lots of praise.

cess and failure. As described above, the first step in training a dog is to find a way to get the dog to do a behavior. If waving an object of attraction will cause your dog to come when called, you then have a useful tool for developing coming on command into a reliable habit.

Choose your object of attraction carefully. It can be almost anything that "turns on" your dog. For most dogs it's a ball, Frisbee, biscuit, squeaky toy, and the like. Barbara and I once had a man call us on *Dog Talk,* our radio show, to say how stubborn his dog was. The man said he could call the dog ten times and the mutt ignored him. All he had to do was grab the Frisbee, wave it around, and then call the dog—who would run right into the house. Our reaction was: Why not use the Frisbee in the first place? If you know that waving a certain object and calling your dog will cause him to come, then *use* that object. Continue using it until your dog forms a solid habit of coming when called. Only then can you test your dog without using the object—and expect him to come at your command.

Another important factor: Every time your dog comes to you, it must be a pleasant experience. If your dog comes to you and you reprimand him, he will associate coming to you as unpleasant. After a while he will avoid coming to you.

Many years ago I made this mistake with my young German short-haired pointer. Jena was nine months old and working on her CD (Companion Dog) obedience title. When I called her, she would approach me until she was about four feet away and not come any closer. I could not understand why. After getting very frustrated, I discussed the problem with my obedience instructor. She asked me about every interaction I had with Jena from morning until night. Finally we hit upon my "socks story."

I would leave my socks laying all over the bedroom floor. Jena would pick up the socks and walk around carrying them. I would say to her, "Jena, come!" When she got to me I would grab the socks from her mouth and tell her, "Bad dog. Don't you eat my socks! Bad girl." Jena never understood that she was being scolded for the socks because the timing was off. Although in my mind I was scolding her for the socks, the behavior she was doing *at the moment* was coming to me. So unfortunately, Jena could only associate the reprimand with coming to me. Any time your dog comes to you, he must think it is the greatest thing he has ever done. Never call your dog to you and then scold him.

An extremely important factor is this: Do not practice *not* coming. What does this mean? Here is a good example. I get phone calls all the time that sound something like this: "My dog will *not* come when we call her. Every morning my husband and I let her out into the yard while we get ready for work. We take a shower, get dressed, and when we call her she refuses to come."

My first question to the owner is, "How long has this been going on?"

"Since she was six months old."

"How old is she now?"

"About ten months old."

These people inadvertently set up a perfect training program. They found a way to get their dog *not* to come: simply let her out in the backyard and call her. They practiced every day for four months. What is the end result? A dog who has been thoroughly trained to ignore the sound *"Come."*

The moral of this story is: *Do not* practice *not coming.* ("Practice" means repeating any behavior until it becomes a habit.) Also, avoid putting your dog in a position where you have learned from past experiences that he will not respond when you use the word *"Come."*

Until your dog is trained to respond reliably, there are only two cases in which he should hear the command *"Come."* The first is when you know from experience that the dog is going to come running to you. For example, whenever my dog hears me fixing his dinner and I call him, he comes running. Fine. Under that set of circumstances I can use the command.

The only other time you should use the command *"Come"* is when you are practicing the formal exercises designed to teach your dog what *"Come"* means. If you are using the word *"Come"* and getting the opposite response, you are practicing *not* coming on command.

Corrections for Not Coming

Unfortunately, there is no good way to punish your dog with proper timing for not coming to you. Picture this situation: You call your dog and he does not come. You call him ten more times, but he still does not come. Finally on the twelfth time he comes, but you scold him for not coming right away. What is his association? He comes to you and he gets yelled at. This is a disagreeable association, so what does the dog learn? To avoid coming to you.

Consider this situation: You call your dog, but he does not come. Instead of calling him again, you sneak up behind him and grab him,

Never call your dog to you and then correct him. He will associate the corrections with coming to you.

yelling "You big dummy! Why didn't you come when I called you?" The next time the dog hears you call him, he is going to look over his shoulder and see you coming and run away.

Again, there is no good way to punish your dog with proper timing for not coming. What you have to do is to make coming to you so agreeable that every time the dog comes to you, he thinks it is the best thing in the world. This, combined with consistent practice of the come-on-command training techniques, will help develop a reliable habit. The only other ingredient required is to never practice *not* coming.

What we are ultimately looking for in the trained dog is a conditioned response to the word *"Come."* Think of this nursery rhyme: "Mary had a little . . ." Guess the next word. Right! "Lamb" is your conditioned response. Why? Because when you were a small child, the person who repeated that rhyme to you always said "lamb." If one day the person said, "Mary had a little lamb," then "dog," then "goat," "cat," or "bag of apples," you would never be sure what Mary had!

The same holds true for your dog. If 80 percent of the time *"Come!"* means run to you and 20 percent of the time it means ignore you, you will never form a conditioned response. Consistency is the key. You must tip the scales so that every time the dog hears the word *"Come,"* he runs to you.

The Long Line

After I explain all of this to my students, they agree that it makes sense. But their dogs have *tons* of energy and need to run for exercise. Going to the beach or park usually means taking the leash off, but then the dogs won't come. What should they do?

This is when I recommend a long line. A long line is twenty-five to

Use your long line to avoid practicing *not* coming.

Pick up the long line and run backward away from your dog. Show him an object of attraction as he runs toward you.

fifty feet of rope or cord clipped to the dog's collar. The long line gives *you* the upper hand. When the dog is free and unclipped from a leash, *he* has the upper hand. If he does not feel like coming when called, all you can do is stand there *practicing not coming* by indiscriminately repeating the *"Come!"* command.

When your dog is clipped to a long line, you call your dog once. If he does not respond, don't even worry about what the dog is doing. Look for the end of the long line. Step on it before you pick it up, and run in the opposite direction holding the line. (Never grab a moving rope. You might get a painful rope burn.) Running in the opposite direction will trigger the chase reflex and cause your dog to come running after you.

Use an object of attraction to induce the dog directly to you. (This prevents him from running right by you.) Praise your dog as he is running toward you. When he reaches you, make him think it is the best thing he has ever done. Give him lots of praise and hugs.

The long line enables you to keep the dog coming to you until a solid habit is formed. If your dog has already learned that the sound *"Come!"* means to run in the opposite direction, you may want to choose a brand-new word that means "Run to me now!"

If all of this sounds like a lot of work, you are right. As I mentioned, if dog training was easy, everyone would have a well-trained dog. Most people don't. But by using the following techniques and avoiding the common mistakes I just described, you can train your dog to do something few dogs do—come reliably at your command.

How to Teach Come on Command

Step 1: Chase Reflex

This technique capitalizes on your dog's instinctive chase reflex. The chase reflex is used in each of the first four steps of teaching come on command. When you start to teach your dog this exercise, keep in mind two important rules.

> *Rule 1:*   *Never* call your dog and then chase him if he does not come to you. This will trigger the flight instinct and condition him to run away when he hears the word *"Come."*
>
> *Rule 2:*   Do *not* put your dog in a position where you have learned from experience that he will not come when you call him. This will only teach him to ignore the word *"Come,"* and you will be practicing *not* coming to you.

• Start with your dog sitting at your *left* side. The training collar and leash should be on the dog. Hold the leash in both hands. The leash should be as loose as possible without wrapping around your dog's legs. Tell your dog to *"Stay."*
• Call your dog's name, followed by the command *"Come!"* As soon as you give the command, run backward away from your dog. Do not turn your body. You should be facing your dog at all times.
• If your dog does not follow after you as you run away from him, give a jerk and release on the training collar. *Jerk gently.* Do not flip the dog over backward.
• If en route to you, your dog becomes distracted and veers off in another direction, give a jerk and release. The leash should either be slack or you should be jerking and releasing. It should *never* be tight. Do *not* pull the dog in like a fish! Keep the leash slack as your dog is moving toward you.
• When your dog reaches you, do not allow him to race by you.

Step 1: Start with your dog sitting at your left side. Hold the leash as you would for controlled walking.

After calling your dog's name and the command *"Come!"* run backward away from him. Use an object of attraction to prevent the dog from running by you.

Induce him to you using food or his favorite object. Do not drag him to you with the leash.

• Praise your dog enthusiastically as he is moving toward you. When he reaches you, squat down on his level. Pet and praise him for one full minute. Make him think this is the best thing he has ever done!

Be sure your command *"Come!"* is clear and pleasant. For best results, practice ten come-on-command exercises a day. They do not have to be done all at one time.

Step 2: Chase Reflex from Six Feet Away

For this step to be effective, your dog must be familiar with sit-stay.

• Start with your dog sitting at your *left* side.
• Use both the verbal command and the hand signal (open palm flashed in front of his face) to tell your dog to *"Stay."* Walk to the end of the leash and turn and face your dog. Do *not* back away from him. (This can cause your dog to follow after you.) Look back over your shoulder to be sure that your dog stays. If he gets up, tell him *"NHAA"* and put him back.
• After you reach the end of the leash and have turned to face your dog, hold the leash in both hands about chest level. The leash should not be tight, but it also should not be very slack. Hold the leash at the point just before it would become tight.

Step 2: When you reach the end of the leash, turn and face your dog with your arms extended. The leash should be held just before the point of becoming tight.

- Call your dog's name and give the command *"Come!"* A second after you give the command, give a jerk and release on the training collar and run *backward* away from your dog. Keep facing your dog as you run away from him.
- Be sure to praise your dog as he moves toward you. Keep the leash loose as he is moving toward you. Do not reel or drag him in like a fish!
- Continue to use your object of attraction to induce the dog directly to you. Do not let him run by you. When he reaches you, squat down on his level. Pet and praise him lavishly. Act as if it is the best thing he has ever done!

As mentioned, for best results, you should do ten come on commands a day, using the training procedures from both steps. Remember rules 1 and 2. Also, if your dog does something wrong, *never* call him to you to scold or punish him.

Reinforcing the "Stay"

Practice this variation of step 2: After you have reached the end of the leash and have turned to face your dog, hold the leash as if you were going to call him. However, instead of calling your dog, walk back to him.

Praise your dog as you walk back to him. Go directly to him. Stand in front of him, knees to nose. Give your dog a small tidbit as a reward for staying. As you do this, praise him lavishly, but do not allow him to break the stay.

Now pivot back so that your dog is at your left side. Then either release him or leave him to do a come on command.

By returning to your dog periodically—as opposed to calling him every time you reach the end of the leash—you will prevent him from anticipating the command before you give it.

Isolating the Sound "Come"

As your dog becomes proficient with step 2, work on getting him conditioned to respond to the specific command *"Come!"* After reaching the end of the leash and turning to face your dog, call your dog's name. If your dog attempts to come to you, say *"NHAA."* Step toward your dog with your right leg and give a jerk and release with the leash to prevent him from getting up. Return back to the end of the leash.

Repeat your dog's name. Do this several times. If he does not move, return to him. Praise him and give him a small tidbit for staying. Pivot back or return around your dog. Stop when he is at your left side.

Practice the following sequence: Call your dog's name several times. Then call your dog's name, give the command *"Come!"* and run backward away from him. Praise your dog enthusiastically when he reaches you.

Practice this procedure with your dog every day. Alternate between calling your dog and returning to him. Keep him on his toes. Work on getting your dog to react specifically to the command *"Come!"*

Step 3: Chase Reflex from Controlled Walking

• While walking with your dog in a controlled walking sequence, call his name and give the command *"Come!"* At the same time run backward away from your dog. Remember not to turn your body. Face your dog at all times.
• Praise your dog as he moves toward you.
• If he does not move toward you, give a gentle jerk and release with the leash.
• Gather up the slack in your leash as your dog moves toward you. However, do not allow the leash to become tight.
• When your dog reaches you, hold an object of attraction up and behind your dog's head and induce him into a sit. Say *"Sit"* as you do so.

Step 3: From a controlled walking sequence, call your dog's name and the command *"Come!"*

As your dog is coming toward you, hold out an object of attraction to prevent him from running by you.

• Command your dog to *"Stay."* Return around him so that he is at your left side.
• Keep him sitting at your left side for ten seconds. Release and praise your dog lavishly.

For best results you should do at least ten come on commands a day. You should alternate among steps 1, 2, and 3. Practicing step 3 will help stop your dog from jumping on you when you call him. Remember: Do not undo all your hard work by practicing *not* coming!

Step 4: When your dog focuses his attention on a distraction, call his name and the command *"Come!"* If he does not respond, give a jerk and release on the collar as you run backward away from him. This will teach your dog to respond to the command *"Come"* even when he is distracted by something.

Step 4: Chase Reflex with Distractions

- Start with your dog standing by your left side on a loose leash.
- Have a friend or family member approach the dog from the front. This person should get your dog's attention with an object of attraction.
- When your dog focuses on the object, call your dog's name and give the command *"Come!"* Run backward away from your dog.
- If your dog does not turn and run with you, give a gentle jerk and release on the leash. Remember not to turn your body.
- Praise your dog as soon as he starts to run in your direction.
- Induce your dog directly to you with an object of attraction.
- When your dog reaches you, induce him into a sitting position and praise him lavishly.

Practice this training technique in conjunction with the other three chase-reflex come-on-command exercises. Your goal is one million repetitions. Do not undo your hard work by practicing *not* coming!

Step 5: Recall

After practicing the four chase-reflex exercises, you should be ready to test your dog. This is done in a controlled testing format called a recall. Be sure to introduce the recall to your dog in an area with minimal distractions. When your dog becomes proficient with this exercise, you can do it in a more distracting environment. *Never* practice recalls near a busy road where a single mistake on your dog's part could result in a tragedy.

Step 5: After telling your dog to *"Stay,"* walk away with your back to him. Watch him over your shoulder.

After walking thirty feet away, turn and face your dog. Hesitate ten seconds before squatting down on your dog's level. Call his name and the command *"Come!"* followed by enthusiastic praise.

- Start with your dog sitting at your left side. Unclip his leash.
- Tell your dog to *"Stay"* using both the verbal command and the hand signal (open palm flashed in front of his face). Watch him for fifteen seconds. If he moves, tell him *"NHAA"* and put him back.
- When your dog looks as if he is not going to move, repeat the command *"Stay."* Leave your dog, walking with your back to him. Do not back away from your dog when you leave him. This may induce him to follow after you. Go about thirty feet away.
- Look over your shoulder as you leave your dog so that you know what he is doing. If you think he is *thinking* about getting up, remind him to *"Stay."* If he breaks the stay, give a firm *"NHAA"* as he is getting up. Return to your dog and sit him. Tell him to *"Stay"* and leave him again.
- When you reach your destination, turn and face your dog. Again, tell him to *"Stay."*
- After you have turned to face your dog, count silently to ten, then squat down on your dog's level. As you are squatting down, you may repeat the command *"Stay"* if you feel it is necessary.
- After you are down on your dog's level, count silently to ten. Using the *same command* and tone of voice you used with the chase-reflex exercises, call your dog's name and give the command *"Come."*
- As soon as you have called your dog, praise him enthusiastically. Do not hesitate.
- Continue to praise your dog as he moves toward you. To prevent

As your dog approaches you, show him an object of attraction to prevent him from running by you.

the dog from veering by you, use his favorite object of attraction to induce him directly to you. When he reaches you, pet and praise him lavishly.

If your dog comes racing toward you and then veers off, do *not* make a wild lunge and try to tackle him. This would only make coming to you disagreeable. If you do this procedure outside, it may be advisable to practice with your dog clipped to a long line to prevent him from running wild.

If your dog just sits there and looks at you after you call him, be sure you are giving the right command in the right tone of voice. If you are sure that it is not an incorrect command or tone of voice, walk back to your dog. Stop when you are about six feet from him. Call his name, give the command *"Come!"* and run backward away from your dog. (Do not turn your back on him.) Running backward reinforces the chase reflex that you have been working on in steps 1 through 4.

After doing three to five repetitions of this "refresher" procedure, try the recall again. If your dog refuses to come, he is probably not ready for the recall. Go back to the first four chase-reflex steps. Practice all four of them for two weeks. Then try the recall again.

Another problem sometimes arises with the recall: The dog will not stay when you leave him. However, this is not a true recall problem, it is a sit-stay problem. Refer to the sit-stay training procedures in Chapter 14 and practice them every day with your dog. While you do so, continue to work on the four chase-reflex steps of come on command. When your dog's sit-stay is reliable and he has received extra practice on steps 1 through 4, your recall will be a success.

If you and your dog are successful with this exercise, do at least eight to ten recalls each day. Also practice one or more of the chase-reflex steps from time to time. This will help reinforce coming on command.

179

Periodically reinforce the "Stay" command by returning to your dog and rewarding him.

Reinforcing the "Stay" During Recall

It is extremely important to reinforce the stay when practicing the testing stage of come on command (recall). If you do not regularly reinforce the stay, your dog will anticipate being called. Your goal is to teach him to respond *specifically* to the command "*Come!*" In this exercise he must learn to wait for the command. A dog who anticipates commands will never be well trained. He will do behaviors when he feels like it—not when you tell him to.

- Repeat the same procedure for leaving your dog on a recall, as described above in step 5.
- When you reach your destination, turn and face your dog. Hesitate for ten seconds.
- As you squat down on his level, tell him to "*Stay.*" Silently count to ten.
- After you have counted to ten, return to your dog.
- Calmly praise your dog as you approach him. You may interject the "*Stay*" command with your praise if the dog looks as if he might move.
- When you reach your dog, stand in front of him in the nose to knees position. Praise your dog and give him a small treat for staying.
- Pivot back or return around your dog. Stop when he is at your left side.
- Release your dog from the stay and praise him. Periodically tell him to stay, leave him again, and practice a recall.

You should return to your dog to reinforce stay often. If your dog seems to want to anticipate coming, reinforce stay more often than you call him. As your dog becomes proficient at waiting to be called and runs to you quickly when he is called, test him further. Call his name as you did in the step 2 chase-reflex exercise.

If your dog comes as soon as he hears just his name, do *not* say "NHAA." The dog was probably *thinking* "Come" at this point, so you do not want a tough correction. Simply walk calmly back to your dog. Gently lead him back by the collar to where he was sitting and place him back into a stay. Repeat the procedure. If he does not move when you call his name, return to him. Praise him warmly.

Periodically during your recall training try this sequence: Call your dog's name several times. Then call your dog's name and give the command *"Come!"* When he comes to you, praise him lavishly. This will help fine-tune your dog's response to the command *"Come!"* If your dog becomes confused, start practicing this procedure three feet away from him. As he gets the idea, gradually increase the distance away from him. Practice this procedure throughout all four testing steps of the recall (steps 5 to 8).

Step 6: Recall with a Sit

To leave your dog for a recall, use the same procedure as described in step 5. Call your dog as described.

• When your dog reaches you, give the command *"Sit."* To induce your dog into a sit, hold the object of attraction above and behind his head.

• You may physically compel your dog into a sitting position. If you do so, do it *gently*. Coming to you must always be *agreeable* to

When your dog is coming to you reliably, begin to sit him when he reaches you using an object of attraction.

your dog. Getting into a wrestling match about sitting is *not* agreeable.

• Praise your dog lavishly while he sits in front of you. Tell him to *"Stay"* and return back to him so that he is at your left side.

• Keep him sitting at your left side for ten seconds. Release and praise your dog.

Step 7: Recall with a Stand

Use the same procedure as described in step 5 to leave your dog and to call him.

• After you have called your dog, praise him as he moves toward you. Stand up as he is about three-quarters of the way to you. You should be standing fully erect at about the same time the dog reaches you.

• As you stand up, tell your dog to *"Sit"* and use an object of attraction to induce him into the sitting position.

• After your dog is sitting in front of you, praise him warmly. Tell him to *"Stay."* Keep him sitting for ten seconds, then return around him so that he is at your left side.

• Keep him sitting at your left side for ten seconds. Release and praise your dog. Remember always to reinforce the stay portion of the recall by returning to your dog periodically and rewarding him for staying.

Step 8: Recall from a Standing Position

• Start with your dog sitting at your left side.

• Tell him to *"Stay"* using both the verbal command and the hand signal.

• After you tell your dog to stay, leave him. Go the same distance you have been going during previous training sessions.

• When you reach your destination, turn and face your dog.

• Do *not* squat down. Stand erect but relaxed. Call your dog's name followed by the command *"Come!"* Be sure to give the command in your usual clear, firm, and pleasant tone. As soon as your dog gets up and starts to move toward you, praise him enthusiastically.

• Continue to praise your dog as he moves toward you.

• As your dog is moving toward you, give the *"Sit"* command. Time the command according to how fast your dog is moving. Show him

Call your dog while you remain in a standing position.

Praise your dog enthusiastically as he approaches you. Get his attention with an object of attraction.

Induce your dog into a sitting position using the object of attraction.

an object of attraction. Hold it above and behind your dog's head to induce him into a sit. At the same time give the command *"Sit."* You may compel your dog into a sit, but be very gentle.

• Praise your dog but do *not* release him. Tell him to *"Stay"* and return so that he is at your left side.

• Keep your dog sitting at your left side for ten seconds. Release and praise him enthusiastically.

If your dog does not come when you call him, repeat the chase-reflex training procedures (see pages 172–173).

Again, be careful during your daily routine not to place your dog in a position where you are not *sure* he will respond to the command *"Come!" Do not practice not coming!* This will undo all your hard work.

During hikes on the beach, walks in the park, or possibly even in your backyard, let your dog drag the twenty-five- to fifty-foot-long line. By doing this for a period of time you will be guaranteed that when you call your dog, you will be able to continue your come-on-command training—even when there are major distractions that might cause your dog not to respond.

Step 9: Come While Running Free

To break the formality of practicing come on command with your dog from a stay position, incorporate this exercise into your training program.

• Take your dog to a schoolyard, football field, or park with open fields.

• Attach the long line to your dog's buckle collar, *not* the training collar. Tell your dog *"GO!"* and let him run.

• Wearing a pair of gloves to protect your hands, hold the end of the long line.

• As your dog is sniffing around, call his name and give the command *"Come!"*

• As soon as you say *"Come!"* run backward away from your dog.

• If your dog does not come running after you, he will when the long line tightens and pulls against his buckle collar.

• As he comes running, squat down on his level and praise him enthusiastically. Use an object of attraction to prevent him from running by you (or over you!).

- When your dog reaches you, induce him directly to you with the object of attraction. Praise and pet him lavishly.

Practice this exercise with your dog every day. When you get to the point where your dog comes dependably, drop the long line and allow your dog to drag it. Stay close enough to your dog so that you can quickly step on the long line, pick it up, and run in the opposite direction.

Keep your dog on the long line for at least one year whenever you exercise him off the leash. If you practice every day and do not undo your hard work by making mistakes, you will condition your dog to come to you dependably when called.

Body Language for Come on Command

Although dogs communicate verbally by barking, growling, and howling, their main mode of communication is through the use of body language. For example, the positions of the ears and tail convey specific messages. So does the body posture. In a wolf pack, a subordinate pack member approaches a more dominant member by keeping his body low to the ground in a groveling manner. A pack leader greets subordinate pack members by standing tall with tail held high and hackles raised.

When training your dog, it is important to be aware of the messages that your own body language communicates. For practical reasons, the techniques in this book are designed to condition your dog to respond primarily to verbal commands. However, your dog will instinctively *first* read what your body language is telling him. To the canine, body language is the stronger signal. It is important to realize this, for you do not want inadvertently to give your dog an incorrect or confusing message.

This is an important factor in come-on-command training. When teaching come on command, you want to condition your dog to associate the *front* of your body with the command *"Come!"* It is unlikely in everyday life that you would ever call your dog with your back to him.

You should also condition your dog to associate your *back* with the *"Stay"* command. This means that every time you command your dog to stay, you must walk away with your back to him. However, you must look over your shoulder and watch him to know if he is about to break the stay. The *only* way to make a timely correction is to be watching your dog!

You would be giving mixed, confusing signals if you trained your dog by backing away from him on a stay and also when you called him. It would be equally confusing if you trained your dog by walking away on a stay with your back to him and then turning your back on him as you called him to you.

If you did this, one body motion would have two different meanings. For example, when you back away facing your dog, should he come or should he stay? Despite a verbal command, your body language would be giving a command also—and it would be a confusing one. No command should have more than one meaning.

My Australian shepherd, Drifter, demonstrates this well. I was always very consistent with my body language when training Drifter to come and to stay. Whenever I called him to me, I faced him. Whenever I told him to stay, I walked away with my back to him.

Now if I leave Drifter on a stay, walk thirty feet away, and give him the command *"Come!"* with my back to him, he will not move a muscle. Even though my voice is saying *"Come!"* my body is saying *"Stay."* Instinctively, Drifter relies on canine language—which is my body language.

If I turn to face Drifter and command "Come!" he quickly runs to me. If I walk around the corner where he cannot see me and call him, he will come running to me. In that situation there is only one signal, the verbal command. When there is only a verbal command and no body language involved, there are no conflicting signals.

This is only one example of how body language can influence training, but it is an important one. Be aware of your body language at all times when training your dog to stay and to come on command.

Come-on-Command Hand Signal

The come-on-command hand signal is useful in situations where your dog may not be able to hear your verbal command. I find it especially helpful on beach walks where the wind and the pounding surf prevent my voice from projecting very far. Older dogs with hearing loss also are good candidates for learning this hand signal.

When used in conjunction with the verbal command, the hand signal provides a body-language cue to the dog. This often produces a more reliable response. The only disadvantage with the hand signal is that the dog must be looking at the handler in order to see the signal.

To give the hand signal to come, start with your *right* arm held at your side. With the palm of your right hand open, make a swinging arc with your arm toward your chest. Return your arm to your side after giving the signal.

Step 1: Teaching the Hand Signal

- Start with your dog sitting at your left side.
- Tell your dog to "*Stay.*" Walk to the end of the leash with your back to your dog. Watch him over your shoulder.
- If your dog attempts to follow you, tell him "*NHAA.*" Gently place him back into a sitting position. Repeat the command "*Stay.*"
- When you reach the end of the leash, turn and face your dog.
- Hold the leash in your left hand. The leash should be neither

The come-on-command hand signal is a sweeping motion across your chest.

tight nor loose. It should be to the point of almost becoming tight.

• Call your dog with the verbal command *"Come!"* Simultaneously, use the hand signal. As soon as you do so, give a gentle jerk and release on the leash toward your chest.

• Run backward away from the dog as you did in step 2 of the chase-reflex exercise. (See pages 173–174.) At this point do not be concerned if your dog is not looking at you.

• As your dog runs toward you, praise him lavishly. Do not reel him in with the leash like a fish on a line.

• Use an object of attraction to induce your dog directly to you. When your dog reaches you, hold the object up and behind his ears to induce him into a sitting position. If you cannot induce your dog to sit, gently compel him to do so.

• Pivot back or return around your dog. Stop when he is at your left side.

• Release and praise your dog, or practice another come-on-command exercise.

Practice many come-on-command hand signals throughout the week. Remember, as with the step 2 procedure of the chase-reflex exercise, do not *always* call your dog when you reach the end of the leash. Sometimes return to him and reinforce the stay so that he does not anticipate the exercise.

Step 2: Eliminating the Verbal Command

After practicing the teaching exercise in step 1 every day for two weeks, you are ready for step 2.

• Start with your dog sitting at your left side. Tell him to *"Stay"* and leave him. Walk to the end of the leash and turn to face your dog.

• Give the come-on-command hand signal with your right arm. Do not use the verbal command. After you give the command, run backward away from your dog.

• Do not be concerned if your dog is not looking at the hand signal. Be sure to give a gentle jerk and release if your dog does not come.

• As your dog is moving toward you, praise him enthusiastically. (Just because you have eliminated the verbal command does not mean you should not verbally praise your dog.)

• Gather up the leash and sit your dog in front when he reaches you. You may compel or induce him to sit. Remember that the leash should never become tight. When your dog reaches you, praise him!

Practice this exercise with your dog every day. When your dog responds dependably to the hand signal, try the same procedure off the leash. When you reach step 7 of come on command, incorporate the hand signal into the exercise. Eventually try step 7 using just the hand signal.

Twenty

The Ten-Point Failure System

With few exceptions, dogs do not fail obedience training. People do. A dog *can* be mentally unsound, although this is very uncommon. A chemical imbalance in the brain, a brain tumor, or a spinal lesion are physical disorders that can affect the central nervous system and cause a dog to be untrainable. If your dog is not responding well to training, have your veterinarian do a complete physical. It is wise to rule out any medical problems before you continue training.

If your dog is mentally sound but you are having training problems, chances are it is something *you* are doing wrong. Dog owners who have not been successful in training their pets have many things in common. Consider the following ten categories.

1. Failure to practice every day
For dogs to develop a conditioned response, repetition is imperative. Dogs rarely learn anything with one experience. You must practice, practice, practice.

2. Failure to adapt to the training program
Inexperienced dog owners train haphazardly. Experienced trainers develop a structured, logical, step-by-step training program and adhere to it. You are fortunate to have a proven program in this book. Stick with it. Do not skip steps.

3. Failure to perform training techniques as designed

Successful end results are achieved only if training techniques are performed correctly. Imagine taking golf or tennis lessons. What would happen if the pro showed you a specific procedure and you did it 30 percent the pro's way and 70 percent your way? Chances are great that you would not achieve the desired results. This is very true with dog training. It is up to you to carry out techniques precisely as they are designed.

Failure to obtain the recommended training equipment also will hamper your success. Imagine taking ice skating lessons on roller skates. You certainly wouldn't get very far. You won't get very far in dog training either if you do not use the proper equipment.

4. Failure to adapt obedience exercises to everyday living

Obedience exercises are not parlor tricks. They are designed to serve as control mechanisms. Use them in everyday life. While walking your dog, make him sit and stay while a neighbor jogs by. When eating dinner, have your dog do a down-stay. These are just two examples. All of the exercises in this book have specific, practical uses. It is important to apply them in their appropriate context.

5. Failure to close your mouth and open your mind

Dealing with self-professed know-it-alls is an amazing and frustrating ordeal for experienced obedience instructors. Whenever obedience instructors attempt to enlighten these individuals with facts and advice, they are contradicted. Instructors have gathered knowledge through years of research and practical experience. The know-it-alls' experiences are based on the untrained dogs they have lived with or known in the past. Do you want to learn something? Close your mouth and listen!

6. Failure to fulfill your dog's need for physical activity

All dogs are different. They have been bred for different, specific purposes. Some high-energy breeds can never succeed with training if they are pent up with energy. My first dog was Jason, an Irish setter. I attribute 50 percent of my training success with Jason to exercise. A daily one-hour run channeled his exuberance. This gave Jason the ability to settle down and concentrate during our training sessions.

7. Failure to match your training approach to your dog

A dog and a handler are a team. Team members have to work together smoothly in order to succeed. Team members must be compatible with one another. If you have a submissive dog and handle him with a heavy macho approach, training will not progress smoothly. If you have a dominant dog and you are an unassertive old softy, you are doomed to failure.

Often complete mismatches in physical strength do not do well. Every dog obedience instructor has had the sweet little old lady with the 110-pound Rottweiler in class. It is your job to choose a dog that you can handle and train successfully.

8. Failure to view the world through a canine point of view

Dogs cannot think or act like humans. But most humans can think and act like dogs. Handlers who develop the ability to do this will communicate effectively with their dogs. Dogs who are labeled stupid or stubborn during training often are just confused. Guess who is confusing them! It is your job as the trainer to learn *"dog talk."*

9. Failure in the dog obedience class setting

I've seen certain traits in handlers who fail group dog obedience classes. Missing classes is a trait that spells failure. If the course you are enrolled in is a structured, step-by-step program, it is imperative to attend all sessions.

Another "failure trait" is chronic lateness. Week after week, this student wanders into class late. Besides disrupting the rest of the group, the late student misses valuable information. This is ironic because this person is usually the one who needs the information the most.

Students who cannot pay attention during class are annoying to instructors. These individuals spend time in side conversations or allow their dogs to pester the dogs next to them. It is disrespectful to any teacher to disrupt a class. Granted, the instructor is responsible for maintaining order in class. But students must also pay attention and conform to the class rules.

10. Failure to maintain your dog's physical health

Dogs who are physically unsound will not respond well to training. For example, a dog with hip dysplasia may be in pain when sitting. If your dog seems to be uncomfortable in the hind end, have him examined by your veterinarian. Your dog should always have vaccinations updated. Be sure he does not have intestinal parasites such as tapeworm, roundworm, or hook or whip worms. Have fecal samples checked at least twice a year. Check your dog's ears for infection. A yearly physical is mandatory.

Routine grooming is also important. Be sure that your dog's toenails are trimmed to the proper length. A matted, uncomfortable coat will inhibit your dog's performance of exercises. Check under your dog's legs and behind his ears. Mats in these places can be especially bothersome to the dog.

Neutering the male dog is advisable for many reasons. Intact males can be aggressive, mark territory, ignore commands when seeking females, and so on. Training such dogs can be highly frustrating. Neutering can help. (See Chapter 29, "Spaying and Neutering.")

Other Factors

Above are the ten most common ways that people fail when training their dogs. If you eliminate these ten problems, your odds for success will increase greatly. However, there are other reasons for failure. If you are working with a dog obedience instructor, be sure that he or she is competent. Obedience instructors cannot effectively teach what they do not know. Without proper experience, they are incapable of developing a workable training program. (See Chapter 28, "Choosing a Qualified Dog Obedience Instructor.")

A physical handicap may inhibit some handlers from success. Being extremely overweight or too weak physically may contribute to failure. A person may simply be too old or infirm to succeed with training a dog. I also have met individuals who were just too unintelligent or uncoordinated to train a dog.

However, never underestimate the individual handler. I competed in obedience trials against a young woman in a wheelchair. Her physical handicap did not prevent her from winning her share of first-place ribbons. People of every shape, size, and age have succeeded in my classes. I personally am not the smartest or most coordinated person in the world, but I have had many years of dog training success. With determination and hard work, you can too.

THE BOYS ON THE BEACH

Part Four

Household Manners

Twenty-one

Around the House

Most dogs spend 99 percent of their lives at home. For this reason, good household manners are essential to a well-trained dog. This chapter covers a number of household behavioral problems and describes how to prevent or correct them.

Obedience exercises such as down-stay, come on command, and controlled walking are control mechanisms. Use these mechanisms in everyday living in order to develop a structured "code of behavior" for your dog. Here are tips on putting the obedience exercises into practice. They will help you solve various problems that you may encounter with your dog.

Barking at the Mail Carrier

Throughout his life, your dog may encounter people and situations that will trigger behaviors that you feel are undesirable. A perfect example of this is a dog's typical reaction to the mail carrier. Every day the mail carrier delivers mail to your house. This triggers your dog's protective instinct. When this happens, your dog goes bananas! He growls and barks like a maniac. He jumps on the window, covers the glass with wet noseprints, and scratches the windowsill.

How do you get your dog to like the mail carrier's daily visits? You *could* invite the mail carrier into the yard every day to feed your dog biscuits. He or she could spend ten minutes playing Frisbee with your dog. Then you could ask the carrier to come into the house for cake and coffee. This would help your dog form a positive association to the mail carrier's visits. But with the busy daily routine of today's mail carriers, this is not a practical solution.

Chances are good that there is no practical way to make your dog *like* his territory being invaded on a daily basis. After all, he is acting on his most basic protective instincts. However, you can control the situation *if* your dog is trained to be quiet on command and to lie down and stay.

If your mail is delivered at the same time every day, place your dog in a down-stay just before the carrier arrives. Stand next to your dog and watch him. When the carrier reaches your house and your dog starts to bark or growl, tell the dog *"Quiet."* If he does not respond to *"Quiet"* or if he attempts to break the down-stay, use the appropriate correction to make him comply with your commands. (See Chapter 17, "Down-Stay," and Chapter 23, "Barking.")

Your dog still may not like the mail carrier's visit. However, a dog cannot go wild and do a down-stay at the same time. You have controlled the situation. With enough consistent repetition, your dog may develop a habit of lying down and staying quietly when the mail carrier approaches.

Begging at the Table

Every dog training book I have ever read says the same thing concerning begging at the table: "Never feed your dog from the table or he will become a beggar." This is ridiculous. Dogs are born beggars! They are very smart, and they are the world's greatest opportunists. They can see and smell the food you are eating. Of course, if you feed

Down-stay will keep your dog under control during a meal, whether it is a formal dinner party or a backyard picnic.

them from the table, you will *reinforce* begging and therefore make it worse.

The way to control begging at the table is the down-stay. Your dog cannot beg at the table and be doing a down-stay at the same time. I live with three dogs who love food. They do a down-stay during all of our meals. This arrangement works quite well and is especially impressive when we have guests for dinner. (In case you are wondering, my dogs do get table scraps. Byron especially likes Mexican food. But all the dogs wait until the meal is over—and they are released from the down-stay—to receive their tidbits.)

Getting on Furniture

To me, *a behavior is a problem only if you do not want your dog doing it.* Quite frankly, I do not mind dogs on my furniture. As a matter of fact, I enjoy snuggling with a dog on the sofa while I watch a movie.

However, my dogs are trained to get on furniture only when invited to do so with a specific command. You do not have to tolerate dogs getting on furniture in your home. You are the pack leader. You make the rules for how your pack will behave in your den.

There are basically four categories of dogs and furniture: (1) the dog who is never allowed on furniture, (2) the dog who is allowed on specific furniture, (3) the dog who is allowed on furniture on command, and (4) the dog who is allowed on furniture at any time.

No Dogs on Furniture . . . Ever!

Let's begin with the first category, the dog who is never allowed on furniture. How is this achieved? Consistency on the part of all family members is the key to success. *Never* let the dog on furniture. This includes the sweet cuddly little puppy that just came to you from the breeder. It is difficult to break a habit in an adult dog that you created when he was a puppy.

Supervise the puppy closely. Well-timed corrections are essential. Correct the puppy as he is *about* to get on the furniture. After he is on the sofa, it is too late to correct him. At this point all you can do is tell him to get off. If you consistently tell the dog to get *off* the sofa, you train him only to get off on command. Your objective is to train the dog not to get on the furniture in the first place!

When your dog is beyond the chewing stage and is no longer crated when you are not home, structure the environment so that he cannot get on furniture. You may have to confine the dog to the kitchen, tip up the cushions on the sofa and chairs, close bedroom doors, or install baby gates that will close off certain rooms. Everyone in the family must be consistent. If certain family members allow the dog on the sofa when the pack leader is not watching, this will undermine the training.

Allowed on Specific Furniture

In certain households there may be rooms, such as a TV room or family room, where the dog is allowed to get on the furniture. In other rooms the dog is not allowed on the furniture. In the "taboo" rooms, employ the same procedures as described above for the dog who is never allowed on any furniture.

If you are going to make distinctions between various rooms in your house, it is your job to be very consistent. Simply never let the dog on the forbidden furniture. Only allow him on the furniture that you deem acceptable.

By Invitation Only

I feel that the best situation is to train a dog to get on furniture *on command*. To succeed with this, you must employ the previously recommended procedures for keeping dogs off furniture. Allow your dog on the furniture only after being invited by you.

As you invite your dog on the furniture, say a specific command, such as *"Up."* Use any command you prefer, as long as it does not conflict with the dog's other learned commands. Be consistent. Never allow the dog to get on any furniture without first giving this command.

On Furniture Any Time

Last but not least is the dog who is allowed on furniture whenever he feels like it. As long as it does not bother you, it is okay. But there are drawbacks to this situation.

You must be careful to supervise the young puppy who is still in the chewing stage. Do now allow him to chew holes in your furniture. Also, a big, wet, furry dog leaping onto a clean sofa can make a mess. Remember, a dog does not know the difference between your old, yard-sale sofa and the brand-new one from the designer showroom. If the dog gets on the furniture only on command, you can keep him off the new one. It is easier to keep furniture clean when you are expecting guests if you allow the dog on it only with your permission. Also, when guests arrive they will not be competing for sofa space with your dog. In addition, it is easier to visit friends and relatives with your dog when you do not have to struggle to keep him off their furniture.

Stealing Food from Counters and Tables

Some dogs are food thieves. I know, I live with one. At times I think my Australian shepherd, Drifter, is part raccoon! He is the world's greatest opportunist. He will steal food whenever he has the chance.

On the other hand, Barbara's two Labrador retrievers never steal food. Our dogs have been raised and trained essentially the same way. As puppies, the Labs, known as "the boys," were corrected approximately three times each for attempting to take food from the table. The correction employed was a firm *"NHAA"* as they were about to do it. They never attempted to do it again. You can leave any kind of food on counters or tabletops. They will not touch it.

Drifter was corrected in the same way *once* when he was a puppy. He has never attempted to steal from the table again . . . as long as I am watching him! The minute I am not watching him, he will steal whatever he can get. It is pointless to correct him after he has stolen food. Such a correction would be ineffective because the timing would be off. He already ate and enjoyed what he had pilfered. (Out of frustration I have tried correcting him after the fact, but to no avail.)

I have nonchalantly left the room as a setup. As soon as Drifter made his move, I came in and corrected him firmly. He fell for that only once. I essentially trained him to be really careful.

During a talk I gave on canine behavior, this subject came up. Someone in the audience suggested that I place a mousetrap on the table near the food. When Drifter got on the table, WHAP! All I could envision was my dog, whom I love dearly, with a broken toe or a bloody, cut nose. Such violent methods are not for me—or my dog.

But what can I do? This is a big problem. Drifter has broken food-stealing records. He once ate an entire key lime pie in less than two minutes. He ate an entire box of my grandmother's prunes, box and all—with no indigestion problems!

I have two options with a dog like Drifter. I can modify the dog's behavior or I can alter the environment. I do not know a practical, nonviolent method to modify Drifter's food-stealing behavior when he is unsupervised. So I must alter the environment. This means that I never give Drifter the opportunity to steal food. If I must leave the kitchen, he leaves the kitchen too. I keep a baby gate in front of the pantry where we store his dog food to prevent midnight food raids.

The point is that some dogs are persistent, clever food thieves. There is nothing an owner can do to stop the dog from liking food and wanting to take it. But there is plenty an owner can do to prevent the dog from getting to the food. The owner can supervise the dog whenever there is food present. The owner can alter the environment by closing cupboard doors, putting lids on trash cans, pushing food far back on counters, and so on.

Or the owner can devise a method that will modify the dog's stealing behavior—as long as it is practical and nonviolent. For example, try feeding your dog two or three smaller meals each day rather than one large meal. Curbing his hunger may diminish his motivation to steal food. Or, if your dog is afraid of crinkled-up newspaper, put piles of it around your trash can. Gimmicks such as this can be highly impractical, although with one or two specific dogs, they just might work.

Grabbing Treats from Your Hand

Some dogs have gentle mouths and do not grab treats from your hand. Other dogs are like sharks. If your dog is a shark mouth, you *can* correct this problem.

First, it is advantageous to teach your dog to take food from your hand on command only. To do this, hold a biscuit firmly in your hand in front of your dog's nose. If he grabs for it, tell him *"NHAA."* Do not let him take the biscuit.

If he does not respond to your verbal correction, repeat *"NHAA"* along with a shake on the scruff of the dog's neck. Continue to hold the biscuit in front of his nose. Wait a few seconds after he stops trying to grab it, then tell him *"Take it."*

If he tries to grab the biscuit roughly, pull it away. Again, do not allow him to take it. Tell him *"Easy."* Allow him to have the biscuit only if he takes it gently from your hand when commanded to do so.

Employ this technique whenever you give your dog a treat. Eventually your dog will take food from your hand gently and only on command.

Even the best dogs in the world need to be supervised around babies and toddlers.

Interacting with Babies and Small Children

To a dog, a new baby entering the home is simply a new member joining the pack. Instinctively, most canines are tolerant of infants, whether they are puppies or human babies. However, dogs who are part of a family before youngsters arrive may not be used to children. As a baby grows to be a toddler, his or her erratic movements can confuse and upset the dog.

What is the best way to handle a child's arrival? Keep in mind that dogs are routine-oriented creatures. If your dog has been the center of attention for several years and suddenly has to play "second fiddle" to a new baby, the dog is likely to experience stress. Your actions and attitude can go a long way toward alleviating his anxiety.

Think about the routines you and your dog have together. If a morning walk after breakfast is a daily habit, make every effort to keep doing that after the baby arrives. Do you always play ball in the yard with your dog after work? Keep it up without fail. Even though your household routines changed dramatically when the baby arrived home, preserve as many old routines for the dog as you can. This will give him a bit of security when his world seems turned upside-down. If you have no "old" routine with your dog, establish one before the baby joins the household and stick with it.

It is advisable to socialize your dog with children before a new baby arrives. Take your dog to visit friends who have children. While supervising closely, evaluate your dog's reactions and attitudes. Make sure that the visit is an agreeable one so the dog will have positive associations with children. Play with a ball, go for a walk together, and so on. Be sure that the children are not rough with the dog. Do not permit games such as tug-of-war or wrestling. Play should not be so vigorous as to inspire nipping.

When the new baby arrives, make sure that the dog again makes positive associations with the youngster. For example, sit the baby on your lap and give the dog a few treats. Take the dog for a walk at the same time you walk the baby in the stroller. Pet the dog while you feed the infant. This assumes, of course, that the dog is not going wild and that you have some control mechanisms over him. That's why obedience training the dog is so important *before* you have your hands full with a newborn.

As the baby matures, the dog may become more assertive with him or her. The dog may try to maintain his position in the pecking order of the pack by growling or snapping at the youngster. An adult dog generally begins such assertive behavior when a child is about one-and-a-half to two years old.

Many people think that their dog is "jealous" of the child. I do not believe dogs are capable of feeling the emotion of jealousy. But I do know that they will compete for attention. An example of this would be the dog who is sitting by the owner's leg, craving attention. Suddenly the two-year-old child climbs into the parent's lap, and the dog growls or snaps at the child. The anthropomorphic dog owner will interpret the dog's competitiveness for attention as jealousy. Whatever it is termed, this behavior should *not* be tolerated. Correct your dog immediately with a firm *"NHAA"* and make him lie down and stay. When you are ready, release him and then give lots of attention and praise.

If your dog is submissive by nature, you may never experience this assertiveness toward your child. Still, it is extremely important for parents to supervise dogs with babies and small children. Even the gentlest, most submissive dog could inadvertently injure a small child. A large, exuberant dog could step on a baby or send a five-year-old crashing to the ground. Even a small dog could scratch a child's face with a toenail.

Remember: A trained dog is a dog you live with for an average of fourteen years and enjoy. No one individual sets the criteria for what makes a dog trained. You decide the criteria with your dog. If "trained" to you means never eating at the table, then never feed him at the table. If "trained" to you means sitting on the sofa watching a movie together, then by all means do so. As long as you can control your dog, you will never have a problem living with him. In fact, you will have many years of real happiness.

Twenty-two

Dealing with Housebreaking and Unwanted Chewing

Two of the most important issues that dog owners must deal with are housebreaking and unwanted chewing. A dog who soils the house or chews up valuable items quickly becomes an unwanted household companion. Unfortunately, eliminating indoors or chewing up a tasty leather shoe are not inherently "wrong" from the dog's point of view. It is up to *you* to teach the dog that these are unwanted behaviors.

In most cases, housebreaking and unwanted chewing are issues of puppyhood—but not always. The following guidelines can be used for a dog of any age. Keep in mind that puppies will probably learn them fastest, since young dogs are eager to learn—and have no longstanding bad habits to undo. Stick to these guidelines and you can expect success.

Housebreaking

The best and most natural way to housebreak your new puppy is to capitalize on the dog's natural instinct to keep his den clean. You will need a kennel crate or a small, chew-proof section of a room for this training. You can make, rent, or purchase a lightweight wire crate. This will become your dog's den.

The first reaction many people have to a puppy-proof, structured environment such as the kennel crate is "Oh, no! I can't lock my poor baby in a cage!" To a human being, a crate represents a jail. But to a canine, it represents a den, cave, or security hole. For this reason, the crate should *never* be used as punishment. It is your dog's safe haven, his own private place. It is also a useful training tool. Use the crate only when you cannot supervise what your pup is doing—much the same as you would use a playpen for a small child.

Consistency is the key to successful housebreaking. The only time your puppy should be free in the house is after he has been outside and has eliminated. This freedom must *always* be supervised. There are three times when accidents are most common: five to twenty minutes after eating or drinking; after vigorous play; and after waking from a nap. During these times, take the dog outside and stay with him. If he relieves himself outside—and be sure to praise him when he does—then he can be free in the house—*supervised.*

If he does not relieve himself outside after five to ten minutes, put him back into the crate. (This is not a punishment for failure to relieve himself. It is simply to prevent him from having the option of eliminating in the house.)

Twenty minutes later take him outside and repeat the procedure. Only after he has relieved himself outside can he be free in the house. Again, freedom at this stage in a puppy's life always means supervised freedom. Keep him in the same room with you.

Continue this procedure—and be consistent. If you are not supervising and you find a mess, it's *your* fault. Clean it up and *do not* scold the pup. Scold him only if you catch him in the act. Your pup will know that he is doing something wrong only if you scold him *as* he is doing an undesirable behavior. Ten seconds later is too late. Even if you think he acts guilty, he does not understand. Be aware of this mistake. (See Chapter 10, "Guilty or Not Guilty.") If you do catch your dog eliminating in the house, tell him *"NHAA"* in a firm voice and take him right outside. When he relieves himself outside, praise him.

Regulating water intake can be a big help in successful housebreaking. Some puppies seem to drink and drink and drink—for the sheer enjoyment of it. When the puppy's weak little bladder fills up like a balloon, then "holding it" becomes extremely difficult. I recommend that you offer the puppy water every hour and let him take a dozen laps. On hot days offer him an ice cube frequently. Keep in mind that puppies do not develop strong control over their bladders until they are about six months old.

Whenever you cannot supervise your puppy, he should be in his crate. However, *do not* leave any dog in a crate for more than three or four hours. Longer periods of confinement constitute misuse of the crate—and abuse of the dog.

At night the dog's metabolism slows down. During this time, the older pup can hold his bladder and bowels for six to eight hours. (Very young puppies cannot usually make it through the night.) For the first three weeks when your puppy cries at night, take him quickly outside and stay with him to confirm that he eliminates. Granted, this is more tolerable in good weather than in bad, but it is absolutely necessary to enforce the pup's instinct against soiling his den. It is also important, in my opinion, that the puppy know that you will take care of him in his distress. Puppies instinctively need to be cared for, and it is your job to fill that need.

Sometimes late-night outings become a habit in older puppies. To help avoid this, remove the pup's water a few hours before bedtime. (Keep an ice cube in the water bowl if the weather is hot.) Avoid vigorous play late in the evening. Take the puppy out one last time before you turn in. Waking up the puppy while *you* are still awake at 11 P.M. makes a lot more sense than a 2 A.M. disruption and an emergency dash to the back door.

If you must get up at night, be sure that your excursions are businesslike. Keep talking to a minimum, and do not play. Allow the puppy to eliminate and then it's back to bed for everyone. The puppy's muscles will soon mature and he will make it through the night.

If you use a crate wisely, keeping your pup in one certainly will not harm him—as long as you fulfill your responsibilities of giving him lots of training, exercise, and love.

Where Should I Put the Crate?

The ideal place to keep the crate is in your bedroom. It is more natural for your puppy to sleep with his fellow pack members than to be isolated by himself. Sharing a den with pack members greatly reduces the chances that your puppy will bark throughout the night. If he does bark or cry, you will hear him and be able to take him out immediately.

There is another advantage to keeping the crate in the bedroom. If you *know* your barking puppy does not have to eliminate, you can use your quiet-on-command training technique. (See Chapter 23, "Barking.") Conditioning the dog to sleep in your bedroom has one more asset. If an intruder enters your home, the best place for an adult dog to be is in your room, warning and protecting you.

Unwanted Chewing

The dog who does not get into a habit of chewing during puppyhood never becomes a destructive chewer. A puppy's urge to chew usually starts around teething time—about sixteen weeks of age. I have found, however, that chewing reaches its peak when the puppy is between six and nine months old. Unless chewing becomes a habit during these months, it will slow down and taper off by the time the dog is a year old.

Dogs generally chew when they are socially isolated and stressed. Chewing is a canine frustration release. For example, if you go out and leave the puppy alone, he will feel abandoned and may chew something in the house. If this happens every time you leave him in the house, chewing will eventually become a habit. Remember, dogs form habits by consistently repeating behaviors.

Do not be anthropomorphic and think your dog is chewing to be "spiteful." Spite is a *human* emotion. Stress, loneliness, or boredom are triggering your dog's chewing.

The best ways to prevent unwanted chewing are a combination of regular exercise, constant supervision, and a puppy-proof house. While your dog is free in the house, give him dog toys to chew. Put the toys in his crate with him when you go out.

If you catch him about to chew, or in the act of chewing, something that is not his, tell him *"NHAA"* in a firm voice. Take the object away from him. About thirty seconds later give him his own toy and praise him. As with a housebreaking accident, punishing or scolding him afterward is too late. It is your fault for not supervising.

Remember, the best time to correct your dog is as he is *thinking* about doing something wrong. Dogs usually give clues to what they are thinking. For example, sniffing a leather shoe is a clue. Tell the pup *"NHAA"* right then and there. The next best time to make a correction is *as* the dog is doing a behavior. The worst—and completely useless—time to make a correction is *after* the dog has done something wrong.

I recommend keeping the unsupervised dog in a crate until he is about a year old—or until you feel very sure that you can trust your dog. Start testing him with short periods of freedom, then extend the time if you are getting good results. It may take several months to build up to long periods of freedom while you are away from the house. And remember, although crates are moderately expensive, they are rarely as expensive as the valuable objects that a dog can destroy in your home.

Twenty-three

Barking: Turning It Off and Turning It On

Barking is a normal and natural behavior in dogs. In fact, it is mentally healthy for dogs to bark. Barking releases frustration. In addition, it is a form of canine communication and a territorial warning device.

This chapter does not aim to teach you how to train your dog *never* to bark. There are electronic gadgets and even surgical procedures designed to eliminate barking. I believe both of these procedures are cruel. Furthermore, they deny the owner a useful aspect of dog ownership. I *want* my dog to bark when a stranger comes to my house or near my car. But I also want my dog to be *quiet on command*. This means the dog should stop barking immediately in response to a signal from the handler.

Quieting the Barker

There are several different techniques used to teach a dog to be quiet on command. The first method I recommend is to hold the dog's muzzle gently closed for a few seconds as you give the command "Quiet." Do not squeeze the muzzle tightly as you do this. If you do, the dog will flag his head back and forth and make whimpering sounds. Simply hold the dog's mouth closed to show what the sound "Quiet" means. Eventually you will not need to hold the dog's muzzle. The command "Quiet" will be all that is needed to quiet your dog.

209

The following analogy will help you understand why this works. Imagine you are visiting China and do not speak the language. If someone asks you to be quiet and you do not understand what she wants, you would probably continue to talk. But if every time you spoke, the person gently puts a hand over your mouth and says *"Quiet"* in Chinese, before long you would know what was wanted. The same holds true with dogs. Dogs do not understand language. They simply form associations with sounds. You must first show the dog what you want from him and then associate a command.

The muzzle-holding technique is not effective with all dogs. If it does not work with your dog, the squirt bottle will come in handy. (See Chapter 8, "Training Tools.") As soon as your dog starts to bark, give the command *"Quiet."* Simultaneously give your dog a squirt in the face with the water bottle. The water will not harm your dog, but the abrupt squirt will quiet him. Be sure to associate the sound *"Quiet"* with the squirt. Before long you will not need the water bottle. Just the command *"Quiet"* will silence your dog when he is barking.

If you are crate training your dog, you have another situation in which to teach quiet on command. If your dog barks while he is in the crate, bang on the top of the crate with something that will make a noise. As you do this, give the dog the command *"Quiet."* The loud

Do not squeeze your dog's muzzle when teaching quiet on command. Gently hold his mouth closed—you are simply showing him what to do.

noise will quiet the dog. At the same time you will be associating the command *"Quiet."* You will not have to bang on the crate forever. Eventually the dog will learn to stop barking when you give the command *"Quiet."*

When doing the crate procedure with a young puppy, be sure that he is not barking to tell you he has to go outside to eliminate. If you know that your dog does not have to relieve himself, repeat the above procedure whenever your dog barks. If you are lazy and try to ignore barking in the crate, you are letting a bad habit develop. The very worst thing you can do is let the dog out of the crate when he barks. This would only reward the dog for barking. Before long, your dog will have you trained to open the crate door at the sound of his bark!

Home Alone

You can try several procedures to solve the problem of the dog who barks in the house when you are not at home. First, practice quiet on command when you *are* home. Use one or more of the above techniques. When you feel your dog understands the command, leave the house and stand outside the door. If your dog begins to bark, give the command *"Quiet"* from where you are standing. This may convince the dog that you are always just outside the door. If he does not respond to the command, quickly step back inside. Use one of the previously mentioned techniques as you repeat the command *"Quiet."*

Some dogs do not begin barking until they hear their owner's car drive away. If your neighbors tell you that your dog does this, you will need a friend to help you change the behavior. Leave your house as usual. Have your friend waiting outside, and him or her drive your car away. When your dog begins to bark, repeat the procedure as described above.

If your dog barks when left alone in the house, you can try leaving the radio on. This will not teach the dog to be quiet on command, but it may keep him quiet. Vigorous exercise also is a big help in keeping your dog quiet. Exhausted dogs do not bark; they sleep.

Quiet for How Long?

One of the frustrations with the dog who is trained to be quiet on command is that you cannot say to the dog "Be quiet now and do not bark for the next hour." A dog in a fenced yard demonstrates this. A child riding by on a bicycle will stimulate the dog to bark. When the owner gives the command *"Quiet,"* the trained dog will stop barking. But five minutes later when another child rides by on a bicycle, the dog will bark again.

It *is* possible to train a dog never to bark at children on bicycles. This would require the owner to have children repeatedly ride their bicycles by the dog. Every time the dog began to bark at them, the owner would have to correct the dog. Eventually the dog would learn to avoid barking at children on bicycles.

However, this would not condition the dog to avoid barking at a neighbor getting into a car, a squirrel sitting on the fence, a stray dog passing by, what have you. The dog that is trained to be quiet on command is conditioned to *stop* barking immediately, regardless of what he is barking at. He is *not* trained never to bark at anything. Teaching quiet on command is more practical than trying to condition your dog not to bark at everything in the world that stimulates him. The only disadvantage with this exercise is that you will have to repeat the command *"Quiet"* whenever your dog begins to bark.

Some dogs learn the quiet-on-command exercise with just a few experiences. Some dogs seem to need a hundred! Remember that all dogs, like all people, are individuals. If you are consistent and persistent with these techniques, you will achieve results.

Barking on Command

Dogs can be trained to be a dangerous threat. They can be trained to bark, bite, and attack. Some breeds adapt more readily to such training than others, but all dogs with vocal chords and teeth have the potential for threatening behavior. Because barking on command is one form of a threat, I want to preface it by a general discussion of protection training.

I do not advocate protection training a family pet. I have seen too many unfortunate incidents involving people who have been talked into this type of training by the local guard dog trainer. During the years that I worked for veterinarians, I encountered an endless number of dogs who had to be euthanized because they had become vicious. Not all of these dogs had been protection trained, but a great many had.

Some guard dog trainers will argue that if the right dog is properly protection trained, he will never become vicious and randomly bite.

While this may be true, the bottom line is that the average family cannot handle an attack-trained dog. Most people find it difficult enough to get their dog to come when called and not drag them down the street at the end of the leash! Attack-trained dogs are very useful to the police and military, and in most cases that's where they belong. The average family certainly does not need a dog who has been conditioned to attack and bite on command.

Most dogs are *instinctively* protective. Rarely does a dog need protection training to be wary of intruders. This is particularly true of dogs who have been selectively bred to guard, herd, or protect. Examples of such breeds are the German shepherd, border collie, and Rottweiler. In the wild, canines naturally protect territory and fellow pack members. The protective instinct is further strengthened when the individual feels that he is an integral part of the pack. Keep in mind that your domestic dog views your family as his pack. If he lives in your home and is part of your family, chances are good that his protective instincts will emerge.

The instinct to protect territory and fellow pack members develops with age. I've talked to many people who are dismayed that their five-month-old dog is not the least bit protective. It is not a puppy's job to be protective! A well-adjusted puppy of any breed should be friendly and love everybody. It is the role of adult pack members to be protective. The puppy instinctively expects you to protect him. With most dogs, the sense of responsibility for being protective of the pack begins at around one year old, give or take a couple of months depending on the breed and the individual dog. At maturity—eighteen months to two years old—the dog should show even stronger signs of the protective instinct.

Although I do not believe that most dogs will instinctively *attack* to protect the family, they will bark. Dogs can be trained to bark on command. When combined with obedience training, barking is a great deterrent to most would-be intruders. If a stranger comes to your front door and you give your 100-pound German shepherd a command to begin barking, that person is going to stop to think. If you then command the barking dog to be quiet and lie down and stay, chances are strong that the stranger will not come through the front door uninvited.

If that stranger turns out to be a friend of a friend and the dog attacks him, you open yourself to serious trouble. The dog who is obedient and barks on command is an asset. The dog who is attack-trained and bites can be a legal liability.

How to Teach Barking on Command

In order to train a dog to bark on command, the trainer must first find a way to cause the dog to bark. Then a command must be associated with the barking. I use the command, *"Who's there?"* with my dogs. I say the command in a low, whispery, excited tone.

Many dogs bark naturally when there is a knock on the door. If this is true of your dog, capitalize on this to cue barking on command. Have a friend knock on the door. As soon as your dog begins to bark, repeat *"Who's there?"* several times. Praise your dog as he barks.

After your dog has barked for about ten seconds, give the command *"Quiet."* If he does not respond, employ a quiet-on-command technique as described earlier in this chapter. Repeat this procedure several times for a few weeks. Eventually your dog will bark when you say *"Who's there?"* Always praise him when he responds by barking. Be sure that he also responds to quiet on command. Remember to praise him again when he complies.

Any time your dog barks, you can associate the command *"Who's there?"* If a stranger coming near your car makes your dog bark, use the command. There may come a day when you see a threat but your dog doesn't. Getting him to bark on command may be a big relief.

Some individual dogs never bark and therefore do not have the potential to be watchdogs. If your dog is one of these, you may never succeed with teaching him to bark on command. Don't despair. He probably has other valuable assets! However, if you are creative you may discover something that will cause your dog to bark and enable you to teach this useful exercise.

Twenty-four

Preventing Biting Problems

Biting is a natural defense mechanism in canines. A wolf in the wild who does not bite would not survive very long. Although biting is a normal behavior in dogs, it is not an acceptable behavior for the family pet. The pet dog who bites is dangerous to family members and their associates. There is also great risk to the dog, because dogs who bite are often euthanized as a result of this behavior.

Dogs must learn as young puppies that biting will not be tolerated. Between the ages of three weeks to seven weeks old, puppies figure out how to dominate fellow pack members. One of the ways in which they do this is to bite. The puppy pack leader is the individual who does the most biting. Submissive pack followers are those who allow other puppies to bite them.

Convince your puppy that you will never tolerate *any* type of biting on you. When a young puppy is mouthing his owner's arms and hands, he is not playing. He is testing a fellow pack member, seeing just how far he can push you around. The puppy must understand that *you* are the pack leader and that biting the pack leader *always* results in a firm correction. (See Chapter 6, "Pack Leader.")

Bite Prevention Tips

Curb biting behavior from the day the puppy enters your home. When your puppy starts to chew on your hand, growl *"NHAA."* If he ignores you, give a gentle shake on the scruff of the neck or a pseudosnap toward his muzzle. Growl *"NHAA"* louder and fiercer as you do this. Do not try to stop biting with one mighty correction. Consistency is the key. Teach the puppy that every time he puts his mouth on you, he will be corrected.

It is a popular technique to distract the puppy from biting by giving him a toy or a bone. It is okay to do this as long as you allow at least a minute to pass after you correct the dog. Otherwise the dog may view the toy or bone as a reward—and think that it is advantageous to keep up his biting behavior.

Each family member has to correct the puppy individually for mouthing. If this is not done, the puppy will soon learn whom he can bite and whom he cannot. Adults have to supervise and come to the rescue of small children. Children under the age of ten should not be allowed to correct the puppy with any technique other than their voice. They should not be allowed to shake or bite puppies.

A puppy also must learn to be handled, groomed, and medicated without biting. Do *not* avoid important procedures such as brushing, clipping toenails, and cleaning ears if they make your puppy bite. Do these procedures even more frequently so that you can correct the puppy and teach him not to bite.

A dog has three options in any situation that he considers threatening. One option is to bite. Another option is to submit—to accept whatever is happening without resistance. The extreme of this behavior is for the dog to roll over on its back, belly up. The dog is saying in canine language, "I give up. Do not hurt me." The third option is called flight instinct. This means to run away from the situation.

Let's say you want to brush an unwilling dog. The dog has three choices. He can growl and bite and try to make you back off. He can submit and allow you to brush him. Or he can run away. If you are holding the dog, he cannot run away, and you have reduced his options to two. If your dog respects you as the pack leader, which he should, he will not bite you. Pack followers do not bite pack leaders. He will submit and allow you to brush him.

Never hit a dog to correct biting. Swatting at a dog is a form of guard dog agitation training. It will cause the dog to snap back and only make the biting situation worse. If you hit a dog hard enough so that he does not dare snap back, the dog will, at best, become hand shy. At worst, you will severely injure your dog. Remember, no training technique should ever cause injury.

A common mistake that pet owners make when correcting a dog

for biting is waving a finger in the dog's face as they are verbally reprimanding him. This finger will trigger him to snap more. Anything flashed in a dog's face is another form of agitation training.

Roughhouse playing with a dog is not constructive play. Games such as tug of war encourage biting. Retrieving a ball or hiking in the woods are more constructive ways to channel your dog's energy.

Corrections to eliminate biting or mouthing often take time and repetition. Perseverance is the key. Although it may seem that you say "NHAA" a hundred times a day, timely corrections for biting are extremely important for the young dog. They will prevent serious problems in the future.

Puppyhood is the time to confront a biting problem head on. Granted, puppy teeth are like little pins, but they cannot hurt you badly. Adult teeth can. If you are not having success on your own with your dog's biting problem, seek the help of a qualified obedience instructor.

By the time dogs reach their full adult personalities at two years old, biting becomes a serious behavioral problem. I believe that biting problems in adult dogs should be handled only by professional dog trainers who have expertise in this field. Even under the tutelage of an obedience instructor, pet owners are not qualified to deal with the problem. Unfortunately, even in the hands of qualified trainers, the prognosis is poor for completely eliminating vicious biting in adult dogs.

Twenty-five

Submissive Urination

Some owners have to deal with a condition in their dogs called submissive urination. Although this condition usually entails a dog urinating in the house, submissive urination is not a housetraining problem. It is caused by a weak bladder that releases when the dog is excited or frightened. The dog is totally unaware that this is happening.

Submissive urination occurs in both male and female dogs, but it is more common in females. The condition is most prevalent among puppies. It usually begins when the dog is about four months old, although in some cases, it begins sooner.

The common scenario in submissive urination is this: You come home from work and your puppy is thrilled to see you. You greet your pup in an excited, exuberant tone of voice. Your puppy's tail is wagging a mile a minute! Then it happens: She squats and lets go. Your puppy seems totally oblivious to the puddle she is creating. To make matters worse, her tail is swishing in the puddle and urine is splattering all over the walls. You instinctively shout *"NO!"*

Unfortunately, your puppy has no idea why your demeanor suddenly has changed from glad to angry. In fact, your anger only causes the dog to urinate more. Her reaction is to roll over submissively, belly up. At this point, urine is spouting out of her like Old Faithful. You show her the puddle she made and tell her that she is a bad dog as you drag her outside.

Submissive urination is a challenging problem because your dog could not have helped what happened, even if she tried. Angry corrections and reprimands are useless solutions to this problem, as the dog is physically incapable of controlling her bladder. Furthermore, she probably associated the angry correction with your arrival at home—not with her urination. If this scenario is repeated too many times, she will get into a pattern of urinating out of fear when she hears you come through the front door.

How can this be avoided? There is no way to *train* a puppy not to urinate submissively. Outgrowing the condition is the only cure. However, in the meantime you can employ certain techniques to minimize your dog's urinating on your rugs, hardwood floors, and the like.

What You Can Do About It

First, you must condition yourself to be conscious of where your dog is located when you greet her. If she is standing in the middle of your living-room carpet, ignore her. Some dogs start to urinate submissively as soon as their owners make eye contact. If your dog typically does this, do not even look at her. Walk through the front door and let your dog follow you out to the yard. Do not hesitate. Keep moving so that your dog keeps moving. Most dogs do not urinate while they are walking.

When you have your dog in the backyard on the grass, say hello to her. Tone down the exuberance of your greeting. Talk to her in a calm tone and give her some loving pats. If she urinates, ignore it.

Squatting down on your dog's level when you greet her also helps. You will then appear less dominant, and your dog will feel more secure. And the secure dog is unlikely to urinate submissively.

When your dog greets friends, neighbors, or even strangers, ask them to follow the same procedures. They should squat down and quietly greet your dog. Remember to have the dog outside, if possible, to avoid having to clean up a puddle.

Intimidation and fear also will cause dogs to urinate submissively. Be careful when you correct your dog during training exercises. Do not overcorrect. As long as the dog stops what she is doing when you tell her "NHAA," you have delivered the message.

If you own a dog who urinates submissively, discuss the situation with your veterinarian. He or she may recommend a urinalysis in order to rule out bladder or kidney disorders.

Although submissive urination can be frustrating, 99 percent of all the female dogs I have known with this condition outgrew it by the time they were a year old. A full 100 percent of the male dogs I have known with this problem outgrew it by about the same age. A little patience and planning on your part will help make this problem a thing of the past. If your dog never outgrows submissive urination, be persistent about using the techniques described above.

Twenty-six

Sound Sensitivity

Some dogs are bothered by loud noises. These dogs may have inherent defects in their nervous system or may have had an unpleasant experience associated with a loud noise. Unfortunately, there is no way for a dog with nervous system problems to be trained *not* to be frightened of loud noises. These individuals have a physical defect that training cannot undo.

On the other hand, many sound-sensitive dogs simply have "learned" that loud sounds are frightening. You can do *many* things to relieve the stress these individuals endure—whether it is during a thunderstorm, fireworks on the Fourth of July, or a first-time outing during hunting season.

Inherent Sound Sensitivity

I lived with one dog for several years who was inherently sound sensitive. Tildy was frightened by thunderstorms and other sudden, loud noises. I found that the best thing I could do for Tildy at such times was to put her into a quiet room and draw all the shades. I would close the windows and turn on the air conditioner if it was hot.

I would set up Tildy's crate and she would curl up inside. She enjoyed the security of the crate that she was trained in as a puppy. I would put on a radio to help calm her and also to drown out the sound of the thunder or fireworks. (Classical music or talk radio seemed to work best.) I stayed with Tildy in the room if it was possible for me to do so. While she was still anxious, she seemed somewhat relieved by my actions.

I was especially careful not to "praise" Tildy for her nervousness. In an effort to soothe a frightened dog, many owners offer words of comfort as they would to a small child. A dog interprets your talking in a gentle, affectionate tone as praise. Even though your *words* say "Don't worry; everything is fine," your *tone* says "Good dog; your behavior is pleasing to me." That's not the message you want to send. Instead, distract your dog, if possible, with a ball or bone. If that does not work, say nothing to the dog. Occupy yourself with some sort of normal activity. Your demeanor should communicate to the dog that everything is fine.

Drug therapy provides another approach to *serious* sound sensitivity. Your veterinarian can prescribe tranquilizers that will relax your dog. However, it takes the drug thirty minutes to one hour to take effect.

This time delay makes drug therapy impractical in some situations. One such situation is the dog who is bothered by thunderstorms, which seem to come up suddenly and disappear just as fast. Aside from confining the dog in a secure, familiar place, there are not many things owners can do to solve this problem.

In predictable situations, however, a tranquilizer can be quite effective. For example, medication plus the above-described procedures can help your dog get through the Fourth of July with minimal stress.

A Conditioning Approach

A large percentage of all dogs who are sound sensitive, especially dogs who are gun shy, were made that way by their owners. Of course the purpose of this book is not to train hunting dogs. It is to have a well-adjusted family pet.

However, in many cases the family pet also serves as a hunting dog. The steps described here for preventing gun shyness serve as a good example of how a conditioning approach to sound sensitivity can work. Regardless of your dog's role—hunting companion or couch coyote— the procedures outlined in this chapter can be adapted easily to condition your dog not to be frightened of *any* kind of loud noise.

The key here is to associate noise with something pleasant. This can start when your puppy is very young. Use a metal feed pan for your dog's dinner. Let him watch you prepare his meal. As you are carrying his dish to the area where he eats, tap gently against the bowl with a metal spoon. Praise your puppy enthusiastically as you do this. Increase the volume of the noise a bit each day. He will soon come to associate all that racket with something great: his dinner! Do this for a couple of months.

If your dog loves to retrieve, you are in luck. Go to a toy store and purchase a pop gun. I have a harmless air gun that makes a slight popping sound when you pull the trigger. Throw a tennis ball or your dog's favorite retrieving object. As your dog is chasing the object, pop the air gun. Praise your dog as he brings back the object.

After several months of practicing with the pop gun, switch to a starter's pistol. Most gun shops carry these and you are not required to obtain a permit. Although a starter's pistol is not a real gun, read the instructions very carefully. *Never* point it at a person or an animal. A small amount of burned powder erupts from the barrel when the pistol is discharged. This could cause a burn.

At this stage in training you will need an assistant. Take your young dog out to a large open field. Have your assistant go about a hundred yards away with the starter's pistol. Throw the tennis ball and send your dog on a retrieve. As the dog takes off after the ball, have your assistant fire the starter's pistol. Praise your dog lavishly as he returns with the ball. Repeat this procedure half a dozen times, every day for at least two weeks.

If your dog appears to be oblivious to the sound of the starter's pistol, gradually move your assistant closer to you. Do this in twenty-yard intervals. When your assitant can stand right next to you, and your dog ignores the sound of the gun, you are ready to simulate authentic hunting.

With or without the help of an assistant, have your dog sit and stay at your side. Throw the ball, but make your dog stay. Do not let him chase the ball. Fire the starter's pistol as if you were trying to shoot the ball. When the ball hits the ground, send your dog. The idea is to associate the sound with the act of retrieving, which the dog loves. You should repeat this procedure as often as you can for a couple of months.

When your dog is fully accustomed to the sound of a starter's pistol, you are ready to introduce him to the sound of a shotgun. I recommend that you follow the same formula that was outlined with the starter's pistol. Have your assistant a hundred yards away. Shoot your gun in a safe direction as your dog is en route to a retrieve. Over two months, gradually move the gunner closer to you and your dog. Be sure that the sound of the gun is always associated with retrieving.

This process may seem extremely methodical to some people. However, a slow, systematic procedure is worthwhile in the long run. Hasty, thoughtless mistakes can make perfectly healthy dogs sound sensitive. The foolish idea of taking young pups or inexperienced dogs into the field and blasting a shotgun over their heads is the main reason for gun shyness. Trying a dog out at a turkey shoot or trap and skeet range is another great way to end up with a sound-sensitive dog.

Whether you plan to hunt with your dog or simply do not want your pet to overreact on the Fourth of July, a systematic conditioning process that associates noise with fun is the key to success.

Twenty-seven

Roaming Free

Allowing your dog to roam free will make training him much more difficult. The primary reason that humans can train dogs is because of the dogs' submissive instinct. As trainers, we develop a structured pack order and use the submissive instinct to condition each dog to think of us as the pack leader. The dog's role in the pack is that of a follower. The dog who is allowed to roam free has a weaker submissive instinct. Roaming free—and doing whatever the dog pleases—is counterproductive to following direction from a pack leader.

Besides making training more difficult, allowing a dog to roam free is like playing a game of Russian roulette with the dog's life. Visit any veterinarian's office and ask for a tour. You will see the painful results of allowing a dog to roam free. In the seven years that I worked for veterinarians, I saw dogs who had been hit by cars, dogs who were attacked by other roaming canines, and dogs who had ingested poison from someone's garbage pail. These are just a few of the hazards that roaming dogs are exposed to. There are many more. Consider the following:

Dogs are very attracted to the smell and taste of radiator antifreeze. At least six times a year, the veterinarians I worked for treated dogs who were poisoned after drinking a puddle of antifreeze that had leaked or been drained from a car. In most cases this proved fatal to the dog.

I have seen dogs with gunshot wounds. These wounds were inflicted

Dogs are naturally attracted to antifreeze. This common chemical is a leading killer of dogs who roam.

illegally by people who did not like dogs and did not want them wandering through their yards. Every year dogs running in packs are shot legally by farmers who, in many states, have the right to protect their livestock.

Dogs who roam free are sometimes caught in traps placed in the woods by hunters. Dogs have been known to lose legs or to starve to death after what we can only imagine was an excruciatingly painful struggle.

In my hometown there are many small ponds and lakes. Every spring roaming dogs drown by falling through the melting layers of ice. This tragedy can be avoided by not allowing your dog to roam.

Injury or death can happen suddenly to *any* dog who roams. The dogs who make it to the veterinary hospital are the lucky ones—if they can be helped. Many never get that far.

Other Problems

Neighbors do not appreciate their yards being ruined by wandering dogs. Male dogs often mark territory by lifting their legs and urinating on trees and bushes. Both males and females urinate and defecate wherever they please when they roam. No one likes to clean up—or step in—defecation from someone else's dog.

Every year pounds and shelters throughout the country put to death several million unwanted dogs. Roaming dogs—both males and females—bear much responsibility for the problem of canine overpopulation. Male dogs are uncanny about finding a way into the pen or

226

fenced yard of a female dog in heat. Many unwanted puppies are born as a result.

In most towns and cities, it is against the law for dogs to roam free. Animal control officers can pick up roaming dogs. If your dog has been picked up, you will not get him back without first paying a fine— sometimes a very stiff one.

Your roaming dog may also bring you unwanted legal trouble. What if he bites a child? Your wandering gypsy may be a sweetheart in your home but a ruffian on the street. You have no way of knowing for sure.

Roaming dogs regularly cause traffic accidents when they run into the street. What if someone is killed or becomes paralyzed as a result? Dogs are not handed lawsuits or given court judgments to pay for damages. Their owners are.

Do not rationalize this situation by claiming that your dog needs the exercise. It is your job as a responsible dog owner to provide your dog with supervised exercise. It is also your responsibility to treat your dog as a family member and to protect him from harm.

If you do not have a fenced yard to keep your pet safe and sound, put your dog on a leash twice a day and take him for a walk. If you are away from home all day, ask a neighbor to walk your dog, or hire a pet-sitting service to do it. Build a secure dog run, or look into electric canine fences, which are often less costly than traditional fencing.

There are many alternatives to letting your dog roam. Pick any one of the options. By keeping your dog under supervision, you will enhance his response to your training efforts. You will also have peace of mind, and your dog will have a much better chance of living a long and healthy life.

BYRON, BENTLEY, AND DRIFTER

Part Five

What Every Dog Owner Should Know

Twenty-eight

Choosing a Qualified Dog Obedience Instructor

In most states, dog training is not a licensed profession. Dog trainers and obedience instructors are not certified or regulated in any way. *Any* individual can advertise as either a dog trainer or an obedience instructor. Unless the person breaks cruelty-to-animal laws, no state or local officials will interfere.

Unfortunately, many so-called obedience instructors subject dogs to inhumane treatment. If you do choose to work with an obedience instructor while you use this book, make every effort to find a qualified individual. Check the credentials of a dog trainer *before* enrolling your pet in a program by asking the right questions.

The first and most important question to ask is:

How did the obedience instructor learn to train dogs?

An individual can acquire these skills in a number of ways. He or she could work for a guide dog organization, training dogs to lead the blind and then teaching their new owners how to handle the dogs. Another option would be to work in the military or police force training guard dogs or bomb and drug detection dogs. A person can also gain experience training dogs by competing in A.K.C. obedience trials, schutzhund trials, tracking tests, or field trials.

Valuable knowledge and experience can be gained by working for a veterinarian as a pet handler or technician, teaching canine patients to behave while they are being treated or examined. Working as a dog groomer or on the staff of a boarding kennel can also provide handling experience. Only by handling hundreds or thousands of dogs can a person truly understand canine behavior and temperament.

Dedicated and successful people with a background in one or more of these fields have a great foundation to teach dog obedience. However, a great trainer of dogs is not necessarily a good teacher of people. The next question to ask is:

What kind of teaching background does the instructor have?

College-level courses offered in a few places around the country are designed specifically to teach people how to be effective obedience instructors. Unfortunately, these courses are few and far between, and not many people have the opportunity to take them.

In contrast, many excellent dog obedience seminars and clinics are held in many states each year. These include the weeklong Volhard Instructor's Clinic and seminars held by other noted instructors. Many teaching skills are learned and practiced at these functions. Does your dog trainer attend them?

Teaching skills can be developed in jobs that require working and communicating with people. Is the instructor articulate and able to express his or her ideas clearly? This is an absolute requirement for a good teacher. In addition, a great number of helpful books are available on the subjects of training dogs and teaching people how to train their dogs. A qualified obedience instructor should be familiar with most of these books.

Some other good questions to ask of an instructor:

How long have you been training dogs? How long have you been teaching people to train their dogs?

Neither of these skills is developed overnight. Be sure your potential instructor has some experience under his or her belt.

Ask if the instructor owns a dog. If so, evaluate for yourself how well the dog obeys. If the instructor's own dog is not obedient, chances are the instructor will not be successful teaching you to train your dog. Also, ask how many different breeds of dogs the trainer has owned or worked with. If the answer is one or two, the instructor may have trouble relating to your particular dog or to your dog's particular training requirements.

Ask the instructor if you can observe one of his or her group classes. What training techniques do you see? Do any of them seem unreasonably harsh? Examples would be "hanging" dogs by their training collars, whipping dogs with the end of the leash, or jerking excessively until the dog yelps. You do not need to be an expert on dogs to know that these procedures constitute cruelty. There is no reason in the world to abuse a dog in order to train it.

On the other hand, how creative is the group class? Do owners walk in endless circles doing nothing but heeling? Are a variety of exercises part of the program? Use your critical judgment to evaluate what you see.

An additional point about the instructor's class:

Is it designed to teach the owners or the dogs?

A group class of any size is not an ideal environment for untrained canines to learn. New smells, different dogs, and a new setting are overwhelming distractions, especially for energetic and curious young dogs.

Imagine what it would be like if you tried to learn a new foreign language while listening to loud rock music—and someone reprimanded you every time you made a mistake! This is what a beginner group obedience class can be like. A dog is best trained in a quiet, familiar environment where he can concentrate and learn. In a properly run group training class, the emphasis should be placed on the owner's handling, not on the way the dog is carrying out the exercises in class.

If an owner (1) understands how to carry out a technique, (2) understands the purpose of the technique, (3) has written material to refer to that describes what was learned in class, and (4) is motivated to go home and work with the dog, then dog and handler will be successful.

Finally, ask if the instructor does obedience work as a professional. As in many other lines of work, only an experienced professional may be able to provide you with professional results. The "hobby dog trainer" who teaches to make a little extra money, or because he or she enjoys dogs, may not be qualified to give you the expert help you need—and to help you effectively and efficiently achieve your goal of an obedient dog.

Also, do not be afraid to ask for references from people this instructor has taught. A qualified professional will be happy to provide them, primarily because he or she should have a long list of satisfied clients who own well-behaved dogs.

Choosing a qualified obedience instructor is one of the most important steps you take in training your dog. Remember—*ask the right questions!*

Twenty-nine

Spaying and Neutering

Who Should Breed Dogs?

I believe that indiscriminately breeding dogs is an atrocity. However, I do not believe dog breeding should be placed exclusively in the hands of kennel club breeders. Kennel club breeders are people who breed purebred dogs for the purpose of dog shows, obedience trials, field trials, and the like.

Every year I meet and work with dozens of wonderful, lovable, trainable, mixed-breed dogs. I would not want to see dogs such as these eliminated from the dog world. However, any time a dog, whether purebred or mixed breed, is bred, the breeding should be planned by knowledgeable people.

The art of breeding good dogs is developed through time, experience, and education. Good breeders understand how genetics influence both physical soundness and temperament in dogs. Crippling hip dysplasia and eye disorders that lead to blindness are serious hereditary canine faults. Good breeders understand these problems and take the proper precautions to detect them in their breeding stock. Prior detection ensures that these faults are not passed down to future generations.

Many temperament traits are also hereditary. Dogs with shy, skittish personalities often produce puppies with similar temperaments. Dogs with vicious personalities can produce vicious offspring.

There is an interesting syndrome among all dog owners. This is the belief that "the dog we own is the greatest dog who ever lived." Unfortunately, many owners also believe that because their dog is *so* wonderful, it should reproduce. It takes a very objective and knowledgeable individual to be aware of this belief and to not let it influence a decision of which dog is appropriate to breed.

The Joy of Birth

One argument I have heard for breeding a pet is that children should experience the joy of birth. This is a woefully poor reason for creating ten or more new lives. Puppies are often born at night, with considerable distress to the mother dog. Birth is accompanied by blood. There may be deformed or dead puppies. And usually a lot of work and attention is required of the humans involved. It is most definitely not the kind of Disney experience you might imagine.

Children can watch videotapes of animals, visit farms, and even be in attendance in the delivery room at some hospitals. Put your efforts into those kinds of experiences. And teach your children that the real miracle and joy is a well cared for pet who lives a long and happy life with a loving family.

The Stud Dog

Often I meet people who tell me that they wanted to breed their male dog but were disappointed to discover that breeders were not interested. Almost all breeders want dogs with show, obedience, or field trial championship titles. Stud dogs are regularly flown all over the country, and there may be hundreds of superior, titled dogs available within a specific breed. Your average, friendly pet—no matter how wonderful he is to you—does not have the credentials that good breeders need for their carefully planned breedings.

The other alternative, of course, is to match your male pet with a neighbor's female pet. Even if both dogs have excellent pedigrees, the results are never guaranteed. Indiscriminately breeding your dog to the female dog across town is nothing more than an inappropriate contribution to the dog population crisis.

Spaying the Female Dog

Serious thought should be put into a decision to breed *any* dog. Every year millions of unwanted puppies are born. A large percentage of these dogs end up abused, abandoned, and euthanized. To help prevent this, I strongly recommend that you have your female dog spayed.

The medical name for the surgery that is performed to spay a dog is an ovarian hysterectomy. This surgery removes the dog's uterus and ovaries. After this surgery, the dog will have no estrus cycles and no periodic bleeding. The lay terminology for estrus cycles is "coming into heat." As a result, the female dog cannot conceive or give birth to puppies.

Health factors indicate that it is wise to spay female dogs who are not going to be bred. Many veterinarians I have interviewed feel that female dogs who are spayed *before* their first heat cycle live longer, healthier lives. (Check with your own veterinarian for the best time to spay your dog.) The incidence of canine breast cancer is high in older, unspayed females. Dogs who are spayed before they ever come into heat do not develop mature breast tissue, and this greatly reduces the incidence of breast cancer.

A life-threatening condition called pyometra, which is an infection of the uterus, can occur in unspayed females. This condition may develop one week to several weeks after the female goes out of heat. Emergency veterinary care is imperative in order to save the dog's life. In almost all cases an emergency hysterectomy must be performed.

Controlling the canine overpopulation problem and minimizing health risks are two good reasons, in themselves, to spay a dog. There is a third reason. Quite simply, dealing with a dog in heat is a major inconvenience. Female dogs come into heat twice a year. These biyearly cycles last for about twenty-one days. Depending on the individual dog, this cycle begins between the ages of six months and fifteen months. Small dogs often come into heat at an earlier age than large dogs. Throughout most of the heat cycle, female dogs are either bleeding or spotting blood. "Doggie diapers" are available, which owners can put on the dog to minimize soiled floors and rugs. However, some dogs do not enjoy wearing them and are persistent in removing them.

During the first nine days of the dog's heat cycle, she will begin to attract male suitors. Try as the suitors might during this phase of the cycle, the female will not, in most cases, accept her admirers. The female will snap, growl, sit down, and jump away when males try to approach. Somewhere between the ninth day and the sixteenth day of the cycle, the female will begin to ovulate. Ovulation lasts about four days. During this phase the female will become receptive and allow males to mount her. In addition, she will become an irrepressible flirt. She may try escaping from the house. I have known receptive females, even if they are small in size, to jump over or dig under the backyard fence. Every wandering male gypsy from miles around will be camping out in her neighborhood.

I had clients who owned a female German shepherd who came into heat. The owners were very careful to keep this dog under lock and key throughout her cycle. On one unusually warm, sunny March day, my client locked her shepherd in a kennel crate in the family room while she went shopping. Because it was such a beautiful day, she closed only the screen door on the side of her house and left the big wooden door open.

When my client returned home an hour later, she found a large tear in the screen door. Inside the house she discovered a large, black, mixed-breed dog wandering around her dining and family rooms. The intruder had not bred her dog because the female was safe in the crate. However, the male had lifted his leg and urinated on every piece of furniture in the two rooms. He was marking his territory to let all the other males in the area know that this was his domain.

This is just one of a dozen horror stories I could relate concerning unspayed female dogs. Until there are no roaming dogs in the world, female dogs in heat will invite potential problems—or disasters. Unless owners are willing to carefully and conscientiously breed their female dog, spaying is imperative.

Neutering the Male Dog

This section is not designed to dictate whether you should or should not neuter your male dog. It is designed to point out circumstances where neutering may benefit your relationship with your dog. It is also designed to help dispel the myths attached to this elective surgery.

Neutering a male dog involves the surgical removal of both testicles. The scrotum is not removed during this procedure, merely opened for testicle removal and then closed. After some post-operative swelling, the scrotum usually shrinks in size and lies flat against the dog's body.

I feel that it is not absolutely essential to neuter *every* male dog who is not going to be bred. I have owned and known a number of male dogs who naturally had a low sex drive. They had no behavioral problems influenced by male hormones, such as leg mounting, urinating indoors, or aggressively defending territory. These dogs were supervised by their owners and always went outdoors into a fenced yard where they had no opportunity to breed a wandering female in heat.

These dogs were probably the exception rather than the norm. In many cases neutering a male dog is necessary and beneficial. First of all, let me state that I have never seen a problem result from neutering any male dog. In my experience, the surgery *has either improved the dog's behavior or had no apparent effect.* Neutering has never made the dog "worse." Even dogs who had the surgery but were not prime candidates for neutering showed no harmful behavior or physical side effects.

There are many good reasons for electing to neuter male dogs that involve both the dog's behavior and physical health. Many of the adverse behaviors of male dogs are sexually based. Although theoretically, female canines come into heat at a specific time of the year, domestic dogs—unlike their cousins, the wolves—do not adhere strictly to this rule. Puppies are born every month of the year. This indicates that some female dogs are in heat every month of the year, potentially keeping male dogs continuously aroused.

Although a large percentage of unwanted behavior results from lack of training, sexual frustration can account for some behavioral problems. Strong anxiety and frustration on the part of unneutered male dogs often lead to undesirable behaviors, such as roaming, lifting a leg to urinate on furniture, and mounting people's legs.

Some undesirable behaviors that are *not* overtly sexual may also be caused by sexual frustration. Neutering may alleviate excessive barking, pacing, and biting.

Consider these health factors when deciding whether or not to neuter your male dog. Veterinarians find that some male dogs develop testicular disease as they get older. Since the testes are removed when dogs are neutered, such dogs can never suffer from testicular disease. Neutered male dogs also have much lower chances for developing some other serious conditions, such as infected prostate glands and cancerous anal growths. I recommend that you discuss all of these ailments with your veterinarian.

The ideal time to neuter your male dog is around one year old. Many veterinarians believe that it is beneficial to allow the dog to reach puberty first, so the dog can develop masculine physical characteristics.

Years ago when I worked as a veterinary technician, it was standard procedure to neuter male dogs at six months old. On the other hand, research has shown positive effects on dogs who were neutered at ten years old. Check with your veterinarian for the ideal time to perform the surgery on your dog. If you have doubts about the recommendation, get a second opinion from another veterinarian.

Myths About Neutering

Many people are very reluctant to neuter the male dog. Most reasons have nothing to do with the factual ramifications of the surgery. Rather they have more to do with the myths that people accept as facts.

Myth Number 1: *My dog will become a wimp.*

Neutering will in no way diminish your dog's strength or stamina. Barbara's yellow Labrador retriever, Bentley, was neutered when he was fourteen months old. I have never met a more athletic individual than this dog. Bentley can run on the beach nonstop for hours. He can run straight up a thirty-foot sand dune without breaking stride. He enthusiastically swims in the frosty Atlantic Ocean in February. This dog is anything but a wimp.

Myth Number 2: *Neutering will affect my dog's "watch dog" ability.*

My Australian shepherd, Drifter, was neutered at a year old. I challenge anyone to get into my car or enter my house uninvited. Believe me, Drifter is an effective watchdog.

Myth Number 3: *Neutering will negatively affect my dog's ability as a hunting dog.*

This is not the case. In fact, neutering may improve his hunting ability. In my years of hunting with my German shorthair pointer, Jena, I witnessed male dogs who spent most of their time in the field trying to mount females and urinate on bushes. Being neutered will allow your male hunting dog to concentrate on the task at hand—finding birds.

Neutering will also improve your dog's concentration with obedience training. The male dog's hormonal instincts will almost always override any amount of training that most people can provide. For example, come on command will mean nothing to the dog who is wandering off in search of females.

Myth Number 4: *Neutering will cause my dog to get fat.*

The surgery does not create fat; calories do. It is true that after neutering, some male dogs do not burn up as many calories as they once did. If your dog had been running around the neighborhood in search of females or pacing back and forth endlessly in the house out of frustration, he may have burned calories with this activity. After these behaviors have been eliminated, you may have to exercise the dog more or feed him less.

Human nature plays a part in perpetuating the myth that neutering a dog makes him fat. Many people would rather blame the surgery for their dog's weight problem than admit that they slip Rover too many doggie biscuits or too many leftover table scraps. Barbara and I own three male dogs who are neutered, and none of them is fat. Exercise and a regulated diet will keep your dog in great shape.

Myth Number 5: I wouldn't want someone to do that to me. I'm not going to do that to my dog.

This macho mentality inhibits many people—men in particular—from neutering their dogs. Unfortunately, men who feel this way never identify with their dogs accurately. Men have wives and girlfriends with whom they can have long-lasting relationships. Dogs do not. For the most part, unneutered dogs go through life frustrated. Men should not regard their male dogs as a projection of themselves.

Moreover, allowing the dog to run loose to fulfill his desires is against the leash laws of most states. (See Chapter 27, "Roaming Free.") Worse than breaking a leash law is contributing to the canine overpopulation problem. As with female dogs, male dogs should be selectively bred only by competent people.

Myth Number 6: My dog will be angry with me for never giving him the opportunity to have a sexual experience.

Or, if he *did* have a sexual experience once, owners may think: *He will know what he is missing and be upset.*

This attitude is simply a form of anthropomorphism. There is nothing at all romantic involved with the canine sex drive. Sex to the dog is one of many instinctive drives. As far as scientific studies can show, dogs do not dwell on sexual behavior unless they are sexually stimulated. Out of sight, out of mind!

Myth Number 7: It is unnatural to neuter a male dog.

Our domestic canines have evolved to a point where they are dependent on humans for food, shelter, and health care. They are no longer wolves.

While it is true that some dogs become feral and live short, sad lives running in a pack, most dogs would not survive a week living this way. We have taken the "natural" life away from domestic canines. They live in a house or an apartment. They must wear collars and walk on a leash. They must learn to come when called and stay when told. People who are obsessed with the dog living a natural life have watched too many *Lassie* episodes.

Individual owners have to decide for themselves if neutering their dog is the right thing to do in their particular situations. However, let facts—not myths, fragile male egos, and old wives' tales—guide your decision.

Thirty

Dealing with Pet Loss

The worst aspect of owning a dog is dealing with the inevitable day when you lose your beloved pet. Although there are many parallels between raising dogs and raising children, one notable difference is that human children normally outlive their parents. This is not so with our "canine children." We usually outlive our dogs. The death of a beloved canine companion is something that, eventually, all dog owners must face.

I have lost dogs whom I loved dearly. You may have too. If so, you can understand the following two stories. If not, my feelings involved with these two experiences may help you cope with that inevitable day.

Woody

I lost my golden retriever, Woody, to cancer when he was five years old. Woody was an exuberant, energetic, eighty-pound canine athlete. He could play Frisbee and chase tennis balls for hours. He would dive into the ocean through four-foot waves to retrieve a stick. If this dog were a human, he would have been a linebacker on a professional football team!

Woody also was very intelligent. He earned his American Kennel Club Companion Dog obedience title when he was only seven months old. He accomplished this in two consecutive weekends, qualifying three times in a row. He won first place twice and second place once. Needless to say, I was tremendously proud of Woody and loved him very much.

One hot July day in Woody's fifth year, he stopped eating. This was unusual, but because of the extreme heat I was not overly concerned. After two days of this, he started to refuse water. In a very short time Woody had become depressed, dehydrated, and had lost weight. I brought him to the veterinarian for an exam.

Initial blood tests showed slight kidney malfunction but no severe problems. Everything else appeared normal. Unfortunately, we still could not get Woody to eat or to drink. He was given intravenous fluids and other medications. He was also X-rayed. Despite all of these treatments, Woody seemed to be going steadily downhill.

Finally Woody was diagnosed as having lymphocarcinoma, a cancer of the lymphatic system. He was placed on high doses of steroids. The drugs made him feel better and renewed his appetite, but only temporarily. On October 15 of the same year, Woody declined severely. The drugs no longer revived him. I brought him to the veterinarian's office and rubbed his ears and talked to him while he was put to sleep.

I was extremely upset over all of this and cried for a long time. My other dog, Jena, a German shorthaired pointer, was ten years old and also had loved Woody immensely. I could tell that she missed him and was upset, partly because I was so upset.

I was fortunate to have friends and family who understood how I felt. They were sympathetic and took my grief seriously. A close friend also loved Woody dearly and allowed me verbally to vent my feelings for hours. This helped tremendously.

There are many clichés, such as "Time heals all wounds" and "You have to roll with the punches." I suppose there is truth to them all. But I was sad.

After a couple of months an interesting thing happened. My sadness turned to anger. I felt ripped off, as if someone had stolen something precious from me. Woody's death seemed so unfair. Why me? This anger would creep up on me at unexpected times. I would be driving along in the car and suddenly think about Woody and feel like pounding the dashboard.

I dealt with these feelings for about a year. Then one day while on a trip to Florida, I pulled into a gas station to fill up my tank. There was a sign on the door: AUSTRALIAN SHEPHERD PUPPIES FOR SALE. I walked inside. Seven little furballs were milling around. The pups were eight weeks old. One of them came strutting over, and I picked him up. It was love at first sight. I handed over the asking price and was out the door with my bundle of joy.

As I drove away, I felt something lift from my body. The grief and the anger were gone. I knew I would never forget Woody, but now I had something positive in which to channel my energy and love.

It had taken me a year before I was ready for another dog. I think in most cases it is not wise to rush out and try to replace the dog you lost. I believe you are better off to take some time to grieve and be sure that you are ready to deal with a new puppy.

When you get a new dog, keep in mind that all dogs, like all humans, are individuals. You will be making a mistake and will be sorely disappointed if you try to duplicate the dog you lost. I have seen people lose a dog and try to replace it with a dog of the same breed. They even give the dog the same name as its predecessor. These people are always disappointed and disillusioned when they discover that this new pup has its own unique personality. After I lost Woody, I knew I would have to get a completely different type of dog. My little Australian shepherd, Drifter, was just the ticket to finding canine love again.

There is no better friend than a loving canine companion who has shared his life with you.

Jena

Five years after losing Woody I lost Jena, my German shorthaired pointer. She was fifteen years old. Again I was sad, but this was different. I did not feel ripped off. I felt that Jena had lived a full life.

Jena had traveled the country with me. She swam in the Atlantic Ocean, the Gulf of Mexico, and dozens of lakes. We camped together many times in the Florida Keys. She had earned two obedience titles. For ten seasons, she fulfilled her passion: hunting pheasants. Jena lived to be a dignified old lady dog.

Although I cried when I lost Jena, the adjustment period was not as long. Again, I had close friends with whom to share my feelings. I was doing my weekly radio show about dogs at the time of Jena's death. I spent an entire show discussing her life and what she had meant to me. Barbara and I took phone calls from listeners who related their own experiences with pets they had lost. Although there were a lot of tears shed during that program, I felt much better by the time we went off the air.

Pet Loss Counseling

Grieving over the loss of something you love is never silly, foolish, or insignificant. I think it is imperative to have someone to talk to. Talking is the best therapy in the world. If you don't feel comfortable talking to a friend, professionals can help. These people are called pet loss counselors.

The goal of pet loss counseling is to provide a supportive atmosphere where you can share your feelings of grief. Such counseling is offered privately or in small groups. Experienced pet loss counselors also can help identify unresolved grief in children, which can take unpredictable and sometimes puzzling forms.

Pet loss counseling can even begin before a pet's death. If you are having trouble deciding about euthanasia, handling your pet's remains, or whether to plan for another pet, you may want to speak to a pet loss counselor. Although this is a relatively new profession, your veterinarian or local mental health department can help you find someone to help you.

Thirty-one

Let's Go for a Swim!

Swimming is a great form of exercise for dogs. It is good for the heart and the lungs. It allows dogs to use many of their muscles without putting excessive stress on hips and shoulders. For this reason, it is a particularly good form of exercise for puppies whose bones are developing and for dogs with structural defects, such as hip dysplasia.

Most dogs can learn to swim if they are properly introduced to water. Some breeds, such as the bulldog, are not very graceful in the water. The bulldog's wide torso and short legs make swimming difficult. And the pushed-in snout seems to cause breathing problems while swimming.

A few other breeds are also not great swimmers. Because of their body conformations, breeds such as the dachshund and basset hound have difficulty in the water. However, there are exceptions to every rule. I am sure that *somewhere* there is a doggie-paddling basset hound!

There are two main reasons why some dogs do not like to swim. One reason is that some dogs have never been exposed to water. The other reason is that many dogs have been improperly introduced to the idea of swimming. The *biggest mistake* owners can make is to throw their dogs into the water in an attempt to teach them to swim. I have met both golden retrievers and Labrador retrievers who hated the water because their owners threw them in. (Instinctively, however, both of these breeds think they are dolphins!)

Dogs of all types can learn to love swimming—if they are introduced to it properly.

Imagine being a small child and having an adult whom you trusted throw you out of a boat to teach you to swim. Your head would go under. You would gulp down mouthfuls of water. Maybe with your arms flailing and legs kicking you would swim back to the boat. You probably would survive, but you sure would not have a pleasant association with water.

Dogs are no different! *Never* undermine your dog's trust in you by throwing him into the water. Even an experienced canine swimmer does not enjoy a sudden, abrupt heave-ho into the drink.

Of all the dogs I have known, my German shorthaired pointer, Jena, was the best swimmer. She swam circles around every Lab or golden I know. But it took Jena dozens of exposures to the water before she actually swam. And it took dozens of more experiences before she swam really well. If you are lucky you will have your dog for an average of fourteen years. What is the rush? Take your time.

How to Introduce Swimming

The sooner in your dog's life that you expose him to water, the greater are the chances that he will learn to enjoy it. Find a gentle pond or stream away from road traffic. Take your dog off the leash and let him explore. Take a seat on the bank and discreetly watch your pup. Read a book or watch a bird. Appear to ignore him. Do not attempt to encourage or coax him into the water. Coaxing just makes an unsure puppy or dog suspicious. Spend half an hour allowing your dog to poke around and explore. Repeat this procedure as often as you can.

When your dog starts to splash around on his own, praise him. Let your dog repeat this experience a dozen different times. When you have accomplished this, take out your dog's tennis ball or another object that will float and that he enjoys retrieving. Throw it a few inches into the water. Encourage him to get it, but do not force him. Use only your voice to motivate him.

If your dog is too nervous to get the object, *you* get it. After you have retrieved the ball, have your dog do a couple of land retrieves. This will build the dog's enthusiasm and confidence. If he does retrieve the object from the water, praise him ecstatically. Using common sense, increase the distance of the retrieves. Take your time. This increased distance should develop slowly over a period of a few weeks.

When your dog first goes out over his head, be sure to praise him enthusiastically when he begins to swim. Two or three successful retrieves are plenty at first. Do not overdo it. Also, do not be concerned if his front feet splash out of the water at first. Most dogs do this. I have never met a dog who did not stop splashing his feet after he became comfortable in the water.

If your dog's feet-splashing technique of swimming seems to persist for a long time, try this: Get a small, somewhat heavy log that your dog can hold in his mouth. Use the log as his object to retrieve in the water. The weight of the log will cause the dog to swim with his front legs under the water. Chances are good that he will figure out he can move quicker and expend less energy swimming this way.

If your dog does not like to retrieve, the best method to teach swimming is for you to go into the water with him. Do not physically take the dog into the water with you. Wade in until you are about waist deep. With your voice and an object of attraction, invite your dog into the water. (You should first introduce the dog to water using the same procedure recommended at the beginning of this section.) If he is not secure enough to follow you, do not force the issue. Chances are good that after a dozen or so experiences, he will follow you in. When he does, praise him lavishly!

A word of caution: Be careful when swimming with your dog. A dog can inadvertently scratch you with his toenails. My ninety-pound Irish setter, Jason, once tried to climb on me in water that was over my head. It took all I had to get away from him and not drown. Although swimming with a dog is great fun, do be careful.

You may know people who were not as methodical when introducing swimming to their dogs. But their dogs love the water anyway! These are the exceptions. The procedures outlined here may be the slow way, but they provide a dependable approach. I have never owned a dog who did not love the water. Along with the many sporting breeds I have owned—and who instinctively took to the water—I have had a bull mastiff, a poodle, and two herding dogs who loved to swim. I taught them to love swimming by introducing them to the water in a way that was nonthreatening and fun.

Thirty-two

Something for Fun: Movie Tricks

Obedience training is designed to teach dogs to respond to commands. This provides their owners with mechanisms of control. Tricks are taught to the dog for fun.

It is not necessary that your dog perform tricks in order to be a well-trained dog. I do not correct a dog for not responding to a trick command. Tricks are simply additional training that you can do with your dog for fun and entertainment. Dogs enjoy learning tricks when they are taught in a purely positive manner. And who knows, you may own the next Benji, Lassie, or Drifter!

Roll Over

In order to teach your dog to roll over, he must first learn to lie down on command. Rolling over should be taught on grass or on a carpeted area.

- Place your dog in a down position.
- Hold a piece of dog biscuit or other tasty treat in your right hand. Stand to one side of your dog.
- Get your dog's attention with the biscuit. Give the command *"Roll"* as you bring the biscuit over your dog's back in the direction that you would like him to roll.

Drifter is on a roll!

It took practice not to get stuck on his back!

- Your dog should follow the biscuit and roll onto his back. When he is on his back, help him keep going with a gentle push. Do *not* frighten your dog by pushing too hard or abruptly.
- As soon as your dog rolls over, praise him profusely and allow him to eat a piece of the biscuit.

Practice several rolls every day. Your dog will eventually associate the sweeping motion over his back as a hand signal to roll. Before long, the command *"Roll"* and the sweeping hand motion will be your dog's cue to roll. As your dog become proficient with this trick, move away from his side so that you are standing in front of him.

Speak!

I do not know a way to *make* your dog speak. Eliciting this behavior from your dog simply requires patience and perseverance on your part.

- Stand in front of your dog holding his favorite dog biscuit in front of his face.
- Give him the command *"Sit."*
- Give the command *"Speak."* If he sits there looking at you with a blank expression on his face, repeat the command.
- Your dog may perform every behavior he knows. Continue to say *"Speak."* You may even try barking at *him* a few times. Chances are good that your dog will eventually bark at you out of frustration.
- As soon as he barks, praise him enthusiastically and let him eat a piece of the biscuit.

Practice this trick every day. Reward your dog for the slightest bark at first. As he gets the idea, encourage him to bark louder. Do this by withholding the reward until he barks louder.

I know dogs who understand *"Little Speak"* and *"Big Speak."* My dog Drifter does the most unusual speak. He simply moves his mouth but no sound comes out! He does this repeatedly, and it is very comical to watch. It is so much fun that I have never encouraged him to make

A great movie dog speaking his lines.

a sound. I have consistently rewarded him at this stage to maintain the behavior.

Some dogs are not very vocal. If after a couple of days your dog does not catch on, move to another trick. He may someday be elected to the House of Representatives, but will never be Speaker of the Dog-house!

Crawling

Step 1

Your dog must know down on command in order to perform this trick. This behavior is very useful when "eluding the bad guys" or "sneaking behind enemy lines"! Teach this behavior on grass or on a carpeted surface.

- Place your dog in a down position. Step in front of him, facing your dog.
- Hold a piece of dog biscuit in your right hand. Place your left hand on your dog's shoulder.
- Place the biscuit six inches in front of your dog's nose. Give the command *"Crawl."*
- As your dog moves forward to get the biscuit, praise him.
- Keep your left hand on your dog's shoulder. If he tries to stand up, give the command *"Down."*
- Do not allow your dog to get the biscuit. Continue to keep it about six inches in front of his nose while you induce him forward.
- After your dog has crawled forward about twelve inches, praise him and allow him to eat a piece of the biscuit.

Practice this step every day. Increase the distance that your dog crawls forward a little each day before you reward him with the food. Be sure to reward him with verbal praise *as* he is crawling. Do not remove your hand from his shoulder. You want to condition your dog to keep his belly on the ground.

Step 2

When your dog will crawl for ten feet using the step 1 technique, you are ready for step 2.

- Place your dog in a down position.
- Step directly in front of your dog, facing him. Do not place your hand on his shoulder. Bend forward slightly toward your dog.
- Show him a dog biscuit. Give the command *"Crawl"* and slowly back up in your tracks.
- If your dog follows after you by crawling forward, praise him.
- If he attempts to get up from the down position, quickly command *"Down."* Then repeat the *"Crawl"* command.
- After your dog has crawled forward for twelve inches, reward him with a piece of biscuit.
- Continue backing up, rewarding your dog at one-foot intervals, until you have gone ten feet.

Practice this step every day. Be sure to stand right in front of your dog. As your dog becomes proficient with this step, have him crawl longer distances between rewards. Eventually do not reward your dog until he has crawled the entire ten feet.

Step 3

When your dog will crawl with your hand off his shoulder for ten feet, you are ready for step 3.

- Down your dog and tell him to *"Stay."*
- Go one foot away and turn to face your dog. Hold a dog biscuit in your hand.
- Give the command *"Crawl."* Simultaneously pat both of your hands, palms open, on your thighs. Your dog will associate this hand patting as a hand signal to crawl.
- Back up six inches as your dog begins to crawl toward you. Verbally praise him as he crawls. Continue to pat your thighs and interject the command *"Crawl."*
- Be sure your dog keeps his belly on the ground. If he starts to stand up, give the command *"Down."*
- When your dog reaches you, pet him and verbally praise him. Let him have a piece of the biscuit.

Practice this behavior every day. Increase the distance away from your dog in one-foot intervals until he will crawl as far as you want. If you have problems, revert back to a prior step.

Playing Dead

This trick is always a big hit when showing off with your dog. The audience particularly loves it when your dog "comes alive" again at the end. Your dog must understand the down and stay commands for this training technique to work.

- Put your dog in the down position and tell him to *"Stay."* Stand to one side of your dog.
- Make your right hand into the shape of a pistol or use an empty toy water gun. (Do *not* use a cap gun or anything that can harm or frighten your dog.)
- Point your pistol-shaped finger at your dog and give the command *"Bang."*
- With your left hand, gently roll your dog onto his side. *Gently* hold his head flat to the floor. Tell your dog to *"Stay."*
- Slowly remove your left hand from the side of his head. If he starts to lift his head, gently push it back down and repeat the command *"Stay."*
- After he keeps his head flat on the ground for a few seconds, tell him *"Okay."* Reward him with a piece of biscuit from your pocket.

Unlike John Wayne, Drifter dies in every appearance.

You may have to practice this behavior repeatedly before your dog catches on. Keep the food rewards in your pocket. Many dogs have trouble concentrating on "staying dead" if they see the food in your hand. Increase the time your dog remains in the dead position by short periods before releasing and rewarding him.

When your dog is responding well to this behavior, repeat the entire teaching process starting with your dog in a sitting position. Eventually you can teach it with your dog in a standing position. Some dogs develop their own unique, dramatic flop-over into the "dead dog" position. Every dog is different, which is what makes this trick so much fun to watch.

Take a Bow

After your dog performs all of his new tricks, he will want to take a bow during his standing ovation. Your dog must understand the stand-stay exercise in order to learn this trick.

- Stand your dog at your left side. Tell him to *"Stay."*
- Place your left arm under your dog's belly, just in front of his hind legs.
- Hold a dog biscuit in your right hand. Wave the biscuit in front of your dog's nose, getting his attention.
- Lower your right hand toward the floor in a slow, sweeping motion. Give the command *"Bow"* as you do this. The sweeping motion of your hand will eventually become a hand signal to your dog.
- Your dog's front end will lower to the ground following the biscuit. Your left arm under his belly will keep his hind end up.
- Tell your dog to *"Stay."* Praise your dog when he is in this position.
- Slowly and gently slide your left arm out from under his belly, repeating the command *"Stay."*
- Praise your dog as you remind him to stay. Release your dog and reward him with tons of praise and a piece of biscuit.

Practice this technique with your dog every day. When he starts to get the hang of it, do the procedure without placing your left arm under his belly. Slowly increase the time that your dog stays in the bow position before you release and reward him. Your goal should be thirty seconds.

A Command Performance

When your dog has mastered all of these tricks, you can incorporate them into a star performance. Here's what I do with my Australian shepherd, Drifter. I set the scene for his audience by telling them that Drifter is an army scout dodging bullets behind enemy lines.

First, I tell Drifter to sit and stay. Then I walk about twenty feet away and turn to face him. I call him: "Drifter, *come!*" As Drifter is running toward me, I give him the command *"Down."* After he goes down, I give him the *"Crawl"* command. (There's imaginary barbed wire to get under!) As Drifter is crawling toward me, I give him a *"Roll"* command. (Bullets are flying past!) After he rolls, I repeat the *"Crawl"* command. I keep alternating between the two commands, causing Drifter to do a series of crawls and rolls. What a brave scout Drifter is!

As Drifter gets close to me, I give him the *"Bang"* command and he plays dead. (His unlucky day.) Then I release him with an *"Okay!"* (He's too tough to die!) Drifter jumps up, full of enthusiasm and seemingly glad to "be alive" again. He gets lots of praise, hugs, kisses, and a piece of biscuit for being my star. He certainly loves it, and so do I. It's really great fun to watch.

There are many other tricks you can teach to your dog that I have not covered in this book. The key with any trick is to *show* your dog gently what you want him to do and, at the same time, associate a command

Drifter takes a bow at the end of his show. Good dog!

with the behavior. Then it takes patience and perseverance on your part as the trainer. Sometimes you may have to repeat a behavior hundreds of times before your dog learns it well.

If a dog biscuit doesn't inspire your dog to work for you, you can try food that is even more appealing. Some trainers use pieces of cheese or hot dog. One famous Hollywood movie dog gets cubes of filet mignon as a reward!

If your dog is not interested in food, you may find trick-training difficult. You can use an object of attraction such as a favorite tennis ball or squeaky toy as a substitute for food.

If your dog is interested in neither food nor objects of attraction, do not try to force him to learn tricks. Even though tricks are fun, they are not necessary in order to have a well-trained dog. Whereas every dog can—and should—be obedience trained, not all dogs are cut out for tricks. I have owned dogs who did tricks and dogs who did not. As long as they were well-behaved family members, they always brought great joy to my life. After all, that's what really counts.

DRIFTER

Now What?

You read the book. You followed the training program. You have a perfect dog, right? Of course not. By now you know that dogs are living creatures—not robots. They cannot be programmed to be infallible any more than you can be. But you and your dog have surely learned a lot. And by working together you have laid the foundation for a lifelong friendship.

Dog Talk training is not meant to be used and then abandoned. It is designed to become a way of life. There is no reason that the standards of behavior you establish for your dog during training cannot stay with him throughout his life. If he starts to "slip up," it means *you* are slipping up. Don't despair. Turn back to the teaching chapters in this book and spend a few days or weeks doing some refresher training. It will do both you and your dog a world of good.

One final piece of advice. Never forget how to love your dog—from a canine point of view. Play with him, exercise him, care for his health, and keep him free from pain in his old age. He will give you a lifetime of companionship and devotion. You owe him no less.

CORK AND GLIN

Training Glossary

Agreeable—Something that feels good, smells good, or tastes good—from the dog's point of view, of course. Dogs repeat behaviors that are agreeable.

Anthropomorphism—Treating your dog as if he were human. This approach usually leads to some very unhappy dog-owner relationships. You must view your dog as a dog and relate to him from a canine point of view.

Biting—Unacceptable behavior. Dogs should not bite humans. No exceptions—except the burglar!

Bonding—Gaining your dog's love and trust. This requires spending time with your dog, treating him fairly, and making him a priority in your life.

Canine point of view—The foundation for all *Dog Talk* training. It means relating to your dog and using training techniques that are meaningful and understandable from the dog's perspective.

Chase reflex—A reaction that all dogs have to chase things that move quickly. This reflex is used to start training a dog to come on command.

Come on command—A big priority in most dog owner's lives. The dog who will come reliably when called is a real joy. However, very few dogs "figure this out" on their own. Coming on command must be taught to a dog using specific training steps. See Chapter 19.

Conditioned response—A predictable behavior in response to a stimulus or signal. A trained dog responds reliably to commands. He has many conditioned responses.

Controlled walking—Walking on a leash without pulling and paying attention to the handler at the other end of the leash. There is a specific way to teach this terrific exercise. See Chapter 18.

Developmental stages—Phases of maturity in a dog's life. Good trainers know what to expect during the various developmental stages, especially throughout puppyhood. They give their puppies time to grow up, reinforcing training skills and obedient behavior on the way to adulthood.

Disagreeable—Something that feels bad, smells bad, or tastes bad. Dogs avoid doing things that are disagreeable.

Dominance—How assertive a dog is, either with people or with other dogs. An extremely dominant dog is usually a challenge to train. Good trainers learn to be assertive themselves. They teach their dogs to follow direction from them—and not the other way around.

Dog abuse—Strictly forbidden. There is no reason in the world to abuse a dog in order to train it.

Dog trainer—That's you. With the help of this book, you can achieve terrific results by working with your own dog.

Down-stay—One of the most important obedience exercises. It requires the dog to lie down and stay in one place until released with a specific signal from the trainer. It allows dogs to be under control in a great many situations, from family gatherings to softball games, from backyard picnics to dinner parties. A dog who knows down-stay usually has a wonderful life—because he gets to go places and do things that an out-of-control dog would never be allowed to.

Equal time rule—A general guideline that applies to undoing unwanted behaviors. First you must eliminate the unwanted behavior and establish a new behavior in its place. You must then devote equal time to practicing the new, desirable behaviors. Dogs are individuals, however, so "equal time" is more a guideline than a rule.

Exercise—Required by all but ill or elderly dogs. Most household pets get too little exercise. Your dog will be easier to train and typically calmer around the house if he gets plenty of exercise. It's good for people, too.

Extrovert—The dog who loves *everyone*. The extrovert is usually a good candidate for learning how to greet people without jumping. See Chapter 15.

Heeling—Walking at the trainer's left side and adapting to whatever pace and direction the trainer takes. Heeling is useful in situations where you need tight control over your dog or where you must move your dog without a leash. For the typical walk around the block, controlled walking is more practical.

Ideal time to train—Same as the "optimum learning period," which is between seven and sixteen weeks old. This is the ideal time to get started. However, dogs of any age are trainable, especially with an organized, step-by-step training program. *Dog Talk* provides just that.

Jerk and release—A technique used with a training collar. It requires a quick tightening and immediate release of the collar. It is used as a correction, never a means of abuse.

Litter mates—Your dog's brothers and sisters who were born at the same time as your dog. Litter mates wrestle and play, learning some of the skills needed to be a well-adjusted pack member.

Long line—A twenty-five- to fifty-foot length of rope used when exercising the dog who is not yet trained to come on command.

"NHAA"—*Dog Talk* for "NO! Stop what you are doing this instant!" This word should sound deep and guttural, like a growl—which, in fact, is exactly what it is. Dogs know what this means. It is what your dog's mother taught him during his first pack experience— whenever he nursed too vigorously or chewed on her ears. A growl means, *"Stop it. NOW!"*

Obedience competitions—Artificial situations in which people show off their dog's precision-oriented obedience skills. Not relevant to the lives of well-mannered family pets.

Pack leader—The most dominant member of the pack (your family). Your job as the trainer is to be the pack leader. Pack leaders should be assertive but never abusive.

Pain tolerance—A dog's sensitivity to pain or discomfort. This is an important component that determines how strong a correction to use during training.

Pattern training—Doing the same training exercises, in the same place, at the same time, every day. Dogs who are trained in this manner learn to do behaviors only in this setting. The end result is that they are unreliable in the "real world." Pattern training is also boring— for both dogs and owners.

Puppy crazies, a.k.a. "the zooms"—Exuberant bursts of energy in which dogs (usually puppies) run, bark, toss toys, shake things, and so on. Unless your dog is damaging things, stand back and watch. It's a lot of fun and your dog is having a great time.

Quiet on command—An obedience exercise in which the dog is trained to stop barking on command. See Chapter 23.

Recall—The testing phase of come-on-command training. The recall is introduced after the dog responds proficiently to the chase-reflex exercises. In a controlled situation, the dog is in a sit-stay and is called to the owner. The dog's response indicates whether he has formed an association between the sound *"Come!"* and the behavior of running quickly to the owner. Repetition of recalls reinforces come-on-command training.

Release word—A word or signal from a trainer to release a dog from a stay position. A release word allows the trainer to reward the dog with praise while the dog is staying.

Roaming free—Something that well-loved dogs should never do. You are not doing your dog a favor by letting him roam. He could be shot, poisoned, lost, injured or killed by a car, hurt in a dog fight, what have you. Take your dog for a walk on a leash instead. Or try a safe, supervised, off-leash hike on the beach or in the woods. You will be strengthening your bond to each other, reinforcing obedience skills, and keeping your dog alive and healthy as long as possible.

Sit-stay—An obedience exercise in which the dog stays in one place, in a sitting position, until released with a specific signal from the trainer. This exercise is useful to prevent dogs from greeting people by jumping on them, charging through opened doors or gates, leaping out of the car, and the like.

Socialization—Giving a dog, especially a puppy, opportunities to meet new people, other dogs, and see new places. A well-adjusted adult dog is one who has been socialized. He knows how to fit into the human world.

Stand-stay—An obedience exercise in which the dog stays in one place, standing, until released with a specific signal from the trainer. This is a great exercise to use at the veterinarian's office, at the groomer's, when drying wet, muddy dog feet, and so on.

Submissive urination—An uncontrolled release of the bladder. It usually occurs in young puppies who become overly excited or intimidated. Most dogs outgrow it by the time they are one year old.

Timing—Essential to effective dog training. You must correct a dog or reward him when you think he is *thinking* about doing a behavior or *as he is doing the behavior* if you want to influence that behavior. Ten seconds later is too late. Good timing comes with practice, but it also requires paying attention to your dog.

Trained dog—A dog you live with, love, and enjoy for his entire lifetime. You set the criteria for good canine behavior in your home. The training techniques in *Dog Talk* will give you the skills to teach your dog those behaviors.

Index

About the Authors

Trainer, instructor, radio host, and author, **John Ross** has been involved professionally with dogs since 1973. His popular obedience courses, taught in Fairfield County, Connecticut, and Nantucket, Massachusetts, are uniquely designed to teach owners how to train their own dogs.

Unlike many dog obedience programs, John's courses are very much pet-oriented. They focus on good household manners and exercises that can be used in everyday living. They take a nonviolent approach and emphasize step-by-step learning. Military precision and drill-style training have no place in the John Ross Dog Obedience School.

Before John developed his current training approach, he was an active competitor in American Kennel Club obedience trials. He earned fourteen obedience titles in six years—one UD, six CDXs, and seven CDs—on nine different dogs of six different breeds. He worked as a veterinary technician for seven years and managed a boarding kennel for one year.

John co-hosts with Barbara McKinney a weekly radio program about dogs. *Dog Talk* radio is a popular and lively one-hour forum. It features training advice, pet-care tips, interviews, and phone calls from listeners.

John has reached a national audience through several *Dog World* magazine articles. He also has instructed at the nationally known summer camp for dogs and their owners, Camp Gone to the Dogs, in Putney, Vermont.

In addition, John trains Drifter, his male Australian shepherd, for various roles as a canine actor. Drifter has appeared on the television programs *PM Magazine* and *USA Today* and has done photo shoots for *Newsweek* and *Town & Country* magazines. Drifter also has appeared in a motion picture, *The Fifth Season,* by Coyote Productions.

Barbara McKinney has been a professional editor since 1979. She specializes in preparing nonfiction and reference material for a general audience. She has an undergraduate degree from Dartmouth College and an M.A. in journalism from the University of Michigan.

Barbara began her involvement with obedience training in 1985 and is now a part-time obedience instructor in the John Ross Dog Obedience School. Barbara is the co-host with John on their weekly radio show, *Dog Talk,* and has co-authored with John a number of magazine articles. Barbara owns two Labrador retrievers. Bentley, a yellow Lab, demonstrates in dog obedience classes. Byron, a black Lab, has appeared in television and print advertisements.

C.B. AND MOLLY